Prosody, Focus, and
Word Order

Linguistic Inquiry Monographs
Samuel Jay Keyser, general editor

1. *Word Formation in Generative Grammar*, Mark Aronoff
2. *X̄ Syntax: A Study of Phrase Structure*, Ray Jackendoff
3. *Recent Transformational Studies in European Languages*, Samuel Jay Keyser, editor
4. *Studies in Abstract Phonology*, Edmund Gussmann
5. *An Encyclopedia of AUX: A Study in Cross-Linguistic Equivalence*, Susan Steele
6. *Some Concepts and Consequences of the Theory of Government and Binding*, Noam Chomsky
7. *The Syntax of Words*, Elisabeth Selkirk
8. *Syllable Structure and Stress in Spanish: A Nonlinear Analysis*, James W. Harris
9. *CV Phonology: A Generative Theory of the Syllable*, George N. Clements and Samuel Jay Keyser
10. *On the Nature of Grammatical Relations*, Alec Marantz
11. *A Grammar of Anaphora*, Joseph Aoun
12. *Logical Form: Its Structure and Derivation*, Robert May
13. *Barriers*, Noam Chomsky
14. *On the Definition of Word*, Anna-Maria Di Sciullo and Edwin Williams
15. *Japanese Tone Structure*, Janet Pierrehumbert and Mary Beckman
16. *Relativized Minimality*, Luigi Rizzi
17. *Types of Ā-Dependencies*, Guglielmo Cinque
18. *Argument Structure*, Jane Grimshaw
19. *Locality: A Theory and Some of Its Empirical Consequences*, Maria Rita Manzini
20. *Indefinites*, Molly Diesing
21. *Syntax of Scope*, Joseph Aoun and Yen-hui Audrey Li
22. *Morphology by Itself: Stems and Inflectional Classes*, Mark Aronoff
23. *Thematic Structure in Syntax*, Edwin Williams
24. *Indices and Identity*, Robert Fiengo and Robert May
25. *The Antisymmetry of Syntax*, Richard S. Kayne
26. *Unaccusativity: At the Syntax–Lexical Semantics Interface*, Beth Levin and Malka Rappaport Hovav
27. *Lexico-Logical Form: A Radically Minimalist Theory*, Michael Brody
28. *The Architecture of the Language Faculty*, Ray Jackendoff
29. *Local Economy*, Chris Collins
30. *Surface Structure and Interpretation*, Mark Steedman
31. *Elementary Operations and Optimal Derivations*, Hisatsugu Kitahara
32. *The Syntax of Nonfinite Complementation: An Economy Approach*, Željko Bošković
33. *Prosody, Focus, and Word Order*, Maria Luisa Zubizarreta

Prosody, Focus, and
Word Order

Maria Luisa Zubizarreta

The MIT Press
Cambridge, Massachusetts
London, England

© 1998 Massachusetts Institute of Technology

All rights reserved. No part of this book may be reproduced in any form by any electronic or mechanical means (including photocopying, recording, or information storage and retrieval) without permission in writing from the publisher.

This book was set in Times New Roman on the Monotype "Prism Plus" PostScript Imagesetter by Asco Trade Typesetting Ltd., Hong Kong.

Library of Congress Cataloging-in-Publication Data

Zubizarreta, Maria Luisa.
 Prosody, focus, and word order / Maria Luisa Zubizarreta.
  p. cm. — (Linguistic inquiry monographs ; 33)
 Includes bibliographical references (p.   ) and index.
 ISBN 978-0-262-24041-3 (hc:alk.paper) - ISBN 978-0-262-74021-0 (pb)

 1. Prosodic analysis (Linguistics) 2. Focus (Linguistics)
3. Grammar, Comparative and general—Syntax. I. Title.
II. Series.
P224.Z83   1998
414'.6—dc21   98-15459
                                                          CIP

The MIT Press is pleased to keep this title available in print by manufacturing single copies. on demand, via digital printing technology.

To my sons, Sébastian and Rafael

Contents

Series Foreword ix

Preface xi

Chapter 1
Introduction 1

1.1 The Assertion Structure 1

1.2 Results Obtained in Chapters 2 and 3: A Preview 16

1.3 The Theoretical Framework 23

Chapter 2
The Relation between Prosody and Focus in Germanic and Romance 37

2.1 Nuclear Stress versus Emphatic/Contrastive Stress 38

2.2 The Domain of the Nuclear Stress Rule in English (and German) 46

2.3 The Nuclear Stress Rule Revisited 49

2.4 Romance 73

2.5 Alternative Analyses 78

2.6 The Nature of the Focus Prosody Correspondence Principle 88

2.7 Summary and Concluding Remarks   90

Appendix: *Wh*-Phrases, the Nuclear Stress Rule, and the Focus Prominence Rule   92

Chapter 3
Clausal Structure, the Position of Subjects, and a Case of Prosodically Motivated Movement in Romance   99

3.1 The Preverbal Field in Modern Standard Spanish   99

3.2 The Preverbal Field in Italian: Some Comparative Remarks   118

3.3 P-Movement in Spanish   123

3.4 P-Movement in Italian: Some Comparative Remarks   135

3.5 The Nature of P-Movement and Where It Applies   138

3.6 Is There P-Movement in French and in English?   146

3.7 Summary and Concluding Remarks   150

Appendix: Intonational, Syntactic, and Interpretive Properties of Right-Dislocation in Modern Standard Spanish   151

Notes   159
Bibliography   199
Index   211

Series Foreword

We are pleased to present the thirty-third in the series *Linguistic Inquiry Monographs*. These monographs present new and original research beyond the scope of the article. We hope they will benefit our field by bringing to it perspectives that will stimulate further research and insight.

Originally published in limited edition, the *Linguistic Inquiry Monographs* are now more widely available. This change is due to the great interest engendered by the series and by the needs of a growing readership. The editors thank the readers for their support and welcome suggestions about future directions for the series.

Samuel Jay Keyser
for the Editorial Board

Preface

The topic of this work has intrigued me for many years. In fact, my first attempt to deal with the issue of word order and interpretation in Spanish dates from twenty years ago, when I was a student in the Linguistics Department at the Université Paris 8 (Vincennes). Despite the encouraging words of my teachers, I was soon disenchanted with my incipient ideas. I was right to be so. At that time linguists did not know enough about the properties of human languages to be able to tackle such complex issues. Since then (especially in the late 1980s and early 1990s) grammatical theory has grown tremendously in depth and sophistication. In 1993, upon publication of Guglielmo Cinque's "A Null Theory of Phrase and Compound Stress," I felt the time was ripe for a second attempt. My first thoughts on the issue were sketched out while I was teaching a seminar at the Instituto Universitario Ortega y Gasset in Madrid in the spring of 1993 and were published in the working papers of that institution and of the Università di Venezia (Zubizarreta 1993). The following year my ideas evolved in a different direction, yielding several preliminary versions of the present manuscript; the third and fourth versions (Zubizarreta 1995b, 1996) circulated widely among colleagues and friends. The notion of *p(rosodically)-motivated movement* put forth in these earlier versions first appeared in print in Zubizarreta 1995b. Other than the notion of p-movement, little has survived from these earlier versions. In particular, my view of the relation between prosody and syntax has undergone radical revisions. Previously, I had conceived of the differences between Germanic and Romance languages with respect to the location of primary prominence in terms of an intonational constraint. A deeper understanding of the phenomenon made me realize that the differences must be stated in terms of a parameterized Nuclear Stress Rule. This in turn has led to important revisions in the conception of the architecture of the grammar itself.

More people than I can mention have assisted me during the conception and many revisions that gave birth to this monograph. I would like to thank Gerhard Brugger and Jean-Roger Vergnaud for extensive comments and discussions on earlier versions. I would also like to express my gratitude for written comments and encouraging words to Ignacio Bosque, Denis Delfitto, Violeta Demonte, Charlotte Galves, Carlos Otero, and Margarita Suñer, and for useful discussions to Pablo Albizu, Joseph Aoun, Alfredo Arnaiz, Filippo Beghelli, Robin Belvin, João Costa, Gorka Elordieta, Olga Fernandez-Soriano, Roland Hinterhölzl, Mary Kato, Rita Manzini, Yuki Matsuda, Marcello Modesto, Martin Prinzhorn, Liliana Sanchez, and Patricia Schneider-Zioga. Last, but not least, acknowledgments are due to two anonymous reviewers for the MIT Press, to the Instituto Universitario Ortega y Gasset for hosting my seminar in the spring of 1993 and the Spanish Ministry of Education for financing it, and to the University of Southern California for a recent sabbatical leave without which this essay would not have been completed. I also thank Anne Mark for invaluable editorial assistance.

Chapter 1
Introduction

This book is about the relation between focus and prosody in Germanic and Romance and about the relation among focus, prosody, and word order in Spanish and Italian. In this introduction I define how the notions of focus and topic are to be understood in this work (section 1.1); I summarize the results obtained in chapters 2 and 3 in informal terms (section 1.2); and I outline the theoretical framework in terms of which those results will be formalized later and explore the theoretical implications of certain aspects of the formalism (section 1.3).

1.1 The Assertion Structure

1.1.1 The Notion of Focus

A fundamental notion throughout this book is *focus*. My intention here is not to review and assess the extensive and growing literature on this notion.[1] Rather, it is to state how the notion is to be understood in this book. Following Chomsky (1971, 1976) and Jackendoff (1972), I will assume that focus is defined in terms of the discourse notion of *presupposition*: that is, *the focus is the nonpresupposed part of the sentence*.[2] The presupposed part of a sentence is what the speaker and hearer assume to be the case (i.e., the shared assumptions) at the point at which the sentence is uttered in a discourse.[3,4] Again following Chomsky and Jackendoff, I will use the question/answer test to determine how a statement is partitioned in terms of focus and presupposition—that is, its *focus structure*. The presupposition in a *wh*-question can be paraphrased by substituting an indefinite for the *wh*-phrase. Thus, the examples in (1) can be paraphrased as in (2). Such paraphrases can be represented in terms of existential quantification, as in (3).

(1) a. What happened?
 b. What did John do?
 c. What did John eat?
 d. Who ate the pie?
 e. What happened to the pie?
 f. What did John do with the pie?

(2) a. *Something* happened.
 b. John did *something*.
 c. John ate *something*.
 d. *Someone* ate the pie.
 e. *Something* happened to the pie.
 f. John did *something* with the pie.

(3) a. there is an x, such that x happened
 b. there is an x, such that John did x
 c. there is an x, such that John ate x
 d. there is an x, such that x ate the pie
 e. there is an x, such that x happened to the pie
 f. there is an x, such that John did x with the pie

To the extent that the answer to a *wh*-question has the same presupposition as the question, the focus in a statement can be identified as the part of the statement that substitutes for the *wh*-phrase in the context question.[5,6] The string in (4) (without phrasal prominence specified) is therefore multiply ambiguous, depending on its context question.

(4) [John [ate [the pie]]].

Following Jackendoff (1972), Selkirk (1984), and others, I will use the diacritic [F] to mark the constituent that is interpreted as focused or as part of the focus. A constituent that is not marked [F] will be interpreted as the presupposition or as part of the presupposition. In other words, a constituent marked [F] must be interpreted as equivalent to [+F], and a constituent not marked [F] must be interpreted as equivalent to [−F].[7] I will refer to a syntactic structure annotated with the diacritic [F] as the *F-structure* of S. Thus, (4) will be assigned the set of F-structures in (5). As we will see below, each F-structure will be associated with one or more distinct Assertion Structures at a later point in the derivation (namely, after LF), and each Assertion Structure is associated with an explicit or implicit context question.[8]

(5) a. [$_F$ John [ate [the pie]]].
   [What happened?]
  b. [John [$_F$ ate [the pie]]].
   [What did John do?]
  c. [John [ate [$_F$ the pie]]].
   [What did John eat?]
  d. [[$_F$ John] [ate [the pie]]].
   [Who ate the pie?]
  e. [[$_F$ John] [[$_F$ ate] [the pie]]].
   [What happened to the pie?]
  f. [John [[$_F$ ate] the pie]].
   [What did John do with the pie?]

As we will see in section 1.2, the F-structure of S plays a crucial role in determining the relation between focus and prosody. This relation, I will argue, must be captured at a point in the derivation prior to LF.

Chomsky (1976) suggests that the focus/presupposition partitioning of a sentence can be represented at LF by applying the rule of Quantifier Raising (QR) to the focused constituent. More precisely, he proposes that the focus of a sentence S is analyzed as a definite quantifier that is adjoined to the presupposition of S at LF. The variable bound by the definite quantifier is assigned a value by the primitive predicate of equality (i.e., the specificational or equative *be*).[9] Thus, the focus structure of (5c) and (5d) is represented as in (6a) and (6b), respectively.[10]

(6) a. the x, such that John ate x, is the pie
  b. the x, such that x ate the pie, is John

The problem with assuming that the focus/presupposition partitioning of a sentence is represented at LF by extracting the focus via QR is immediately brought out by examples like (5e), where the focus does not correspond to a syntactic constituent. In effect, in this example (as in others in which the verb is part of the focus), the focus is an event and the part of the event for which the equative relation provides a value does not correspond to a syntactic constituent. Note that it would not do to assume that what is extracted via QR is the presupposition rather than the focus. Although such a move would solve the problem with the representation of (5e), it would in turn raise problems with the representation of multiple *wh*-questions and their corresponding answers, in which the [−F] part of the sentence is not a constituent.[11,12]

(7) Q: Who invited whom to go where?
   A: [$_F$ John] invited [$_F$ Mary] to go [$_F$ to the movies], [$_F$ Peter] invited [$_F$ Jane] to go [$_F$ to the beach], ...

Examples like (5e) suggest that the focus structure of a sentence S should be captured in terms of a more abstract representation derived from LF via some interpretive mechanisms.[13] I will refer to this representation as the *Assertion Structure (AS)* of S. I will not explore the properties of AS in any detail, but will only make some preliminary suggestions. In particular, the suggestion I will make below will solve the "constituency problem" in (5e) by introducing a predicate in the presupposition of this sentence that is not part of its LF.

I suggest that the AS of a statement is represented "in context." In other words, in the case of question-answer pairs, the presupposition provided by the context question is part of the AS of the answer statement. More precisely, I propose that the focus-presupposition structure of such statements is represented in terms of *two ordered assertions*.[14] The first assertion (A_1) is the existential presupposition provided by the context question. The second assertion (A_2) is an equative relation between a definite variable (the restriction of which is the presupposition provided by the context question) and a value. Under this view, the ASs of the examples in (5) are as given in (8). I use the equality symbol to represent the equative relation; I will refer to A_1 as *the presuppositional part* or *background assertion of the statement* and to A_2 as *the main assertion of the statement*. As in (8a), in (8b), (8e), and (8f) the focus is a proposition that consists of a predicate and its two arguments. In (8b) it is the content of the predicate and its theme argument that is assigned a value by the equative relation; the value of the agent is specified by the presupposition and is picked up by the pronoun *he* in the main assertion. In (8e) it is the content of the predicate and its agent that is assigned a value by the equative relation; the value of the theme is given by the presupposition and is picked up by the pronoun *it* in the main assertion. In (8f) it is the content of the predicate that is assigned a value by the equative relation; the values of the agent and the theme are specified by the presupposition and are picked up by the pronouns *he* and *it*, respectively, in the main assertion.[15]

(8) a. A_1: there is an x, such that x happened
   A_2: the x, such that x happened = [John [ate the pie]]

b. A_1: there is an x, such that John did x
   A_2: the x, such that John$_i$ did x = [he$_i$ [ate the pie]]
c. A_1: there is an x, such that John ate x
   A_2: the x, such that John ate x = the pie
d. A_1: there is an x, such that x ate the pie
   A_2: the x, such that x ate the pie = John
e. A_1: there is an x, such that x happened to the pie
   A_2: the x, such that x happened to the pie$_i$ = [John [ate it$_i$]]
f. A_1: there is an x, such that John did x with the pie
   A_2: the x, such that John$_i$ did x with the pie$_j$ = [he$_i$ [ate it$_j$]]

Suppose we assume that discourse also provides an order among the assertions introduced by the sentences it is composed of: if a sentence S_i precedes sentence S_j, then the AS of S_i precedes the AS of S_j. We can then establish the following analogy: the relation between the indefinite variable in A_1 and the definite description in A_2 in the ASs given in (8) is comparable to the relation between a so-called E-type pronoun and its antecedent (see Evans 1980); see (9). In both cases the definite description in A_2 picks up the referent introduced by A_1.

(9) a. Some sailor walked into the room. He was wearing a red shirt.
   b. A_1: there is an x (x = a sailor), such that x walked into the room
      A_2: the x (such that x = a sailor & x walked into the room) was wearing a red shirt

Although the determiner that binds the focus variable in the cases examined above is definite, there are other cases where it is not; see, for example, (10a), due to Herburger (1993, 1997). This sentence (which must be pronounced with main prominence on *cooks*) implies that "among the people who came to the party, few were cooks," which indicates that the variable that binds the focus in this case is *few*; see (10b). In effect, it is a property of weak determiners (such as *few* and *many*) that when their restriction is focused, they can be "stripped" apart from their variable in the background assertion and inserted as head of the quantificational structure in the main assertion.

(10) a. Few cóoks came to the party.
   b. A_1: there are x, such that x came to the party
      A_2: few x (such that x came to the party) = cooks

As Herburger notes, although the focusing of weak DPs affects the truth conditions of the sentence in the way indicated above, the focusing of strong DPs does not.

(11) Every cóok came to the party.

Indeed, the sentence in (11) cannot be interpreted as "among those who came to the party, everyone was a cook." The stress in this example must therefore be understood as purely emphatic and not as focus-related. (On emphatic stress, see section 2.1.2.)

In other words, strong determiners cannot be "stripped" apart from their variable in the presupposition in the way that weak determiners can. This distinction is probably related to the semantic property of "symmetry" that distinguishes the two types of determiners; see Keenan 1987.[16,17]

Another property worth mentioning is that there is one and only one focus per sentence. This is suggested by the fact that multiple *wh*-questions and their corresponding answers obligatorily have a linked interpretation; see (12) and its AS in (13).

(12) [$_F$ Mary] bought [$_F$ the newspaper], [$_F$ Peter] bought [$_F$ the book], ... [Who bought what?]

(13) a. there is an (x,y), such that x bought y
 b. the (x,y), such that x bought $y =$ (Mary, the newspaper), (Peter, the book), ...

If every assertion in the AS of a nonconjoined sentence must be ordered with respect to every other assertion, it follows that there cannot be more than one semantic focus per sentence. In effect, the main assertion part of a statement is ordered with respect to its background assertion (the latter always precedes the former by definition). If there were more than one focus per sentence, there would be multiple main assertions unordered with respect to each other because there is nothing in the AS that would impose such an ordering relation. In other words, ordering between foci is not part of the primitive ordering relations defined by the AS.

Let us briefly consider the notion of contrastive focus. The context for contrastive focus is provided by a preceding statement in the discourse (call it the *context statement*). Contrastive focus has two effects. On the one hand, it negates the value assigned to a variable in the AS of its context statement (as indicated by the explicit or implicit negative tag associated with contrastive focus), and on the other hand, it introduces an alternative value for such a variable. As an example, consider the follow-

Introduction

ing contrastive utterance and its context statement (capital letters indicate contrastive stress; the context statement is in square brackets):[18]

(14) John is wearing a RED shirt today (not a blue shirt).
   [John is wearing a blue shirt today.]

The sentence in (14) is a conjunction of two ordered propositions, *John is not wearing a blue shirt today* and *John is wearing a red shirt today*, which give rise to a conjunction of two main assertions.

(15) A_1: there is an x, such that John is wearing x
   A_2: it is not the case that the x (such that John is wearing x) = a blue shirt & the x (such that John is wearing x) = a red shirt

Although the semantic nature of the focus is the same in cases of contrastive and noncontrastive foci in that they both introduce a value for a variable, contrastive focus has another dimension that makes it comparable to emphasis as well. Like emphasis, contrastive focus makes a statement about the truth or correctness of the assertion introduced by its context statement. As noted above, contrastive focus negates certain aspects of the assertion introduced by its context statement. Emphasis may negate the assertion introduced by its context statement, as in (16) ('It is not the case that someone lied to me'), or it may reassert the assertion introduced by its context statement, as in (17) ('It is the case that Mary lied to me').

(16) NOBODY lied to me.
   'there is no x, such that x lied to me'
   [Someone lied to you.]

(17) You are right; Mary DID lie to me.
   'there is an x, such that x (= Mary lied to me) happened'
   [I think Mary lied to you.]

As we will see in chapter 2, the phrasal stress rule that governs emphasis and contrastive focus is distinct from the phrasal stress rule that governs noncontrastive focus.

1.1.2 The Notion of Pragmatic Sentence Topic

The post-LF Assertion Structure would seem to be the natural place in the grammar to incorporate Reinhart's (1982) notion of *pragmatic sentence topic*. Reinhart develops a theory of pragmatic "aboutness" based on Stalnaker's (1978) discourse notion of *context set*:

[Stalnaker] defines the *context set* of a given discourse at a given point as the set of propositions which we accept to be true at this point.... These propositions may be viewed as the speakers' presuppositions, and in a nondefective or happy discourse the speakers are assumed to share the same context set. The effect of each new assertion in a discourse is to add the proposition expressed by it to the presuppositions in the context set. (p. 23)

Reinhart supplements the notion of a context set with the notion of a set of possible (and distinct) assertions of a given *proposition* (drawing on Strawson's (1964) principles of verification and relevance):[19]

[E]ach declarative sentence is associated with a set of possible pragmatic assertions (PPA), which means that that sentence can be used to introduce the content of any of these assertions into the context set. (p. 25)

The proposal is clearly and succinctly summarized as follows in Reinhart 1995:[20]

Each sentence is associated with a set of ... Possible Pragmatic Assertions (the PPA set). The members of this set are, first the bare proposition (in case there is no topic), and then, all possible pairs of an entity and the proposition (similarly to the cards of [Discourse Representation Theory]). The set is restricted by sentence level considerations: While a normal SVO sentence has three members in its PPA set (SVO, S/SVO, O/SVO), there are structures where only some of the construals are possible. E.g. *there* sentences do not have a PPA with the subject as a topic. Passive sentences allow only (the bare proposition and) the subject as a topic. Left dislocation sentences mark the topic explicitly, hence have only one member, etc. In actual context, one member of the PPA set is selected, relative to that context. (p. 86)

Following Strawson, Reinhart argues that the notion of a PPA set is relevant in accounting for truth value judgments and truth value gaps. The assessment procedure involves checking predication, where any expression in the sentence can be taken as the argument and the rest as the predicate. The argument within such a predication relation is the expression that is considered to be the topic in a given discourse. Thus, in the PPA set mentioned above (SVO, S/SVO, O/SVO), the first assertion is topicless, and the second and third are topic-related. This means that, in a given discourse context, if the propositional content of a given sentence is assessed via the PPA S/SVO, then to assess the sentence we have to verify whether the set defined by the subject has the property defined by the predicate. On the other hand, if the propositional content is assessed via the PPA O/SVO, then to assess the sentence we have to verify whether the set defined by the object has the property defined by the predicate. Reinhart provides the examples in (18).

(18) a. Two American kings lived in New York.
b. There were two American kings in New York.

She reports that when members of a class were asked to assess the sentences in (18), about half judged (18a) as false; the others judged it as undefined. On the other hand, in the case of (18b), there was no variation in judgments: all participants judged it as false. This intuition can be captured via the PPA set. The sentences in (18a) and (18b) are associated with the PPA set in (19) and (20), respectively.

(19) a. Two American kings lived in New York. (topicless assertion)
b. two American kings $(x) \setminus x$ lived in New York
c. New York $(y) \setminus$ two American kings lived in y

(20) a. There were two American kings in New York. (topicless assertion)
b. New York $(x) \setminus$ there were two American kings in x

In an out-of-the-blue context, any member of the PPA can be arbitrarily selected. Consider (18a). The reason why some speakers may judge it as undefined is that (19b) is a member of its PPA set (when the sentence appears in an out-of-the-blue context). For those speakers who select (19b) as the representation on the basis of which the assessment is computed, the assessment starts with the empty set *American kings*. Therefore, the predication relation cannot be established, the assertion cannot be assessed, and the speakers judge the sentence as undefined. On the other hand, speakers who select the representation in (19c) will judge the sentence as false, since the predicate *American king* does not apply to any New York resident. Next consider (18b). As mentioned in the previous quotation, the indefinite in the *there*-construction cannot function as a topic. This is shown by the fact that such DPs cannot give rise to backward pronominalization: for example, **Because he is hungry, there is a dangerous tiger in my garden*. Since the indefinite in the *there*-construction (in this case *two American kings*) cannot function as a topic, no representation comparable to (19b) is available for (18b). Only (20b), comparable to (19c), is available for (18b), if it is analyzed as a topic-related assertion. It therefore follows that no undefined judgments should be attested for (18b).

Let us assume with Reinhart that the partitioning of the sentence into topic/comment is represented in terms of predication, where the topic is the subject and the comment the propositional predicate in the predication relation.[21] Suppose furthermore that the topic/comment partitioning is represented in the AS of the sentence. An interesting consequence then follows: the topic can never be identified with the focus, because by definition, the topic is the subject of the propositional predicate and the focus is contained within that predicate. As an illustration, consider the AS of the sentence in (21), where *the beans* is the topic, as indicated by its context question. As shown in (22), *the beans* is the subject of the predicate in the presuppositional part of the statement (A_1) and is carried over as such to the main assertion (A_2). It follows, therefore, that *the beans* cannot serve as the second term of the equative relation as well.

(21) [$_F$ Fred] ate the beans.
    [What about the beans? Who ate them?]

(22) A_1: the beans$_y$ \ there is an x, such that x ate y
     A_2: the beans$_y$ \ the x (such that x ate y) = Fred

1.1.3 Summary

To summarize briefly: I have suggested in sections 1.1.1 and 1.1.2 that there is a post-LF representation (the Assertion Structure) where certain grammatically relevant aspects of the assertion structure of the sentence, such as the focus-presupposition partitioning, are represented. The main motivation for representing the focus structure of a sentence in terms of its AS rather than at LF is that the focus need not constitute a syntactic constituent. I suggested that in such cases (as well as in others), a context-dependent presupposition provides a predicate that is not part of the LF representation.

I suggested furthermore that the focus structure of a sentence is articulated in the form of two ordered assertions. The first assertion represents the background assertion, that is, the presuppositional part of the statement. The background assertion, provided by the context question (explicitly or implicitly associated with the statement), has the form of an existential quantification. The second assertion represents the main assertion of the statement; it assigns a value to the variable introduced by the background assertion. Contrastive focus resembles noncontrastive focus in that it introduces a variable and a value for that variable, but differs from it in that its background assertion is provided by a statement (rather than by a *wh*-question). Like emphasis, contrastive focus makes a statement about the truth or correctness of (certain aspects of) the presupposition provided by its context statement.

Introduction 11

I noted that the AS is also the natural place to encode the topic/comment articulation of the sentence, in the sense of Reinhart 1982. The topic of the assertion is the subject of an open propositional predicate (where the propositional predicate is the comment). Because the focus assigns a value to a variable contained within the comment, it follows that the topic must be distinct from the focus.

1.1.4 Quantifier Binding and the Assertion Structure

I now turn to data on quantifier binding that provide some support for incorporating the AS of a sentence, with the properties summarized in section 1.1.3, as part of its grammatical representation. As first noted in Zubizarreta 1993, the QP object *each/every N* may bind the pronoun contained within the subject if and only if the subject is focused in English as well as in other languages (e.g., French and Spanish). In other words, although the English and French counterparts in (23) are not possible under a wide focus interpretation (i.e., as answers to *What will happen*?), they are possible if the subject is focused, as shown in (24). (This interpretation requires main prominence on the subject, a property to which I will return in section 1.2.)

(23) a. [_F_ *His* mother will accompany *each/every boy* the first day of school].
   b. [_F_ *Sa* mère accompagnera *chaque enfant* le premier jour d'école].
      [What will happen?]
      [Bound reading: *]

(24) a. [_F_ *His* mother] will accompany *each/every boy* the first day of school.
      [I would like to know who will accompany each/every boy the first day of school.]
   b. [_F_ *Sa* mère] accompagnera *chaque enfant* le premier jour d'école.
      [Je voudrais savoir qui accompagnera chaque enfant le premier jour d'école.]
      [Bound reading: OK]

I suggest that one important ingredient of the representation of (24) is the indefinite status of the focused subject in its AS. In effect, a distributive QP object can take scope over an indefinite subject.

(25) A person should accompany each/every boy.
   [Distributive reading: OK]

The indefiniteness of the focused subject is to be attributed to the existential presupposition associated with such sentences, which is provided precisely by their context questions.

(26) for each/every *y*, *y* a boy, there is an *x*, such that *x* will accompany *y* ...

Another property is relevant to the well-formedness of (24), namely the type and status of the QP object. If the QP object is a negative phrase, it cannot bind into a focused subject (compare (24) with (27)). This follows immediately from the fact that the context question does not allow a bound reading either.

(27) a. [F *His* mother] will accompany *no boy* the first day of school.
  [I would like to know who will accompany no boy the first day of school.]
  b. [F *Sa* mère] n'accompagnera *aucun enfant* le premier jour d'école.
  [Je voudrais savoir qui n'accompagnera aucun enfant le premier jour d'école.]
  [Bound reading: *]

This observation is of course immediately related to the fact that a negative object can never have scope over an indefinite subject (see Hornstein 1995, Beghelli 1995).

(28) Someone/A person should accompany no boy.
  [Distributive reading: *]

Furthermore, a QP object *each/every N* can bind a pronoun contained within an indefinite subject, but a QP negative object (e.g., *nobody/no person*) may not do so.

(29) a. Someone that *he* can trust should accompany *each/every boy*.
  [Bound reading: OK]
  b. Someone that *he* can trust should accompany *no boy*.
  [Bound reading: *]

Given such facts, it would seem that we could provide an LF account of the contrast between (23) and (24), on the one hand, and of the contrast between (24) and (27), on the other hand. Along the lines pursued by Hornstein (1995), we could say that focused subjects (like indefinite subjects) are "reconstructed" at LF to their VP-internal position and that d-linked objects in the sense of Desetsky 1987 (like *each/every N*) move out of the VP (to [Spec, Agr$_O$]) at LF. The subject would then be c-commanded by the QP object in such cases. This account would thus capture both the fact that the QP object *each/every N* can distribute over an indefinite subject and the fact that the QP object *each/every N* can bind a pronoun contained within an indefinite subject. Note that this analysis claims that there is an intimate link between quantifier scope and quantifier binding. Interestingly, a closer look at the analysis and the data reveals important shortcomings. On the one hand, the account is unilluminating because it fails to explain why focused DP subjects behave like indefinite subjects. On the other hand, it is empirically inadequate precisely because it claims that there is an intimate link between quantifier scope and quantifier binding. Consider the contrast in (30). In effect, all speakers consulted (including those who readily allow the bound reading in (31)) agreed, on the one hand, that the QP object *everybody* can have scope over an indefinite subject (see (30a)) and, on the other hand, that the QP object *everybody* cannot bind a pronoun contained within an indefinite or focused subject (see (30b–c)).[22]

(30) a. Someone/A person will accompany everybody.
 [Distributive reading: OK]
 b. Someone from *his* entourage will accompany *everybody*.
 [Bound reading: *]
 c. [$_F$ *His* mother] will accompany *everybody*.
 [Bound reading: *]
 [I would like to know who will accompany everybody.]

(31) *Everybody* promised *he* would arrive on time for the meeting.
 [Bound reading: OK]

The same contrast is found with French *tout le monde*.

(32) a. Quelqu'un accompagnera tout le monde.
 [Distributive reading: OK]
 b. Quelqu'un de *son* entourage accompagnera *tout le monde*.
 [Bound reading: *]
 c. [$_F$ *Sa* mère] accompagnera *tout le monde*.
 [Bound reading: *]

(33) *Tout le monde* a promis qu'il arriverait à l'heure pour la réunion.
 [Bound reading: OK]

The difference between *each/every N* (*chaque N*) and *everybody* (*tout le monde*) lies in the fact that the former is descriptively richer than the latter. I suggest that this is precisely why *each/every N* (*chaque N*), but not *everybody* (*tout le monde*), can function as a sentence topic in the AS and why the topic status of such QPs plays a fundamental role in the pronominal binding facts in (24).[23]

More precisely, I am claiming that there are two parts to the analysis of sentences like (24).

(34) a. There must be a distributive reading; that is, the QP object must have scope over the focused subject.
 b. The QP object functions as a topic; as such, it can bind a pronoun within its scope.

As an illustration, consider the AS analysis of (24a) given in (35). A_1 encodes the scope relation between the object and the subject (see (34a)), and A_2 encodes the fact that the pronoun is bound by the QP that functions as the topic of the main assertion (see (34b)).

(35) A_1: for each/every y, y a boy, there is an x, such that x will accompany y ...
 A_2: for each/every y, y a boy, (the x, such that x will accompany $y = his_y$ mother)

The proposal that there are two conditions that must be met in order to ensure the felicity of the binding relation in (24) (as summarized in (34)) receives further support from the three-way contrast in (36). The QP object is *chaque enfant* 'each child' in (36a), *aucun enfant* 'no child' in (36b), and *aucun de ces enfants* 'none of those children' in (36c). The last example gives a somewhat marginal result with respect to the intended pronominal binding reading: worse than (36a) but clearly better than (36b). I suggest that the reason is that *aucun de ces enfants* (being a negative phrase) cannot have scope over the indefinite subject (as indicated by the lack of a linked interpretation in the corresponding question). On the other hand, because *aucun de ces enfants* is a partitive (which, moreover, contains a demonstrative determiner), it can function as a topic.[24] Thus, (36c) lacks property (34a), but it has property (34b), giving rise to the less than perfect judgment with respect to pronominal binding.

(36) a. [$_F$ *Sa* mère] accompagnera *chaque enfant* le premier jour d'école. (cf. (24b))
 [Je voudrais savoir qui accompagnera chaque enfant le premier jour d'école.]
 [Bound reading: OK]

b. [_F_ *Sa* mère] n'accompagnera *aucun enfant* le premier jour d'école. (cf. (27b))
   [Je voudrais savoir qui n'accompagnera aucun enfant le premier jour d'école.]
   [Bound reading: *]
c. [_F_ *Sa* mère] n'accompagnera *aucun de ces enfants* le premier jour d'école.
   . [Je voudrais savoir qui n'accompagnera aucun de ces enfants le premier jour d'école.]
   [Bound reading: ?]

1.1.5 Conclusion
In this section I made explicit how the notion of focus should be understood in this work: basically, in the way defined by Chomsky (1971, 1976) and Jackendoff (1972), as the nonpresupposed part of the sentence. I argued that the focus/presupposition partitioning of the sentence (or *focus structure*) should be represented in the AS of the sentence. I based the suggestion on the fact that the focus structure of a statement must be represented in tandem with its (implicit or explicit) context question or statement. The context provides the background assertion in the form of an existentially quantified proposition, and the main assertion of the statement provides a value for the variable introduced by the background. The background is therefore ordered prior to the main assertion by definition. I suggested furthermore that the notion of pragmatic sentence topic should also be represented in the AS, in terms of a subject/predicate relation. I provided some new data on the interaction of focus and quantifier binding as empirical motivation for the representation of focus and topic with the above-mentioned properties (see (24) and its associated AS in (35)). Although I have concluded from such data that quantifier binding may be defined in the AS in some cases, this conclusion must not be interpreted as entailing that LF is irrelevant to quantifier binding. As we will see in chapter 3, Spanish provides evidence that there are asymmetries with respect to quantifier binding that cannot be attributed to differences in AS. In effect, in this language QPs in preverbal subject position and QPs in postverbal subject position differ in their ability to bind a pronoun contained within a fronted object; compare (37a) with (37b).

(37) a. A   su   hijo, *cada madre*   lo   acompañará
         ACC her son each mother   ACC.CL will-accompany
         el primer día de escuela.
         the first day of school
         [Binding: OK]
         'Each mother will accompany her son the first day of school.'
   b. A   *su*   hijo, lo   acompañará   *cada madre*
         ACC her son ACC.CL will-accompany each mother
         el primer día de escuela.
         the first day of school
         [Binding: *]
         'Each mother will accompany her son the first day of school.'

Although it is true that a preverbal subject can function as a sentence topic and a postverbal subject cannot, this cannot be the cause of the asymmetry in (37).[25] This is shown by the fact that in (38a–b) the preverbal but not the postverbal subject *ningún padre* may bind the pronoun contained in the fronted object and that negative phrases (unless they are partitives) cannot be interpreted as sentence topics, whatever their position in the sentence might be.[26]

(38) a. A   su$_i$ hijo, ningún padre$_i$ lo   quiere castigar.
         ACC his child no   father ACC.CL wants to-punish
         'No father wants to punish his own child.'
   b. ?*A   su$_i$ hijo no lo   quiere castigar   ningún padre$_i$.
         ACC his child not ACC.CL wants to-punish no   father
         'No father wants to punish his own child.'

We may conclude therefore that quantifier binding may be licensed either in the LF representation or the AS of the sentence.

1.2 Results Obtained in Chapters 2 and 3: A Preview

As noted at several points in section 1.1, the prosody of a sentence is intimately related to its F-structure. Thus, (39a) (with main prominence on *pie*) is compatible with the F-structures in (5a–c) (repeated in (40a–c), (39b) (with main prominence on *John*) is compatible with the F-structure in (5d) (repeated in (40d)), and (39c) is compatible with the F-structures in (5e–f) (repeated in (40e–f)).[27]

(39) a. John ate the píe.
   b. Jóhn ate the pie.
   c. John áte the pie.
   d. He ate the píe.
   e. John áte it.
   f. He áte it.

(40) a. [_F John [ate [the pie]]].
      [What happened?]
   b. [John [_F ate [the pie]]].
      [What did John do?]
   c. [John [ate [_F the pie]]].
      [What did John eat?]
   d. [[_F John] [ate [the pie]]].
      [Who ate the pie?]
   e. [[_F John] [[_F ate] [the pie]]].
      [What happened to the pie?]
   f. [John [[_F ate] the pie]].
      [What did John do with the pie?]

The main goal of chapter 2 is to describe the correspondence between F-structure and phrasal prominence in Germanic (in particular, in German and English) and in Romance (in particular, in Spanish and French). The novelty of the analysis to be proposed lies in its empirical scope. Previous studies that have dealt with the focus-prosody relation in Germanic did not examine Romance. I claim that in order to attain an accurate view of this relation, it is important to examine both groups of languages. With Chomsky (1971) and Jackendoff (1972), I defend the position that in Germanic and Romance, it is phrasal prominence that is relevant in determining the F-structure(s) of a sentence, a claim that has not gone unchallenged. Gussenhoven (1984) and Selkirk (1984, 1995) defend the view, based on an analysis of Germanic, that it is the distribution of pitch accents rather than phrasal prominence that is relevant in determining the F-structure(s) of a sentence. Under this view, the Nuclear Stress Rule (NSR) is a late rhythmic rule insensitive to the F-structure of the sentence. I argue that this view cannot be sustained when Romance is taken into consideration, as well as Germanic.

I hypothesize that the assignment of primary stress can be dissociated from the assignment of subsidiary stresses. Furthermore, with Chomsky (1971) and Jackendoff (1972), I distinguish phrasal prominence related to contrastive focus or emphasis from phrasal prominence related to noncontrastive focus (see section 1.1.1). The former is generated by the Emphatic/Contrastive Stress Rule and the latter by the NSR.

Below I lay out some of the basic facts in Germanic and Romance and the empirical generalizations that underlie them, which any adequate theory of nuclear stress (NS) must account for. I argue that in Germanic the position of NS (marked by ´) is the result of an intricate interplay of two rules, one sensitive to an ordering defined in terms of selection and another sensitive to an ordering defined in terms of asymmetric c-command (on the latter notion, see section 1.3.4). In both (41) and (42) (with a wide focus interpretation), it is the "lowest" constituent that receives NS, but in the two cases "lowest" is defined along different dimensions. In (41) the "lowest argument" defined in terms of a primitive notion of "selectional ordering" (based on the lexicosyntactic structures proposed in Hale and Keyser 1991, 1993) receives NS. In (42) the "lowest constituent" defined in terms of asymmetric c-command receives NS. I will refer to the former as the *selection-driven NSR* (or *S-NSR*) and to the latter as the *constituent-driven NSR* (or *C-NSR*).[28]

(41) a. A bóy has danced.
 b. A dóg disappeared.
 c. John ate the píe.

(42) a. A boy has dánced.
 b. A dog mysteriously disappéared.
 c. John ate the pie in the kítchen.

The examples in (43) and (44) (with a wide focus interpretation) illustrate the S-NSR and the C-NSR, respectively, for German. In (43) it is the "lowest argument" in the "selectional ordering" that receives NS, and in (44) it is the "lowest constituent" in the "asymmetric c-command ordering" that receives NS.

(43) a. Es heißt, daß ein Júnge getanzt hat.
   it is-said that a   boy   danced has
   'It is said that a boy has danced.'
 b. Das Táxi kommt.
   the taxi is coming
 c. Karl hat an einem Papíer gearbeitet.
   Karl has on a   paper worked
   'Karl has worked on a paper.'

(44) a. Es heißt, daß ein Junge getánzt hat. (cf. (43a))
  b. Das Taxi kommt spǎt.
    the taxi is coming late
  c. Karl hat an einem kleinen Tisch geárbeitet.
    Karl has on a small table worked
    'Karl has worked on a small table.'

The modularized NSR in (45) will be shown to account not only for Germanic, but also for the differences between Germanic and Romance.

(45) *Revised NSR*
  S-*NSR*: Given two sister categories C_i and C_j, if C_i and C_j are selectionally ordered, the one lower in the selectional ordering is more prominent.
  C-*NSR*: Given two sister categories C_i and C_j, the one lower in the asymmetric c-command ordering is more prominent.

The main difference between Germanic and Romance lies in the fact that phrasal prominence in Romance is sensitive only to the C-NSR. Thus, the Spanish and French counterparts (46a) and (47a), but not (46b) and (47b), are well formed with a wide focus interpretation. Compare these examples with (41a) and (43a). (I mark NS in Romance with underlining, in order to avoid confusion between accent marks in these languages and the conventional orthographic mark for word stress.)

(46) a. Un niño ha <u>bailado</u>.
    a boy has danced
  b. *Un <u>niño</u> ha bailado.
(47) a. Un garçón a <u>dansé</u>.
  b. *Un <u>garçon</u> a dansé.

To recapitulate: In chapter 2 I show that both the S-NSR and the C-NSR are active in German and in English and, furthermore, that in German the S-NSR has primacy over the C-NSR (the latter being more general than the former). In Romance, on the other hand, only the C-NSR applies. I also argue that, given the nature of the revised NSR, it is natural to assume that it applies in the syntactic component of the grammar. More specifically, it applies at the point of Spell-Out, in other words, at the end of the syntactic derivation (see the architecture of the grammar in section 1.3.3).

There is another dimension along which languages vary. Whereas in German, English, and French defocalized and anaphoric constituents (as well as functional categories) are "metrically invisible" with respect to the NSR, in Spanish and Italian all phonologically specified elements are "metrically visible." This difference accounts for the facts below. The German, English, and French examples in (48), (49), and (50) (with NS on the initial phrase) may be associated with a noncontrastive focus interpretation, as shown by the fact that such sentences are compatible with the context question given immediately below each example. (The metrically invisible constituents are marked with italics.)

(48) Den Húnd   *hat Karl*   geschlagen.
 the dog(ACC) has Karl (NOM) beaten
 'Karl beat the dog.'
 [What did Karl do?]

(49) Jóhn *ate an apple*.
 [Who ate an apple?]

(50) Jean *a   mangé une pomme*.
 Jean has eaten an apple
 [Who ate an apple?]

On the other hand, sentences with main prominence on a phrase-internal constituent in Spanish and Italian are not compatible with a noncontrastive focus interpretation. This is shown in (51a) and (52a); such examples are not appropriate answers to the specified context questions. Main prominence on a phrase-internal constituent in these languages is necessarily interpreted as contrastive or emphatic; see (51b) and (52b) (contrastive/emphatic stress is marked with capitals).

(51) a. *Juan *comió una manzana*.
  Juan ate   an apple
  [Who ate an apple?]
 b. JUAN comió una manzana (no Pedro).
  Juan ate   an apple (not Pedro)

(52) a. *Gianni *ha mangiato una mela*.
  Gianni has eaten   an apple
  [Who ate an apple?]
 b. GIANNI ha mangiato una mela (non Piero).
  Gianni has eaten   an apple (not Piero)

The generalization that NS must be rightmost in the phrase in Spanish and Italian is further confirmed by the examples in (53) and (54), which

Introduction 21

are incompatible with a focus-neutral interpretation. Compare these with the French and English examples in (55).

(53) a. *María puso el <u>libro</u> *sobre la mesa.*
María put the book on the table
[What did María put on the table?]
b. María puso el LIBRO sobre la mesa (no la revista).
María put the book on the table (not the journal)

(54) a. *Maria ha messo il <u>libro</u> *sul tavolo.*
Maria has put the book on-the table
[What did Maria put on the table?]
b. Maria ha messo il LIBRO sul tavola (non il periodico).
Maria has put the book on-the table (not the journal)

(55) a. Marie a mis le <u>livre</u> *sur la table.*
Marie has put the book on the table
[What did Marie put on the table?]
b. Mary put the bóok *on the table.*
[What did Mary put on the table?]

The contrast between the French examples in (47b) (which shows the incompatibility of phrase-internal NS with a wide focus interpretation) and (50)/(55a) (phrase-internal NS with narrow focus on the subject and on the object, respectively) is very revealing. It shows that the ill-formedness of (46b) in Spanish and of (47b) in French indeed cannot be accounted for by an intonational constraint that requires that the nuclear pitch accent in Romance be right-adjacent to the intonational phrase boundary (as suggested in Zubizarreta 1995b, 1996). Such facts, I believe, are hard to reconcile with a pitch-based account of focus (see Gussenhoven 1984, Selkirk 1984, 1995).

As mentioned above, the F-structure of the sentence is constrained by the location of main prominence. I suggest that this is captured by the *Focus Prominence Rule*.[29]

(56) *Focus Prominence Rule (FPR)*
Given two sister categories C_i (marked [+F]) and C_j (marked [−F]), C_i is more prominent than C_j.

The coexistence of the FPR and the NSR in the grammar gives rise to cases in which the output of the NSR contradicts the output of the FPR. How does the grammar resolve such contradictions? In Germanic (and in

French) this is done by treating defocalized constituents (i.e., constituents marked [−F]) as metrically invisible for the NSR; see (48)–(50) and (55).

But how is it done in Spanish and in Italian, where all phonologically overt constituents are metrically visible? This question is addressed in chapter 3, where I argue that the defocalized constituent undergoes movement (i.e., copying and deletion). I refer to this process as a case of *prosodically motivated movement (p-movement)*. Thus, the appropriate form of the answer (using a complete sentence) to the context questions in (51a) and (52a) and to the context questions in (53a) and (54a) is as shown in (57) and (58), respectively. As these examples illustrate, p-movement of the defocalized phrase leaves the focused phrase in a position to receive NS via the C-NSR (i.e., the focused phrase ends up as the lowest constituent in the asymmetric c-command ordering).

(57) a. Comió una manzana Juan.
          ate   an apple   Juan
     b. ?Ha mangiato una mela Gianni.

(58) a. María puso sobre la mesa el libro.
          María put   on   the table the book
     b. Maria ha messo sul tavolo il libro.

P-movement is subject to the condition known as Last Resort, like other movement rule (on Last Resort, see section 1.3.2). Given that p-movement feeds the NSR, p-movement must also apply prior to Spell-Out, a conclusion that is shown to be empirically correct. More precisely, I suggest that the three prosodically related rules—the NSR, the FPR, and p-movement—apply at the end of the syntactic derivation (i.e., just before the derivation branches); see section 1.3.3.

Although VOS order in Spanish and VOS order in Italian are generated by p-movement, they have slightly different properties. In Italian, but not in Spanish, VOS is sensitive to the relative heaviness of VO with respect to S; see the contrast between (57a) and (57b). I suggest that this is due to the fact that VOS has different sources in the two languages. Abstracting away from the details of the clausal structure of these languages (see chapter 3), I propose that in Spanish, VOS is derived from VSO via leftward movement of O across S, whereas in Italian (which lacks VSO), VOS is derived from SVO (via leftward movement of VO across S). This syntactic analysis of Italian VOS, in conjunction with the Relative Weight Constraint in (59) (also discussed in Guasti and Nespor 1996), accounts for the less than perfect status of the Italian example in (57b). Compare

Introduction 23

this with the perfect status of *Ha mangiato una mela GIANNI* (where the subject *GIANNI* carries extra-heavy pitch) or of *Ha mangiato una mela solo Gianni* (where the subject *solo Gianni* 'only Gianni' is branching).

(59) *The Relative Weight Constraint*
P-movement of constituent A across constituent B is degraded if A is "metrically heavier" than B.
A is "metrically heavier" than B if A is branching and B is not (where only metrically visible material counts for computing "branchingness"), unless B has heavier pitch than A.

To recapitulate: In chapter 3 I uncover a new type of movement—namely, a prosodically motivated movement—which plays the same kind of role as metrical invisibility does with respect to the NSR.[30]

1.3 The Theoretical Framework

1.3.1 The Minimalist Program

The guiding ideas assumed in this book are those outlined by Chomsky in "Categories and Transformations" (1995), referred to as the *Minimalist Program*. A grammar is defined to be

a generative procedure that constructs pairs (π, λ) that are interpreted at the articulatory-perceptual (A-P) and conceptual-intentional (C-I) interfaces, respectively, as "instructions" to the performance systems. π is a PF representation and λ and LF representation, each consisting of "legitimate objects" that ... receive an interpretation... (p. 219)

A generated representation consisting entirely of such objects is said to satisfy the condition of *Full Interpretation (FI)*. Under minimalist assumptions, there are no levels of linguistic structure apart from the two interface levels PF and LF.[31] The grammar determines a set of derivations. Chomsky states that "[a] derivation *converges* at one of the interface levels if it yields a representation satisfying FI at this level, and *converges* if it converges at both interface level, PF and LF; otherwise, it *crashes*" (pp. 219–220).[32]

It appears that a linguistic expression cannot be defined just as pair (π, λ) formed by a convergent derivation. In addition, its derivation must be *optimal*, satisfying various natural economy conditions: locality of movement, the "Shortest Movement" Condition, and so on. A grammar thus generates three relevant sets of computations: the set of derivations, the set of convergent derivations (a subset of the former determined by

FI), and the set of admissible derivations (a subset of the former determined by the economy conditions). A derivation starts with some *array* of lexical items. The computational component of the grammar maps such an array to a pair (π, λ). The LF representation λ is a constituent structure of the standard type. The elementary relations at play in such a constituent structure are defined in the usual way. Two constituents X and Y can be joined into a bigger one as follows:

(60) $Z = \{_\alpha X, Y\}$

The constituent Z in (60) is a *set* with elements X and Y. Z has a mark α, called its *label*, that indicates which one of the constituents X and Y Z is a projection of. Suppose Z is a projection of X. If X is a minimal category, then the label α of Z is X itself. Otherwise, α is the label of X. The category H with which α is identified is called the *head* of Z (see Chomsky 1994; 1995, 241–249). The elementary constituent structure just discussed falls under what is called *X-bar theory*. If X is a minimal category and Z is a projection of X, then Y is called the *complement* of X. If X is a branching constituent, Y is called the *specifier* of Z.[33] In addition to the grammatical relations defined by X-bar theory, there is the *adjunction relation*. A category Y may be adjoined to a category X with label α to yield the category W with label $\langle \alpha, \alpha \rangle$ as in (61).

(61) $W = \{_{\langle \alpha, \alpha \rangle} Y, X\}$, α the label of the head of the structure

In the structure in (61), X does not count as a category, but only as a *segment* of the category W. W thus has two segments, X and itself.

As an illustration of these formal notions, consider the sentence in (62).

(62) There is someone in the room.

The initial array for (62) is given in (63).

(63) {room, the, in, someone, is, there, T}

The lexical categories in (63) are *room*, *in*, *someone*, *is*, and *there*. The functional categories are the determiner *the* and T(ense). Following Chomsky (1995), I am assuming that there is no category Agreement (see in particular pages 349–377); but, following Sportiche (1992), I will be postulating additional functional categories for clitics (see section 3.1.3). The derivation of the representation (π, λ) for (62) starts with joining the determiner *the* and the noun *room*, producing the constituent in (64) with label *the*.

(64) $\{_{the}$ the, room$\}$

Introduction

The joining of *the* and *room* is a particular instance of the operation called *Merge*, one of the central procedures for combining syntactic objects in the computational system (see Chomsky 1995, 226, 243, 246–248, 289–290).

A representation equivalent to (64) is (65).

(65)
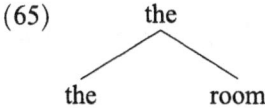

In this book I will follow the established practice of using the simplified representation in (66) or one of the equivalent representations in (67).

(66)
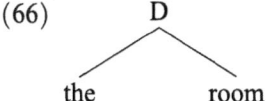

(67) a. [$_D$ the room]
     b. [$_{DP}$ the room]

In other words, a subpart of the set of features that constitute the head determiner *the* is to used to label the category projected from it—specifically, in (66) and (67a), the categorial feature D. A lexical entry such as *the* is made up of three collections of features (see Chomsky 1995, 230–235, 276–312):

(68) a. phonological features such as [*ends with a vowel*]
     b. semantic features such as [*antecedently presented*]
     c. formal features such as [*determiner*]

The distinction between formal and semantic features refers to a difference in behavior with respect to the computation: formal features are accessible in the course of the computation, semantic features are not.

Returning to the derivation of the representations (π, λ) for the sentence in (62), we can take the next step to be the merging of *in* with the syntactic object in (64) (= (65)) into the new combined syntactic object in (69).

(69)
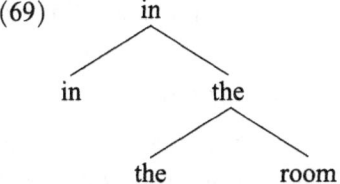

After (69) is created, *in* and *the* mutually check their Case features. This is achieved by adjoining the set FF(*the*) of formal features of *the* to the head *in*. This adjunction is an instance of the second central operation in the computational system, *Move α*, now recast as *Move f(eature)* (see Chomsky 1995, 249–276).[34] In the case of (69) the movement required for Case checking is *covert*.

After this covert Case checking, the object in (69) is merged with *someone*, yielding (70).

(70)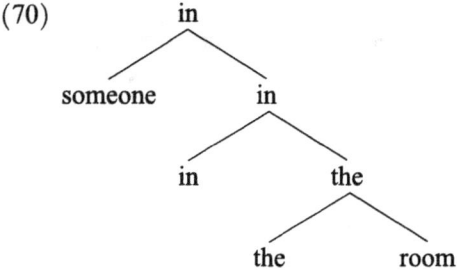

I leave open whether the structure (70) is an adjunction structure, with label ⟨*in, in*⟩, or a *specifier-head-complement* structure with label *in*. (70) is a *small clause* in the sense of Stowell 1981.

The next step is to merge the small clause with *is*. The subject *someone* of the small clause bears a Case feature that must be checked. However, the verb *is* has no Case feature, so no movement takes place within the structure (70).

Next, T is merged with [$_V$ *is someone in the room*]. T has four collections of formal features that need to be checked; the feature affix-of-V, a Case feature, φ-features, and the feature D. The feature D is what Chomsky (1995) calls a *strong feature* (see pp. 232–235). In essence, a strong feature is a feature that must be checked overtly. There are two possibilities for checking the strong feature D on T. The first is to move the item *someone* overtly to the specifier position of T. The second possibility is to merge [$_T$ *is someone in the room*] with the item *there* from the array. The item *there* has no semantic features and bears only one formal feature, D. In other words, *there* is the collection of features in (71) (see Chomsky 1995, 287, 340–348).

(71) [P$_{there}$, D], with P$_{there}$ the phonological matrix for *there*

The grammar prefers to insert *there* rather than overtly move *someone* because of a principle called *Procrastinate*, which favors *covert movement* over *overt movement* (see Chomsky 1995, 254, 264, 266). Note that merging *there* and T will not provide for the checking of the Case features or φ-features of T. The latter features will be checked by adjoining covertly to T the set of formal features of *someone*, FF (*someone*).

The final step in the derivation of the structural description of (62) is the overt adjunction of the auxiliary *is* to T to check the feature affix-of-V of T. In the end, the LF representation created by the derivation is as shown in (72) (The overt part of the structure is highlighted in boldface.)

(72) **[$_T$ there [**$_T$[$_T$ FF(*someone*) [$_T$ is T]] **[$_V$ {***is***}** [someone **[$_P$**[$_P$ FF(*the*) in] **[$_D$ the [$_N$ room**]]]]]]

The complex [$_T$ FF(*someone*) [$_T$ *is* T]] in (72) is the outcome of the two adjunctions to the functional category T performed to check the formal features of T other than D. Similarly, the complex [$_P$ FF(*the*) in] is the outcome of the adjunction required for the mutual checking of their Case features by *in* and *the*. Movement is copying (see Chomsky 1993; 1995, 202–212). The element {*is*} is the trace (invisible at PF) left by the movement of *is*. Following Chomsky (1995), I assume that the set FF(*LI*) of formal features of a lexical item LI has no PF representation. Then, *overt movement is pied-piping*: overt movement occurs when an element bigger than FF(*LI*) is moved. It is furthermore assumed that *only categories—that is, heads and maximal projections (excluding segments)—can undergo overt movement*.

Consider next the sentence in (73).

(73) Someone is in the room.

The initial array for (73) is the same as the one for (62), less the item *there*.

(74) {room, the, in, someone, is, T}

The derivation of the LF representation for (73) will proceed as above, except that, in the case of (73), *someone* has to check the strong feature D of T. In other words, in the case of (73), *someone* raises overtly to the specifier position of T. This displacement allows for the concomitant checking of the Case features and of the φ-features on T. The LF representation for (73) is the structure in (75), where {*someone*} is the copy (invisible at PF) created by the raising of *someone*.

(75) **[$_T$ someone [**$_T$[$_T$ is T] **[$_V$ {***is***}** [{*someone*} **[$_P$**[$_P$FF(*the*) in] **[$_D$ the [$_N$ room**]]]]]]

The PF representation of (62) (resp. (73)) is derived by applying *Spell-Out* to the structure in (72) (resp. (75)). A central part of Spell-Out is an operation that associates a phonological matrix to each lexical item. There are various ways of carrying out that mapping. One method, suggested by Chomsky (1995, 229–233), assumes that each lexical item comes into the syntactic tree with its phonological features and that those features are *stripped away* by Spell-Out. A possibly different method is found within the framework of *Distributed Morphology* (Halle and Marantz 1993), where the semantic and formal features of each lexical item are mapped onto a level of *Morphological Structure (MS)*. MS representations are subsequently associated with phonological matrices. I will leave the question open here, since nothing in my discussion or proposals hinges on any particular choice of framework. I now turn to a more general discussion of Move and the architecture of the grammar.

1.3.2 On Move f, Last Resort, and the Minimal Link Condition

On general minimalist assumptions, the operation *Move* is driven by the necessity to ensure convergence at LF and at PF. In particular, it is driven by morphological considerations: the requirement that some feature f must be checked in order for LF to satisfy FI. The necessity of checking itself arises from the fact that some formal features are not legitimate objects at LF. This is the case, for example, for the feature affix-of-V, the feature D and the ϕ-features when carried by the category T, and for Case features in general (see Chomsky 1995, 277–286). A checked feature becomes invisible at LF and, in general, inaccessible to the computation (pp. 279–286). Thus, in the examples discussed in section 1.3.1, the displacements that occur are driven by the necessity to check the Case features on the pairs of items (*in, the*) and (T, *someone*), as well as the feature D, the ϕ-features, and the feature affix-of-V on T. For the purpose of LF convergence, then, the minimal operation raises just lexical features: Move α is Move f. Of course, more material may need to be moved to ensure convergence in specific cases. In general, Move is subject to the following economy condition (see Chomsky 1995, 262):[35]

(76) The operation Move carries along just enough material for convergence.

In other words, to paraphrase Chomsky 1995, Move "seeks to raise just f." Whatever additional material is required to move for convergence involves some kind of generalized pied-piping. Output conditions determine what is carried along, if anything, when f is raised. There are empirical reasons for assuming that, when the operation Move f applies to f belonging to the lexical item LI[f], it automatically carries along FF(LI[f]), the set of formal features of LI[f] (see Chomsky 261–312, 340–378). On minimalist assumptions, Move f is a *last resort* operation in the following sense:

(77) Move f raises f to target K only if f enters into a checking relation with a feature of the head of K or with a feature of some element adjoined to the head of K.

The application of Move f is governed by the *Minimal Link Condition* (see Chomsky 1995, 294–312, 355–367, and in particular 358).

(78) *Minimal Link Condition (MLC)*
α can raise to target K only if there is no legitimate operation Move β targeting K, where β c-commands α.

The MLC is a particular rendering of the requirement that each displacement be the "shortest possible." The formulation of the MLC can be made more natural by reinterpreting movement as "attraction": the raising of α to target K is formalized as the attraction of α by K. *Attract f* is defined in terms of the condition (79), incorporating the MLC and Last Resort (see Chomsky 1995, 297–312).

(79) K *attracts f* if f is the closest feature that can enter into a checking relation with a feature of the head of K or with a feature of some element adjoined to the head of K.

As mentioned in section 1.2, I will argue in chapter 3 that not all movements are motivated by feature-checking considerations. In particular, I will argue that there exists a *p(rosodically motivated) movement*, the object of which is not to check features but to resolve a prosodically contradictory situation; this operation also obeys Last Resort. The question arises whether the proposed analysis can be made compatible with the formalization developed for feature checking, namely, a formalization in which Last Resort is incorporated into the definition of the movement operation itself. I will address this question in section 3.5.

1.3.3 The Focus-Prosody Relation and the Architecture of the Grammar

Let us now return to the question raised in note 32 concerning the status of the FPR within the Minimalist Program. As mentioned in section

1.3.1, I follow Chomsky in adopting the hypothesis that the only PF-LF interactions relevant to convergence are those that are consequences of the derivation itself (see Chomsky 1995, 220). In other words, convergence is determined by independent inspection of the interface levels. At first sight, this *Modularity of Convergence Hypothesis (MCH)* appears to be invalidated by the existence of a rule such as the FPR. In general, the hypothesis is invalidated whenever properties of "surface structure" play a role in determining semantic interpretation; see Chomsky 1971. Another feature of the FPR also makes it incompatible with the principles put forward in Chomsky 1995: it violates the *Inclusiveness Principle*. This principle states that outputs consist of nothing beyond properties of items of the lexicon, in other words, that the interface levels consist of nothing more than arrangements of lexical features (see Chomsky 1995, 225). However, the feature [F] mentioned in the FPR is not a lexical feature; nor is the relation of relative prosodic prominence that is mentioned in the rule. The Inclusiveness Principle gives significance to the MCH. In effect, the MCH has content only within a fairly disciplined formal approach: it is clear that, if one can make free use of diacritics in the course of the derivation, it will be possible to respect the letter of the MCH and still circumvent its intent. One consequence of the Inclusiveness Principle is precisely to forbid free usage of such diacritic features. On the one hand, I will suggest that the Inclusiveness Principle must be weakened in order to allow for the features [F] and [prosodic prominence] at the interface levels. On the other hand, I will suggest that the architecture of the grammar must be slightly revised if the constraint expressed by the FPR is to be amenable to a treatment in terms of convergence at a single interface, as required by the MCH. Indeed, if the MCH is to be respected, there must exist a phrase marker in the derivation where the properties related by the FPR—namely, [F] and [prosodic prominence]—are jointly defined. As I will show, a proper understanding of the nature of the feature [F] leads to a conception of the grammatical architecture that indeed provides a stretch in the derivation where [F] and [prosodic prominence] may be defined over the same phrase marker.

The features [F] and [prosodic prominence] share a characteristic: they both denote global relational properties of the phrase marker. The feature [F] corresponds to a semantic contrast between two classes of categories in the structure, and [prosodic prominence] refers to a phonological contrast between sister categories (see the formulation of the NSR in section 1.2). By definition, then, these two relations cannot be defined in terms

Introduction

of arrangements of lexical features. They are irreducible properties of the derived phrase marker and, indeed, cannot be defined until the derivation has reached a point where the structure involved is a single phrase marker. Let us call the earliest point in the derivation where this happens Σ-*Structure*.

(80)

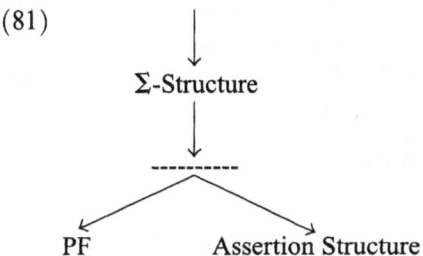

We can take [F] and [prosodic prominence] to be defined over Σ-Structure. The computation continues after Σ-Structure, in particular involving the features [F] and [prosodic prominence]. This is the postcyclic stretch of the derivation, where the NSR and the FPR apply. If these two rules have contradictory outputs, p-movement will also apply (see section 1.2) in that stretch of the derivation. The MCH implies that this part of the computation takes place before the derivation branches (see discussion above). We then have the architecture in (81).

(81)

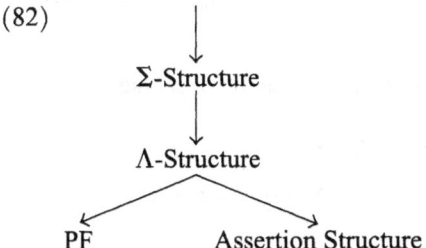

Let us call the last phrase marker in the derivation before it branches Λ-*Structure*. The diagram in (81) is now revised to (82)).

(82)

       ↓
   Σ-Structure
       ↓
   Λ-Structure
   ↙   ↘
PF   Assertion Structure

I will show in chapter 3 that p-movement has an impact on LF. This implies that LF either is Λ-Structure or follows it in the derivation (somewhere on the right branch in the diagram in (82) or (83)).

(83)

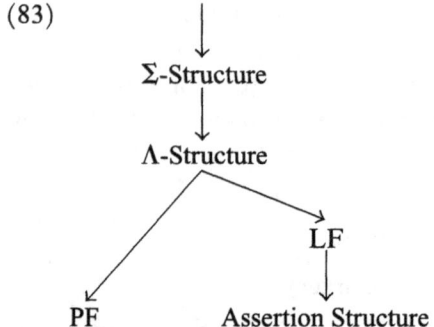

Whether LF is Λ-Structure or some later structure on the path to semantic interpretation is an empirical issue that relates to the nature of covert movement. Recall that movement is formalized as follows in the Minimalist Program. For checking purposes, Attract seeks to raise some feature f from the lexical item LI[f] in accordance with the condition in (79). Attract automatically carries along FF(LI[f]), the set of formal features of LI[f]. Additional material is pied-piped only if required for convergence. Thus, the unmarked case is that of covert movement, since FF(LI[f]) has no PF associated with it. Overt movement occurs as a last resort, when an element bigger than FF(LI[f]) needs to be pied-piped for convergence. We therefore have the equations in (84).

(84)

Let us assume the empirical adequacy of this theory.[36] Then, we can assume that all the feature-checking-driven movement (overt and covert) applies prior to Σ-Structure, and we identify the LF level with Λ-Structure. Accordingly, we revise (83) to (85).

(85)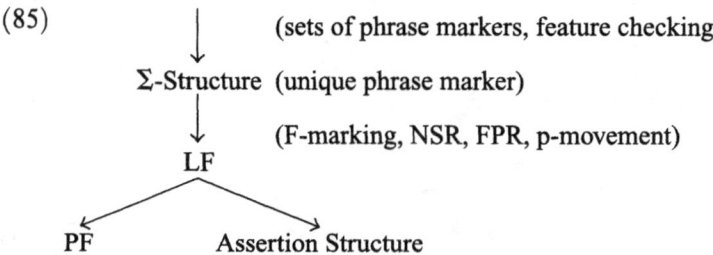

Introduction

We see that, in the end, it is not possible to totally reconcile the FPR with Inclusiveness. We must weaken the principle as follows:

(86) *Inclusiveness Principle (revised)*
The interface levels consist of nothing more than arrangements of lexical features and interpretations of the arrangement of categories within the phrase marker in terms of the focus/nonfocus distinction and in terms of relative prosodic prominence.

Indeed, this revision of the Inclusiveness Principle is required because there is a part of the sound-meaning pairing in a sentence that cannot be reduced to the atomic sound-meaning pairings defined by the lexical items in the sentence. That nonlexical part of the sound-meaning pairing refers to the phrase structure. For example, it includes the FPR. To account for this fact, one must postulate an architecture in which the syntactic derivation proper and the PF interpretation accompany each other for a stretch, namely, the stretch that starts with Σ-Structure and ends with LF. Technically, then, Spell-Out starts before the derivation branches at LF. However, for the sake of simplicity, I will follow the convention of using *Spell-Out* to refer to the part of the interpretive process that branches off the syntactic derivation and leads to PF.

1.3.4 On Asymmetric C-Command

The notion of asymmetric c-command plays an important role in this book. As mentioned in section 1.3.1, I suggest that a subpart of the modularized phrasal NSR (namely, the C-NSR, which has as its ancestor the NSR in Chomsky and Halle 1968) is in essence a correspondence between the asymmetric c-command ordering of the syntax and the prosodic (partial) ordering defined by the assignment of relative prominences to syntactic categories (see chapter 2). Of relevance to my proposal is the view of syntax put forward by Kayne (1994). Asymmetric c-command plays a central part in Kayne's theory, in particular, in relation to the structural organization of the set of terminals. In this theory the following condition holds:

(87) Given two terminals α and β, α precedes β iff there exists a constituent A dominating α and a constituent B dominating β such that A asymmetrically c-commands B.

This principle implies (88).

(88) Given two terminals α and β, there must be a constituent A
dominating α and a constituent B dominating β such that A
asymmetrically c-commands B or vice versa.

In this book I will assume that at least the weaker version of the principle in (87) (adopted in Chomsky 1994, 1995) holds. This weaker version takes the linear ordering of terminals to reflect asymmetric c-command in the following manner:

(89) Given two constituents A and B, if A asymmetrically c-commands
B, then every terminal that A dominates precedes every terminal
that B dominates.

The relation just postulated between linear ordering and asymmetric c-command will ultimately make it possible to formulate the C-NSR as an algorithm that relates prominence and asymmetric c-command, as in (45), repeated here.

(90) *C-NSR*
Given two sister categories C_i and C_j, the one lower in the
asymmetric c-command ordering is more prominent.

The joint requirement of sisterhood and of asymmetric c-command in the structural description of the C-NSR is, of course, contradictory if the classical definition of asymmetric c-command is assumed. It is desirable to preserve a formulation that refers to sisterhood (over one invoking some notion like "local asymmetric c-command," for example), because this is the most natural way of describing prosodic prominence. As I will show in chapter 2, the notion of sisterhood has to be extended to accommodate a phenomenon called "metrical invisibility," and this extension goes some way toward resolving the above-mentioned contradiction. There remain cases that fall outside this extension, though, and that clearly point to the need for a revision of the notion of asymmetric c-command.

The classical notion can be defined as follows. We define *c-command* in terms of *sisterhood* and *domination*:

(91) α c-commands β $=_{\text{def}}$ (a) α and β are sisters or (b) there exists a χ
such that α and χ are sisters and χ dominates β.

The elements α, β, and χ in this definition are taken to be nodes in the syntactic tree. Therefore, for the purpose of that definition, no distinction is made between *categories* and *segments* in the sense of Chomsky 1986 and May 1985 (see section 1.2.1). In particular, the notion of domination

Introduction   35

assumed here is the traditional notion defined over tree diagrams. That notion is to be distinguished from the more restricted notion of *domination by a category* introduced in May 1985 and Chomsky 1986, but it can be equated with the notion of *containment* defined in the same works. The notion of asymmetric c-command is then defined as in (92).

(92) α asymmetrically c-commands β $=_{def}$ α c-commands β and β does not c-command α.

As I will show in chapter 2, we want to able to say that, for example, a specifier asymmetrically c-commands its sister and all the categories contained within it. Accordingly, I will revise c-command as follows. I will assume a narrower notion of c-command, according to which the relation holds only between nodes that are "visible" for the syntactic computation in the sense of Chomsky 1986; in other words, it is restricted to heads and maximal projections (excluding segments). More precisely, I posit the following definition:

(93) α c-commands β $=_{def}$ α and β are visible to the syntactic computation (i.e., are either heads or maximal projections (excluding segments)) and (a) α and β are sisters or (b) there exists a χ such that α and χ are sisters and χ dominates β.

I also introduce the natural convention stated in (94).

(94) If α c-commands β, then α c-commands χ, χ a projection of β that does not contain α.

In other words, whereas (93) defines a *direct relation of c-command* between two nodes, (94) defines an *indirect relation of c-command* between two nodes. To see this, consider the structure in (95), with ZP the specifier of XP and YP the complement of X.

(95)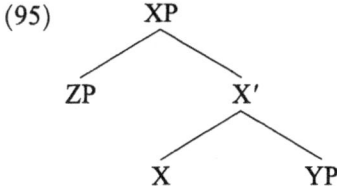

The category ZP in (95) c-commands X and hence indirectly the projection X' of X, but is not c-commanded by the latter (which is not visible for the computation). Then, ZP in (95) asymmetrically c-commands X'.[37] The C-NSR can therefore apply between a specifier and its sister. The only problematic case would be one in which the sister of the specifier is a head, but that configuration may not arise given standard assumptions concerning verbs and argument structures.[38] A similar result holds for adjunction structures. Consider the structure in (96), with segments XP_1 and XP_2.

(96)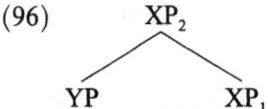

The category YP in (96) c-commands the head of XP_1, but no c-command relation holds directly between YP and XP_1, because the latter node, being a segment and not a category, is not visible for the computation. Then, YP c-commands XP_1 indirectly by (94) and asymmetrically c-commands XP_1. The C-NSR can therefore apply to an adjunct and its sister. The only problematic case again would be one in which XP_1 in (96) is a head. However, this is a configuration of head adjunction, whose stress pattern is governed by morphophonological rules that need not concern us here.[39]

Chapter 2
The Relation between
Prosody and Focus in
Germanic and Romance

Natural languages use different means to identify the focus in the sentence: prosody, morphology, or a syntactically specified position. A given language may use one or more of these means. In this chapter I will discuss the manner in which prosody identifies the focus, based on what I believe to constitute the core data in Germanic languages (such as English and German) and Romance languages (such as French and Spanish). Building on initial insights by Chomsky (1971) and Jackendoff (1972), I put forth an analysis in which phrasal prominence (as determined by the Nuclear Stress Rule) plays a crucial role in determining the relation between focus and prosody for languages of the Germanic/Romance variety (sections 2.1–2.4). I argue that the proposed analysis (based on a revised and modular version of the NSR, formulated in terms of syntactic notions such as asymmetric c-command and selectional ordering) can adequately account for crosslinguistic variations; in particular, it can account for differences between Germanic and Romance. Finally, I discuss alternative analyses proposed by Schmerling (1976), Selkirk (1984, 1985), Gussenhoven (1984), and Cinque (1993) (section 2.5). Of particular importance is the comparison between my approach and approaches such as those of Selkirk and Gussenhoven, in which the distribution of pitch accents (rather than the degree of phrasal prominence) is relevant in determining the scope of the focus. Although these alternative analyses (especially Gussenhoven's) go a long way in describing the Germanic data, they offer no insight concerning the differences between Germanic and Romance. I close this chapter with a discussion on the nature of the principle that governs the relation between focus and prosody (section 2.6), and with a summary and some concluding remarks (section 2.7).

2.1 Nuclear Stress versus Emphatic/Contrastive Stress

2.1.1 The Nuclear Stress Rule: A Preliminary Formulation

In pioneering work on the relation between focus and prosody in English, Chomsky (1971) and Jackendoff (1972) proposed the following well-formedness principle, which I will refer to as the *Focus Prosody Correspondence Principle.*

(1) *Focus Prosody Correspondence Principle (FPCP) (Part 1)*
    The focused constituent (or F-marked constituent) of a phrase must contain the intonational nucleus of that phrase.

To the extent that in German and Romance the intonational nucleus is identified as the rhythmically most prominent word in the intonational phrase, (1) may be rephrased as (2) for these languages.[1]

(2) *FPCP*
    The F-marked constituent of a phrase must contain the rhythmically most prominent word in that phrase.

It is assumed furthermore that the NSR (first formulated in Chomsky and Halle 1968, hereafter *SPE*) is responsible for locating the rhythmically most prominent word within the phrase (except for cases involving emphasis or contrastive focus, to be discussed below). Under this view, then, this phrasal rhythmic rule mediates the relation between intonation and focus. It has since been argued that rhythmic patterns should be represented in terms of a metrical grid (see, e.g., Liberman and Prince 1977, Halle and Vergnaud 1987, Selkirk 1984, Dell 1984), possibly bracketed as in Halle and Vergnaud 1987. The NSR can then be viewed as one rule among others responsible for the construction of the metrical grid.

The NSR, as formulated in *SPE*, is an algorithm that interprets phrasal boundaries as metrical domains and assigns stress to the rightmost word within those domains in a cyclic (bottom-up) fashion. Given the assumption that a noun phrase and a clause constitute cyclic domains, this algorithm generates not only primary stress on the rightmost word in the VP but also secondary stress on the rightmost word of the NP subject. Thus, the NSR assigns primary stress to *rats* and secondary stress to *hat* in (3). (It is assumed that functional words such as determiners, complementizers, and auxiliaries do not define metrical domains of their own.)

(3) ((The cat (in the blue hàt)) (has written (a book (about ráts)))).

Subsequent research on rhythmic patterns has shown that primary stress has distinct characteristics from nonprimary stress (i.e., secondary and tertiary stresses). Although the location of primary stress is intimately related to the focus structure of the sentence, it is never influenced by rhythmic considerations such as number of syllables. On the other hand, although the location of nonprimary stress does not affect the focus structure of the sentence, it may be influenced by, among other factors, the length of the material that precedes and follows it (see Dell 1984, Nespor and Vogel 1986). I illustrate the properties of nonprimary stress with examples from Dell 1984. In (4) the location of secondary stress may vary (i.e., it can be either on the subject or on the verb), without affecting the focus structure of the sentence.

(4) a. (Sa fille (a pris (des haricots verts))).² 'His/Her daughter had
       2   3   1   some green beans.'
   b. (Sa fille (a pris (des haricots verts))).
       3   2   1

Although the two members of the pairs in (5) and (6) have identical constituent structure, they vary in terms of length (measured in number of syllables). This plays a role in determining the possible rhythmic patterns that can be associated with each form. In effect, the (ii) pattern is less natural in (5b) than in (5a), and it is perfectly acceptable in (6b) but marginal in (6a). Such contrasts are attributed to eurhythmicity.³

(5) a.   (un' chos' (facile à voir)) 'a thing easy to see'
    i.   2   3   1
    ii.   3   2   1
   b.   (un' chos' (facile à récupérer))
    i.   2   3   1
    ii.   3   2   1
(6) a.   (son pantalon rouge) (plein (d'grains (d'tabac)))
    i.   0 2   0   3   1
    ii.   0 0   2   0   1
        'his/her red trousers covered with grains of tobacco'
   b.   (son pull) (plein (d'grains (d'tabac))) 'his/her pullover covered
    i.   2   0   3   1   with grains of tobacco'
    ii.   0   2   0   1

On the basis of the above-mentioned considerations, it seems justified to assume that the NSR only specifies the position of primary stress within the relevant phrase. Other rhythmic rules (or well-formedness principles) determine the possible locations of nonprimary stresses within the phrase. Furthermore, the stress generated by the NSR (or by the Emphatic/ Contrastive Stress Rule; see below) is the only rule relevant to determining the well-formedness relation between F-structure and intonation.

The phrasal NSR advanced in *SPE* may be viewed as an algorithm that yields a prosodic interpretation of asymmetric c-command in the sense of Kayne 1994 and of Chomsky 1994, 1995. As remarked in section 1.3.4, asymmetric c-command plays a central role within the view of syntax developed by Kayne (1994), in particular, in relation to the structural organization of the set of terminals.

(7) Given two terminals α and β, there must be a constituent A dominating α and a constituent B dominating β such that A asymmetrically c-commands B or vice versa.

I assume that at least a weaker version of (7) (adopted in Chomsky 1994, 1995) holds. Under this weaker version, the liner ordering of terminals is taken to reflect asymmetric c-command as follows:

(8) Given two constituents A and B, if A asymmetrically c-commands B, then every terminal that A dominates precedes every terminal that B dominates.

Accordingly, I formulate the phrasal NSR as follows:

(9) *NSR*
Given two nodes C_i and C_j that are metrical sisters, the one lower in the syntactic asymmetric c-command ordering is more prominent.

In the spirit of Liberman 1975, the NSR is formalized as a local rule that applies to a pair of sister metrical constituents and assigns relative prominence to one of them (I assume that branching is binary). The location of the nuclear stress (NS) in some given structure is completely determined by the pattern of relative prominences between sister categories so established. Specifically, as will become clear when I illustrate the application of the NSR in section 2.3, NS falls on the terminal element that is dominated solely by prominent constituents (i.e., constituents with the feature specification *[strong]* in the sense of Liberman 1975). This terminal element will then be designated as the rhythmically most prominent element in the metrical grid associated with the utterance.

(10) The terminal element dominated solely by prominent constituents within a phrase is designated as the rhythmically most prominent one within that phrase.

I make the following assumption:

(11) The NSR applies to the syntactic tree that is the input to Spell-Out (in the sense of Chomsky 1995).

As I will show, (11) is the optimal assumption given the nature of the structural conditions governing the application of the rule. I will argue (see in particular sections 2.3 and 2.7) that it is necessary to make this assumption on empirical grounds as well. The structural description of the NSR includes two conditions, one concerned with asymmetric c-command and one with "metrical sisterhood." The import of the distinction between metrical sisterhood and syntactic sisterhood is that metrical sisterhood is a less restricted version of syntactic sisterhood, in the sense that it may ignore intervening syntactic constituents that are not metrically branching, that is, that immediately dominate metrically invisible (or "prosodically silent") material. See the discussion pertaining to (13). Typically, constituents that are phonologically silent, such as traces, are metrically invisible for the purpose of applying the NSR. In addition, in some languages certain types of phonologically realized constituents may also be metrically invisible. This is the case for constituents with reduced or null stress. These are functional categories such as determiners, light lexical categories such as auxiliaries and certain prepositions, defocalized and anaphoric constituents; see section 2.2. Obviously, the existence of metrically invisible constituents in the above sense requires that the following convention be added to the formulation of the NSR in (9):

(12) Relative prominence between two constituents is established by the NSR iff they are both metrically visible (i.e., iff they each dominate at least one metrically visible head).[4]

To illustrate the notion of metrical sisterhood, consider the structure in (13), where each C_i, $i = 1, 2, 3, 4$, e is a head and C_e stands for a metrically invisible constituent.

(13) $[_{C_1} C_1 [_{C_e} C_e [_{C_e}[_{C_4} C_4 C_e] [_{C_e} C_e [_{C_2} C_2 [_{C_3} C_3 C_e]]]]]]$

The pairs of metrical sisters in (13) are listed in (14).

(14) a. C_1 and $[_{C_e}\ C_e\ [_{C_e}[_{C_4}\ C_4\ C_e]\ [_{C_e}\ C_e\ [_{C_2}\ C_2\ [_{C_3}\ C_3\ C_e]]]]]$
 b. C_1 and $[_{C_e}[_{C_4}\ C_4\ C_e]\ [_{C_e}\ C_e\ [_{C_2}\ C_2\ [_{C_3}\ C_3\ C_e]]]]$
 c. C_e and $[_{C_e}[_{C_4}\ C_4\ C_e]\ [_{C_e}\ C_e\ [_{C_2}\ C_2\ [_{C_3}\ C_3\ C_e]]]]$
 d. $[_{C_4}\ C_4\ C_e]$ and $[_{C_e}\ C_e\ [_{C_2}\ C_2\ [_{C_3}\ C_3\ C_e]]]$
 e. $[_{C_4}\ C_4\ C_e]$ and $[_{C_2}\ C_2\ [_{C_3}\ C_3\ C_e]]$
 f. C_2 and $[_{C_3}\ C_3\ C_e]$
 g. C_2 and C_3
 h. C_4 and C_e

Of the pairs in (14), only those in (14a,c,d,f,h) are sisters in the standard syntactic sense. The pairs that are not strict syntactic sisters (i.e., those in (14b,e,g)) are sisters in the extended metrical sense because the elements in each pair are separated only by metrically invisible constituents within the syntactic tree. A natural way to formalize this extension of sisterhood is to define sisterhood over equivalence classes of constituents. Specifically, two constituents will count as equivalent from the point of view of the relation of metrical sisterhood just in case they differ only by metrically invisible heads.[5] I introduce the relevant notion of *metrical nondistinctness* in (15).

(15) Constituents A and B are *metrically nondistinct* $=_{def}$ A and B dominate the same set of metrically visible heads.

The notion of metrical sisterhood can then be formalized as in (16).

(16) Constituents X and Y are *metrical sisters* $=_{def}$ there exist two constituents Z and W such that (a) Z and W are sisters and (b) Z (resp. W) is metrically nondistinct from X (resp. Y).

This definition implicitly involves a notion of *metrical nondistinctness of structural analyses*, which I formalize in (17).

(17) Two analyses ..., C, ... and ..., K, ... of the syntactic tree are *metrically nondistinct at* (C, K) $=_{def}$ the constituents C and K are metrically nondistinct.

The definition in (16) can now be revised as follows:[6]

(18) Constituents X and Y are *metrical sisters* $=_{def}$ there exists an analysis of the syntactic tree ..., Z, W, ... such that (a) Z and W are sisters and (b) the analysis ..., Z, W, ... is metrically nondistinct from the analysis ... X, ..., Y, ... at (Z, X) and at (W, Y).

As I will show in section 2.3, the fact that the NSR must be stated in terms of a generalized notion of sisterhood is merely an instance of a more general characteristic of that rule. Namely, as it will turn out, sets of metrically nondistinct constituents in general constitute equivalence classes for all aspects of the structural description of the NSR. This means that, in the particular case of the NSR, the standard conditions for meeting a structural description must be generalized. More precisely, in cases in which two or more metrically nondistinct analyses are available, the structural description of the rule will apply to all of them or to none of them. Consequently, I adopt (19) as a general convention for the application of the NSR.[7]

(19) *Convention for the application of the NSR*
Given two analyses of the syntactic tree $\ldots, C_i, \ldots, C_j, \ldots$ and $\ldots, K_i, \ldots, K_j, \ldots$ such that $\ldots, C_i, \ldots, C_j, \ldots$ and $\ldots, K_i, \ldots, K_j, \ldots$ are metrically nondistinct at (C_i, K_i) and at (C_j, K_j) and (C_i, C_j) meets some condition P of the structural description of the NSR in the standard sense, then (K_i, K_j) is taken to meet P as well.

As an illustration, consider the two pairs of categories $(C_2, [_{C_3} C_3 C_e])$ and (C_2, C_3) in (14f) and (14g), respectively. Recall that the notion of metrical nondistinctness allows us the define C_2 and C_3 in (14g) as metrical sisters: on the one hand, the categories C_2 and $[C_3 C_e]$ are syntactic sisters and, on the other hand, $[C_3 C_e]$ and C_3 are metrically nondistinct. In other words, C_2 and C_3 are sisters in the derivative sense defined above. The notion of metrical nondistinctness, extended in (19) so as to apply to all aspects of the structural description of the NSR, also allows us to derivatively define an asymmetric c-command relation between the two members of each pair in (14). The categories C_2 and $[C_3 C_e]$ are syntactic sisters and, therefore, strictly speaking, no asymmetric c-command relation holds between them. But because, on the one hand, C_2 asymmetrically c-commands C_3 and, on the other hand, $[C_3 C_e]$ and C_3 are metrically nondistinct, C_2 asymmetrically c-commands $[C_3 C_e]$ derivatively, as far as the NSR is concerned. The NSR will therefore apply to the pair of categories C_2 and $[_{C_3} C_3 C_e]$, as well as to the pair of categories C_2 and C_3.[8,9]

Note that given the above system of conventions, the formulation of the NSR can be simplified to (20).

(20) *NSR*
Given two sister nodes C_i and C_j, the one lower in the asymmetric c-command ordering is more prominent.

That is, the rule need no longer refer to the notion of metrical sisterhood since this aspect of its structural description is subsumed under an independent convention, namely, (19). For the cases discussed to this point, the formulation of the NSR that applies locally to sister categories according to the convention in (19) might seem unnecessary. The following would have sufficed:

(21) The lowest constituent in the asymmetric c-command ordering in the phrase is the most prominent in that phrase.

But as we will see in section 2.3, certain basic facts of English and German require a revision of the NSR. The revision needed to accommodate this richer array of data can be naturally stated as an extension of (20), but not as an extension of (21).

2.1.2 Emphatic/Contrastive Stress

As is well known, not only lexical words, but also function words and even subparts of words, may be the locus of main prominence. With Chomsky (1971) and Jackendoff (1972), I assume that such cases are generated by an independent rule. As is commonly done, I refer to these as case of *emphatic stress* (whose presence I will indicate with capital letters).

Emphatic stress has a purely metagrammatical function, as when it signals correction or repair.[10]

(22) a. I said CONfirmation (not AFFirmation).
 b. I said I drink my coffee WITH sugar (not WITHOUT sugar).

This is also the case when stress is used to reassert or deny the hearer's presupposition, as in (23a) and (23b), respectively (the context is given in brackets below each example).

(23) a. You are right; she DID write a book about rats.
 [I am pretty sure this cat wrote a book about rats.]
 b. NOBODY wrote a book about rats.
 [Who wrote a book about rats?]

Cases of emphatic stress are abundant in the literature. I cite here a few examples from Gussenhoven 1984, 52–54.

(24) a. I TOOK the garbage out.
 [Why didn't you take the garbage out?]
 b. But I DO love you.
 [I wish you loved me.]

c. In this hospital, no organs will BE transplanted!
   [Simple! We'll transplant a new kidney!]
d. We ARE in France.
   [I wish we were in France.]
e. No, I DON'T watch television.
   [Mark Rufus, you watch television.]

I will have nothing more to say in this work about stress with a purely metalinguistic function.

So-called *contrastive stress* is partly metagrammatical and partly focus-related, as illustrated by the examples in (25). It is metagrammatical in that it serves the function of denying part of the hearer's presupposition (as indicated by the explicit or implicit negative tag), and it is focus-related in that it introduces a variable and a value for it. (See also section 1.1.1.)

(25) a. The CAT wrote a book about rats (not the dog).
     b. The cat wrote a BOOK about rats (not a squib).

Stress associated with contrastive focus is freely assigned, but as we will see in section 2.4, in such cases the relation between F-structure and stress is more restricted than in the case of noncontrastive focus. Looking ahead, in the case of contrastive focus, the correspondence relation between F-structure and stress may be formulated as follows (compare with the FPCP in (2)):

(26) *Focus/Contrastive Stress Correspondence Principle*
     A word with contrastive stress must be dominated by every F-marked constituent in the phrase.

2.1.3 Summary

In line with the view outlined in Chomsky 1971 and Jackendoff 1972, I assume that

(27) a. Rhythmic prominence mediates the relation between focus structure and intonation in Germanic and Romance (see the FPCP in (2)).
     b. There are two distinct main prominence assignment rules: the NSR and the Emphatic/Contrastive Stress Rule.
     c. Contrastive stress is freely assigned, but the correspondence between contrastive stress and F-structure is more constrained than the relation between NS and F-structure (compare (26) with (2)).

d. The NSR is a phrasal rhythmic rule that reflects asymmetric c-command, as defined on the syntactic tree. See (20), which applies according to the convention in (19) (the formulation of the NSR will be extended in section 2.3).

2.2 The Domain of the Nuclear Stress Rule in English (and German)

2.2.1 Defocalized Phrases

As predicted by the NSR in conjunction with the FPCP, (3) can have any of the F-structures shown in (28): the entire sentence, the VP, the object, or the PP complement of the object. (3) can thus serve as an answer to any of the questions in (29).

(28) [$_F$ The cat in the blue hàt [$_F$ has written [$_F$ a book [$_F$ about ráts]]]].

(29) a. What happened?
    b. What did the cat in the blue hat do?
    c. What has the cat in the blue hat written?
    b. What has the cat in the blue hat written about?

On the other hand, if NS is on the subject as in (30a), the F-structure must be as in (30b). In other words, (30a) can have (30c), but not (29a–d), as its context question.

(30) a. The cat in the blue hát has written a book about ràts.
    b. [$_F$ The cat in the blue hát] has written a book about ràts.
    c. (I would like to know) who has written a book about ráts.

This fact suggests that in English (as well as in German; see section 2.3.1), the domain of the NSR is determined by the F-marking of the sentence. In other words, only F-marked constituents are "visible" for the NSR. (See Meredith 1990 for a similar proposal.) I therefore postulate (31). Note that (31) actually entails the FPCP. In effect, in languages in which the domain of the NSR is determined by the F-marking of the sentence, it follows that the NS will be contained within the focused part of the sentence.

(31) Defocalized constituents are metrically invisible for the NSR in English and German.

The NSR will therefore correctly assign primary stress to the last word of the subject constituent in (30a) and to the last word in the VP in (28). From now on I will indicate those elements that are metrically invisible

Prosody and Focus in Germanic and Romance 47

for the NSR, when relevant, by writing them in italics. These are the defocalized phrases, on the one hand, and the function words, on the other hand.

Let us now return to the example in (30), repeated in (32). This example has an interesting property. The secondary stress located in the defocalized VP is *not* focus neutral. (I indicate the secondary stress contained within a defocalized phrase with the symbol ^ to distinguish it from secondary stress within a non-defocalized phrase.) Although the position of secondary stress in (4) and (5) does not affect the focus-related meaning of the sentence (see also note 3), the position of secondary stress in (32a) does. In effect, if stress within the defocalized phrase is on *book* in (33a), its context question must be (33b), rather than (32b).

(32) a. [F The cat in the blue hát] *has written a book about râts*.
 b. (I would like to know) who has written a book about ráts.
 (NS on *rats*)

(33) a. [F The cat with the blue hát] *has written a bôok about rats*.
 b. (I would like to know) who has written a BOOK about rats.
 (contrastive stress on *book*)

I suggest that the stress within the defocalized phrase has been copied from the context question directly. I will refer to it as the *echo stress* and postulate that:

(34) A word that bears an echo stress within a phrase is rhythmically subordinate to the word that bears a nonecho stress within the same phrase.

2.2.2 Anaphoric DPs: The So-Called Default Accent Cases
It is a property of pronouns that when they bear phrasal stress, they give rise to a contrastive focus meaning associated with them. Compare (35a) and (35b). In the latter example, with NS on the pronoun, the implication is that John kissed Mary rather than some other person present in the context.

(35) Mary walked in.
 a. John kíssed *her*.
 b. John kissed hér (and not Martha).

Examples with distressed pronouns abound in the literature. For example, Gussenhoven (1984, 181) cites the following examples:[11]

(36) a. Talking about the lid, did you take the lid óff *it*?
 b. Then he put the screen in frónt *of it*.
 c. Carefully he put the mouse on tóp *of it*.
 d. Have you heard fróm *him*?
 e. Did you scrape this fróm *it*?

The contrast in (35) suggests that anaphoric phrases are also metrically invisible for the NSR in English. (The same observation holds for German.)

(37) Anaphoric phrases are metrically invisible for the NSR in English and German.

It is tempting to treat certain examples analyzed by Ladd (1980) in terms of the notion of "default accent" as a subcase of anaphora (see Williams 1997 for a proposal along these lines). We can then account for such cases in terms of (37). Close examination of the examples cited by Ladd as cases of default accent reveals that they do not constitute a unitary phenomenon. Consider the example in (38), in which NS falls on the verb rather than on the DP object. Ladd (1980, 81) comments, "The accent in [(38)] is in no sense 'contrastive', as it is often said to be: the meaning of B's reply is not the explicit contrast 'John doesn't read books, he writes (reviews, collects, burns, etc.) them'. Rather the point of the accentual pattern is that *books* is deaccented; the focus is broad, but the accent falls on *read* by default."

(38) A: Had John read *Slaughterhouse Five*?
 B: No, John doesn't READ books.

Although (38) is not a case of contrastive focus, it is clearly a case in which stress has a metagrammatical function. In effect, the answer denies the presupposition entailed by the question, which is that John reads books. Consequently, we can safely assume that the stress in the answer is not a case of NS. Instead, it is a case of emphatic stress (see section 2.1.2).[12]

But there are other examples cited by Ladd that are not cases of emphatic stress (see also Selkirk 1984, Gussenhoven 1984). These examples share properties with pronominal anaphora in that they involve noun phrases with a discourse antecedent. In effect, in (39) and (40) the noun phrases in italics (*the measure, the feed, the till*) all have a discourse antecedent. It is therefore reasonable to treat them in the same fashion as we treated the pronouns in (35a) and (36). Because they are anaphoric, they are metrically invisible by virtue of (37).[13] (I underline the relevant part of the examples. (39) is taken from Ladd 1980, 81; (40) is cited in Gussenhoven 1984, 179.)

(39) A bill was sent to Congress today by President Carter which would require peanut butter sandwiches to be served at all government functions. At a press conference today, a group of Senators led by Republican Barry Goldwater of Arizona denóunced *the measure*. Goldwater said ...

(40) a. Farmers also use it to feed their animals. They add considerable quantities of salt tó *the feed*.
b. When you emptied the till, did you count the money ín *the till*?

To summarize: I have proposed that the domain of the NSR is restricted in English (and German) to focused and nonanaphoric constituents. (31) and (37) can thus be collapsed as in (41).

(41) Defocalized and anaphoric constituents are metrically invisible for the NSR in English and in German.

In section 2.4 I will show that the domain of the NSR in other languages is not restricted in the same fashion. In effect, although (41) applies to some Romance languages as well (in particular, to French and Brazilian Portuguese), it does not apply to others (e.g., Spanish and Italian).

To the extent that prominence must be borne by a terminal element, we may assume that phonologically empty categories are also metrically invisible (in all languages).

(42) Empty categories are metrically invisible.

2.3 The Nuclear Stress Rule Revisited

2.3.1 German

As has long been acknowledged, German V-final structures constitute a prima facie counterexample to the *SPE* formulation of the NSR, which relies solely on constituent structures. The data examined below suggest that selectional relations play a major role in determining the location of NS in such structures, an observation that has not gone unnoticed (Schmerling 1976, Gussenhoven 1984, Selkirk 1984, 1995, among others).[14]

In German V-final transitive structures, NS falls obligatorily on the direct object, if it is not defocalized.[15]

(43) Hans hat das/ein Búch gelesen.
    Hans has the/a   book read

(44) Karl hat das/ein Búch gekauft.
    Karl has the/a   book bought

If the verb selects an object and a PP (directional) complement, NS falls obligatorily on the PP complement (if it is not defocalized).

(45) Karl hat ein Buch ins   Regál gestellt.
    Karl has a book on-the shelf put

(46) Karl hat die Milch in den Kühlschrank gestellt.
    Karl has the milk in the refrigerator put

The relevance of selectional relations is further supported by the contrast between the unaccusative verb *kommt* 'comes' in (47) and the unergative verbs *getanzt/gelacht* 'danced/laughed' in (48)–(49). Although in the former case NS falls obligatorily on the subject (if it is not defocalized), in the latter cases it can fall either on the verb or on the subject.[16]

(47) Es heißt, daß der/ein Júnge kommt.
    it is-said that the/a boy   comes

(48) a. Es heißt, daß ein Junge getánzt hat.
       it is-said that a boy   danced has
    b. Es heißt, daß ein Júnge getanzt hat.

(49) a. Es heißt, daß ein Junge gelácht hat.
       it is-said that a boy   laughed has
    b. Es heißt, daß ein Júnge gelacht hat.

Another piece of evidence for the sensitivity of NS to selectional properties in German is provided by a number of modifier/complement asymmetries in V-final structures (noted by several authors and reported by Truckenbrodt (1993), from whom I borrow the examples cited below). Typically, in a [...PP V] structure, the PP will attract NS if it is an argument of the verb, but not if it is an adjunct. Consider (50) (attributed to Krifka (1984) by Truckenbrodt), in which the sole location of stress disambiguates a sentence. In (50a) the PP, which carries NS, is interpreted as an argument of the verb. In (50b) NS falls on the verb and the PP is interpreted as a locative adjunct.[17]

(50) a. Peter hat an einem Papíer gearbeitet.
    Peter has on a paper worked
    'Peter worked on a paper.'
  b. Peter hat an einem kleinen Tisch geárbeitet.
    Peter has on a small table worked
    'Peter worked on a small table.'

Another minimal pair (also attributed to Krifka by Truckenbrodt) is provided by secondary predicates and resultatives. If the PP is a temporal adjunct, then NS falls on the verb (see (51a)), but if the PP is a resultative complement of the verb, then NS falls on the PP (see (51b)).

(51) a. Er hat sie [$_{VP}$ im Schlaf [$_{VP}$ gekűßt]].
    he has her in-the sleep kissed
    'He kissed her while sleeping.'
  b. Er hat sie [$_{VP}$ in den Schláf gekűßt].
    he has her in the sleep kissed
    'He made her sleep as a result of kissing her.'

If a locative is unambiguously an argument of the verb, then NS must fall on the PP.

(52) a. in einen Séssel sitzen
    in an armchair sit
  b. in einer grossen Stádt wohnen
    in a big city reside

If the PP is unambiguously an adjunct (whether a manner (53a), time (53b), or locative (53c) modifier), then NS must fall on the verb.

(53) a. Maria kann [auf eine bezaubernde Art [flírten]].
    Maria can in a charming way flirt
  b. Peter ist [an diesem Tag [wéggefahren]].
    Peter is on that day driven-away
  c. [in den Bergen [skífahren]]
    in the mountains skiing

Note that the adjunct/argument distinction with respect to the position of NS is manifested only in V-final contexts. In particular, it does not manifest itself in verb-second (V2) contexts. Thus, there is no contrast between (54a) and (54b) (the V2 counterparts of (50a) and (50b), respectively). NS falls on the final PP in both cases, whether the PP is an argument or an adjunct. (The same remarks extend ceteris paribus to the examples in (51), (52), and (53).)

(54) a. Hans arbeitet   an einem Papíer.
       Hans is-working on a   paper
   b. Hans arbeitet   an einem kleinen Tísch.
       Hans is-working on a   small   table

And, if both the PP argument and the PP adjunct are present, NS falls on the last one in the sequence.

(55) Hans arbeitet   an einem Papier in seinem Zímmer.
     Hans is-working on a   paper in his   room

Similarly, whereas NS falls on the subject of the unaccusative verb in (56a) (*Taxi*), it falls on the adjunct in (56b) (*spät*).

(56) a. Das Táxi kommt.
       the taxi is-coming
   b. Das Taxi kommt   spǎt.
       the taxi is-coming late

The generalization is then that when the verb is not in final position, NS falls on the last constituent in the structure.

    The German data suggest that the NSR has two parts. One part manifests itself in non-V-final structures; this is the standard NSR, formulated in (9) in terms of asymmetric c-command (i.e., the last constituent in the asymmetric c-command ordering receives NS). The other part, which manifests itself in V-final structures, reflects a different kind of ordering, namely, the one established by the ordered sequence of selected heads, which I will refer to as the *selectional ordering*. This ordering is shown in (57).

(57) $(C, T, V_1, \ldots, V_i, P/V_m, D_m)$, with possibly m = 1
     $(C, T, \ldots, V_i, D_i)$, for $i = 1, 2, \ldots, m - 1$ (for the cases where $m > 1$)
     where $D_i, i = 1, 2, \ldots, m - 1$ is the nominal argument of V_i (for the cases where $m > 1$) and D_m is the nominal argument of the lowest (possibly only) verb or prepositional predicate (P/V_m) in the selectional ordering.

The functional category C(omp) selects the functional category T(ense), which in turn selects a verbal projection. The selectional ordering within the verbal projection is given by the lexicosyntactic structure of the verbal predicate. More specifically, the sequence $V_1, \ldots, V_i, \ldots, P/V_m$ is the ordered analysis of the lexical verb into elementary verbs or prepositions (see Hale and Keyser 1991, 1993, Chomsky 1995). D_m is the nominal argument of the last (possible only) element P/V_m in the selectional ordering, and $D_i, i = 1, 2, \ldots, m - 1$ is the nominal argument of V_i when V_i exists.[18] Thus, in the most general case, a partially ordered system of categories results. This system is represented in (57) as a set of maximal selectional chains. A category C_r to the right of some other category C_q in the selectional ordering in (57) is said to be *lower than* C_q in the selectional ordering. Note that, given that the ordering is defined strictly in terms of selection, no ordering is established among coarguments. Ordering holds only between selectors and selected constituents.[19] The partial ordering in (57) can be represented as the tree in (58).

(58)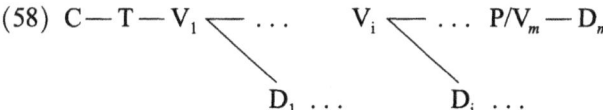

Although the selectional ordering in (57) (=(58)) is defined in terms of heads, we may assume that it naturally extends to the projections of selected heads: if the head C_q is selected by C_r, so are the projections of C_q, and, therefore, if the head C_q is lower in the selectional ordering than C_r, the projections of C_q are also lower than C_r in the selectional ordering. An important aspect of the selectional ordering so generalized, then, is that it is asymmetric in the sense that a selector is necessarily a head, but a selected constituent may be a head or some projection thereof. This asymmetry plays a central role in the account to be presented below.

Let us examine the lower (i.e., verbal) part of the selectional sequence of heads in (57) (=(58)), since it is this part that is relevant for the NSR. The number and sequence of verbal heads is given by the lexicosyntactic properties of the verbal predicate. Following Hale and Keyser (1993), I assume the syntactic structures in (59a), (59b), and (60) for transitives, unergatives, and unaccusatives, respectively. The transitive structure contains two verbal heads, each of which selects an argument. The unergative structure is analyzed as a type of covert transitive: it contains two verbal heads, each of which selects an argument. What differentiates the transitive from the unergative is that in the latter case the lower V selects a cognate object, which is incorporated into its selecting head. Note that according to (57) (=(58)), D_2 is the lowest constituent in a selectional chain in a transitive structure.

(59) a. *Transitives*

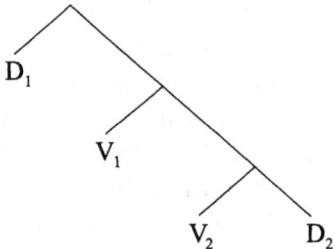

b. *Unergatives*

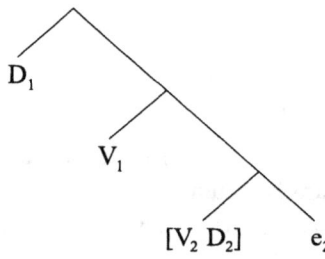

The unaccusative differs from the transitive and the unergative in that it contains only one verbal head, which selects one nominal argument. This nominal argument constitutes the lowest constituent in the selectional chain.

(60) *Unaccusatives*

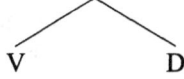

In the case of dirtransitive directional predicates like *put*, I will assume that V_2 selects the prepositional predicate P_3. P_3 in turn selects a nominal argument D_3, which constitutes the lowest constituent in a selectional chain.[20]

(61) *Ditransitive directional predicates*

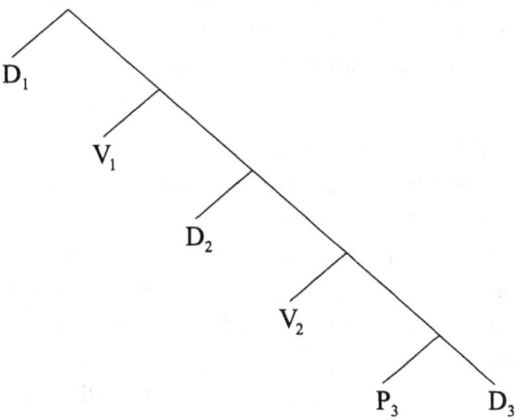

Let us examine how such structures are realized in German V-final structures. First, if we follow Kayne's (1994) hypotheses that asymmetric c-command is a central relation in the syntactic organization of the sentence and that word order reflects asymmetric c-command, it must be the cast that in German, as in English, the complement is uniformly projected to the right of its selecting head and that it subsequently moves leftward for licensing reasons. This line of analysis is worked out and defended by Zwarts (1993) for Dutch and German. We may then assume the structures in (62), (63), and (64) for V-final transitives, directional ditransitives, and unaccusatives, respectively, obtained via leftward movement of arguments to their respective licensing positions. Note that in structures consisting of two elementary verbal elements, such as (62), (63), and (65), I have chosen to analyze the past participle as associated syntactically to V_2, a plausible although not necessary assumption for present concerns.[21] (I ignore the details of the syntactic analysis of the Aux in final position in (65). I also omit the incorporated object for the sake of simplicity.)[22]

(62) [$_{CP}$ Karl$_1$ [*hat* [e_1 [v_1 [*ein* Buch$_2$ [$_{V_2}$ *gekauft* [e_2]]]]]]] (see (44))

(63) [$_{CP}$ Karl$_1$ [*hat* [e_1 [v_1 [*ein* Buch$_2$ [e_2 [*ins* [*Regal*]$_3$]]$_4$ [$_{V_2}$ *gestellt* [e_4]]]]]]] (see (45))

(64) [$_{CP}$ *daß* [*ein* Junge$_1$ [$_V$ *kommt* [e_1]]]] (see (47))

(65) [$_{CP}$ *daß* [*ein* Junge$_1$ [v_1 [$_{V_2}$ *gelacht hat*]]]] (see (49))

I can now formulate a revised version of the NSR that will work for German.

(66) *Revised NSR*
Given two sister nodes C_i and C_j, (a) if C_i and C_j are selectionally ordered, in the sense of (57) (=(58)), the one lower in the selectional ordering is more prominent; (b) otherwise, the one lower in the asymmetric c-command ordering is more prominent.

The first part of the NSR, which establishes prominence in terms of selectional ordering, will be referred to as the *S-NSR*. The second part of the NSR, which establishes prominence in terms of asymmetric c-command, will be referred to as the *C-NSR*. As we will see, the algorithm as stated in (66), in which the S-NSR has primacy over the C-NSR, correctly accounts for the facts in German. Given this particular formulation of the NSR, the C-NSR applies to a pair (C_i, C_j) iff the S-NSR fails to apply to such a pair (i.e., iff C_i and C_j are not selectionally ordered in the sense defined in (57) (=(58)). Furthermore, the modular formulation of the NSR in (66) can accommodate crosslinguistic differences between Germanic and Romance. In effect, as I will show later, whereas Germanic languages compute main prominence in terms of the S-NSR and the C-NSR, the Romance languages compute prominence in terms of the C-NSR only.

For convenience, I repeat the convention in (19) that governs the application of the (revised) NSR and the associated definitions in (17) and (15).

(67) *Convention for the application of the NSR*
Given two analyses of the syntactic tree $\ldots, C_i, \ldots, C_j, \ldots$ and $\ldots, K_i, \ldots, K_j, \ldots$ such that $\ldots, C_i, \ldots, C_j, \ldots$ and $\ldots, K_i, \ldots, K_j, \ldots$ are metrically nondistinct at (C_i, K_i) and at (C_j, K_j) and (C_i, C_j) meets some condition P of the structural description of the NSR in the standard sense, then (K_i, K_j) is taken to meet P as well.

(68) Two analyses $\ldots, C, \ldots$ and $\ldots, K, \ldots$ of the syntactic tree are *metrically nondistinct at* $(C, K) =_{def}$ the constituents C and K are metrically nondistinct.

(69) Constituents A and B are *metrically nondistinct* $=_{def}$ A and B dominate the same set of metrically visible heads.

I repeat in (70) the important subcase of (67), originally stated in (18), that is concerned with sisterhood.

(70) Constituents X and Y are *metrical sisters* $=_{def}$ there exists an analysis of the syntactic tree $\ldots, Z, W, \ldots$ such that (a) Z and W are

Prosody and Focus in Germanic and Romance 57

sisters and (b) the analysis ..., Z, W, ... is metrically nondistinct from the analysis ..., X, ..., Y, ... at (Z, X) and at (W, Y).

Finally, I repeat the convention originally stated in (10).

(71) The terminal element dominated solely by prominent constituents within a phrase is designated as rhythmically most prominent within that phrase.

I now return to the structures in (62)–(64), repeated here, and examine how the revised NSR works for them.

(72) a. [$_{CP}$ Karl$_1$ [*hat* [e_1 [v_1 [*ein* Buch$_2$ [$_{V_2}$ gekauft [e_2]]]]]]]
 b. [$_{CP}$ Karl$_1$ [*hat* [e_1 [v_1 [*ein* Buch$_2$ [e_2 [*ins* [Regal]$_3$]]$_4$ [$_{V_2}$ gestellt [e_4]]]]]]]
 c. [$_{CP}$ *daß* [*ein* Junge$_1$ [$_V$ kommt [e_1]]]]

Consider the structures in (72) in the light of the convention and definitions above. In (72a) the metrical sisters D_1 (= *Karl*) and [D_2 V_2] (= [*ein* Buch$_2$ [*gekauft*$_2$ [$_{D_2}$ e]]], metrically nondistinct from [*ein* Buch$_2$ [*gekauft*$_2$]]) are not selectionally ordered, according to the definition of selectional ordering in (57) (=(58)): no metrical sister to D_1 is a head and, hence, a selector. On the other hand, they are ordered with respect to asymmetric c-command; therefore, the C-NSR applies, assigning prominence to the rightmost constituent, namely, to [D_2 V_2]. The algorithm reapplies to the metrical sisters D_2(= *ein Buch*) and V_2(= [*gekauft*$_2$ [$_{D_2}$ e]], metrically nondistinct from *gekauft*$_2$). These are selectionally ordered (derivatively, because of the metrical nondistinctness between [*gekauft*$_2$ [$_{D_2}$ e]] and the selecting head *gekauft*$_2$). Hence, the S-NSR applies, assigning prominence to D_2, the nominal argument of the last V in the selectional chain. Observe that there is no indeterminacy in the application of the revised NSR in that case, because, as noted, although the pair of metrical sister constituents [$_{D_2}$ *ein Buch*] and [$_{V_2}$ *gekauft* [$_{D_2}$ e]] does not meet the structural description of the S-NSR directly, it meets it derivatively by (67) (=(19)), that is, by virtue of the fact that [$_{V_2}$ *gekauft* [$_{D_2}$ e]] is metrically nondistinct from *gekauft*$_2$ and that the rule applies to the set of metrically equivalent constituents. Furthermore, recall that the S-NSR takes precedence over the C-NSR, given that the context of application of the latter constitutes the "elsewhere case."[23] Given that *Buch* (metrically nondistinct from *ein Buch*) is the unique terminal element that is dominated only by prominent constituents, it is interpreted unambiguously as the most prominent terminal element in that sentence.[24]

In (72b) D_1 (= *Karl*) and $[D_2 [[P\ D_3]_4\ V_2]]$ (= *ein Buch ins Regal gestellt*) are metrical sisters. They are not ordered with respect to selection (see above), but they are ordered with respect to asymmetric c-command. The constituent $[D_2 [[P\ D_3]_4\ V_2]]$ is lower with respect to asymmetric c-command and is therefore assigned prominence. The rule applies again to the metrical sister constituents D_2 (= *ein Buch*) and $[[P\ D_3]_4\ V_2]$ (= *ins Regal gestellt*), which are not selectionally ordered but are ordered with respect to asymmetric c-command. In effect, given that D_2 is the specifier of $[[P\ D_3]_4\ V_2]$ and a specifier asymmetrically c-commands its sister (see section 1.3.4), D_2 asymmetrically c-commands $[[P\ D_3]_4\ V_2]$. The constituent $[[P\ D_3]_4\ V_2]$ being lower, the C-NSR assigns it prominence. The rule reapplies to the metrical phrasal sisters $[P\ D_3]_4$ (= *ins Regal*) and V_2 (= $[gestellt\ [e_4]]$, metrically nondistinct from *gestellt*), which are selectionally ordered. PP_4 being lower in the selectional chain than V_2, PP_4 receives prominence. Again, there is no indeterminacy in the application of the revised NSR here, because the pair $[ins\ [Regal]_3]_4$ and $[_{V_2}\ gestellt\ [e_4]]$ meets the structural description of the S-NSR derivatively by (67) (= (19)), that is, by virtue of the fact that $[_{V_2}\ gestellt\ [e_4]]$ is metrically nondistinct from *gestellt* and that the rule applies to sets of metrically nondistinct constituents. The algorithm reapplies to the metrical sisters P (*in*) and D_3 (= *das Regal*, metrically nondistinct from *Regal*). D_3 being the nominal argument of P (*in*) in the selectional chain, D_3 is assigned prominence by the S-NSR. The terminal element *Regal* (metrically nondistinct from *das Regal*) is dominated only by prominent constituents. It is therefore interpreted as the most prominent element in that sentence.

In (72c) D_1 (= *ein Junge*) and V (= $[kommt\ e_1]$, metrically nondistinct from *kommt*) are metrical sisters. Furthermore, they are derivatively selectionally ordered, by virtue of the fact that the phrase $[kommt\ e_1]$ and the head *kommt* are metrically nondistinct; see (67) (= (19)). The S-NSR assigns prominence to D_1, the nominal argument of the only verb in the selectional chain. *Junge* (metrically nondistinct from *ein Junge*) is therefore unambiguously the most prominent terminal element in that sentence.

Let us turn next to the structure in (65), repeated here.

(73) $[_{CP}\ daß\ [ein\ Junge_1\ [_{V_1}\ v_1\ [_{V_2}\ gelacht\ hat]]]]$

Recall that such a structure gives rise to an ambiguity in the position of NS: it can fall either on the subject or on the past participle (see (49)). It must therefore be the case that such a structure is ambiguously analyzed for the purpose of applying the revised NSR. This ambiguity can be attributed to the fact that in such structures some projection of the elementary verb V_1 and some projection of the elementary verb V_2 are metrically nondistinct. I therefore propose the following auxiliary statement to the interpretive convention that governs the application of the NSR in (67) (= (19)):

(74) *Auxiliary to convention (67) for application of the NSR (optional)*
If some projections of the verbal components V_i and V_j of the lexical verb are metrically nondistinct, then V_i and V_j are analyzed as metrically nondistinct for the purpose of applying the interpretive convention in (67) (= (19)).

I assume that the clause in (74) is optional. Consider the structure in (73) in this light, looking first at the case where (74) does not apply. The NSR applies to the phrasal sisters D_1 (= *ein Junge*) and V_1 (= [$_{V_1}$ v_1 [$_{V_2}$ *gelacht hat*]], metrically nondistinct from [$_{V_2}$ *gelacht hat*] or [$_{V_2}$ *gelacht*]). Given this metrical interpretation of the syntactic structure, D_1 and V_1 are not selectionally ordered. In effect, although D_1 is a nominal argument of the head [$_{V_1}$ *e*] and, as such, is selectionally ordered with respect to [$_{V_1}$ *e*], no selectional ordering holds between D_1 and [$_{V_2}$ *gelacht*] (see (58) or (57)). Furthermore, D_1 and [$_{V_1}$ *e*] are not metrical sisters. The S-NSR then fails to apply. The C-NSR applies instead and assigns prominence to the lower constituent in the derivative c-command ordering, namely, to V_1 (= [$_{V_1}$ v_1 [$_{V_2}$ *gelacht hat*]], metrically nondistinct from [$_{V_2}$ *gelacht hat*] or [$_{V_2}$ *gelacht*]). Ultimately, the terminal element *gelacht* is interpreted as bearing main prominence.

Consider next the case where (74) does apply to the structure in (73). The NSR applies to the sisters D_1 and V_1 (= [$_{V_1}$ v_1 [$_{V_2}$ *gelacht hat*]]). Given (74), V_1 stands for the class: [$_{V_1}$ v_1 [$_{V_2}$ *gelacht hat*]], [$_{V_2}$ *gelacht hat*], [$_{V_2}$ *gelacht*], [$_{V_1}$ *e*]. In effect, because [$_{V_1}$ v_1 [$_{V_2}$ *gelacht hat*]] and [$_{V_2}$ *gelacht hat*] are metrically nondistinct, their heads [$_{V_1}$ *e*] and [$_{V_2}$ *gleacht*] are interpreted as metrically nondistinct, by virtue of (74). By transitivity, the phrase [$_{V_1}$ v_1 [$_{V_2}$ *gelacht hat*]] is metrically nondistinct from the head v_1 as well. Therefore, under this analysis the sisters D_1 and V_1 are derivatively interpreted as selectionally ordered. The S-NSR applies and assigns main prominence to the lowest constituent in the selectional ordering, namely, to D_1 (= *ein Junge*, metrically nondistinct from *Junge*). The terminal element *Junge* is therefore interpreted as the most prominent one in (73).

The auxiliary convention in (74) is independently supported by structures involving defocalized constituents, in particular, V-final transitive structures in which the object (i.e., D_2) has been defocalized. Whether the defocalized object has undergone long scrambling (as in (75) and (76)) or not (as in (77)), the position of the NS is equally ambiguous: it falls either on the subject or on the verb.[25] (The context question is given in brackets below each pair of examples.) A caveat about the data must be pointed out. Some speakers strongly prefer that defocalized objects undergo long scrambling. For such speakers (77) is not an option.[26] (Examples like (75a) are cited in Prinzhorn 1994.)

(75) a. weil   *ihn/Hans* ein Verwándter angerufen *hat*
       because him/Hans a   relative   called   has
       'because a relative called Hans/him.'
    b. weil *ihn/Hans ein* Verwandter ángerufen hat
       [Why is Hans happy?]

(76) a. *Hans*   *hat* gestern *eine* Fráu   geküßt.
       Hans(ACC) has yesterday a   woman(NOM) kissed
       'A woman kissed Hans yesterday.'
    b. *Hans hat* gestern *eine* Frau geküßt.
       [Why is Hans happy?]

(77) a. Ich glaube, *daß ein* Júnge *das Buch* genommen *hat*.
       I   believe that a   boy   the book   taken   has
       'I believe that a boy took the book.'
    b. Ich glaube, *daß ein* Junge *das Buch* genómmen *hat*.
       [What happened to the book?]

Recall that in section 2.1.2 I hypothesized that defocalized constituents (like functional categories) are metrically invisible in English and German (see (31)). (Here, as before, I have indicated the metrically invisible constituents in italics.) Owing to the invisibility of the defocalized object, there is a projection of V_1 that is metrically nondistinct from V_2 in the structures associated with (75), (76), and (77); see (78a), (79a), and (80a). Given the auxiliary statement in (74), there are two options. Either V_1 and V_2 are analyzed as metrically nondistinct, or they are not. In the former case we obtain the metrically equivalent classes given in (78b), (79b), and (80b). In the latter case we obtain the metrically equivalent classes given in (78c), (79c), and (80c). If the metrical analysis is as in (78b), (79b), and (80b), the phrase V_1 is metrically nondistinct from the head $[_{V_1} e]$. It is therefore derivatively selectionally ordered with respect to D_1. The S-NSR applies and assigns main prominence to D_1. The stress patterns in (75a),

(76a), and (77a) are thus obtained. If the metrical analysis is as in (78c), (79c), and (80c), the phrase V_1 is metrically nondistinct from the lexical head V_2, but metrically distinct from the head $[_{V_1} e]$. Hence, there is no selectional ordering between D_1 and its metrical sister (the phrase V_1); the S-NSR fails to apply. The C-NSR applies instead and assigns main prominence to the phrase V_1, which is metrically nondistinct from the lexical head V_2 (*angerufen, geküßt, genommen*). We thus obtain the stress patterns in (75b), (76b), and (77b).

(78) a. [weil [*ihn/Hans*$_2$ [$_{V_1}$ *ein* Verwandter$_1$ [$_{V_1}$ e_1 [v_1 [$_{V_2}$ e_2 [$_{V_2}$ angerufen$_2$ e_2 *hat*]]]]]]]]

　b. {[$_{V_1}$ e_1 [v_1 [$_{V_2}$ e_2 [$_{V_2}$ angerufen$_2$ e_2 *hat*]]]], [v_1 [$_{V_2}$ e_2 [$_{V_2}$ angerufen$_2$ e_2 *hat*]]],
　　[$_{V_2}$ e_2 [$_{V_2}$ angerufen$_2$ e_2 *hat*]], [$_{V_2}$ angerufen], [$_{V_1}$ e]}

　c. {[$_{V_1}$ e_1 [v_1 [$_{V_2}$ e_2 [$_{V_2}$ angerufen$_2$ e_2 *hat*]]]], [v_1 [$_{V_2}$ e_2 [$_{V_2}$ angerufen$_2$ e_2 *hat*]]],
　　[$_{V_2}$ e_2 [$_{V_2}$ angerufen$_2$ e_2 *hat*]], [$_{V_2}$ angerufen]}

(79) a. [*Hans*$_2$ [*hat* [gestern [$_{V_1}$ *eine* Frau$_1$ [$_{V_1}$ e_1 [v_1 [$_{V_2}$ e_2 [$_{V_2}$ geküßt e_2]]]]]]]]

　b. {[$_{V_1}$ e_1 [v_1 [$_{V_2}$ e_2 [$_{V_2}$ geküßt e_2 *hat*]]]], [v_1 [$_{V_2}$ e_2 [$_{V_2}$ geküßt e_2 *hat*]]],
　　[$_{V_2}$ e_2 [$_{V_2}$ geküßt e_2 *hat*]], [$_{V_2}$ geküßt e_2 *hat*], [$_{V_2}$ geküßt], [$_{V_1}$ e]}

　c. {[$_{V_1}$ e_1 [v_1 [$_{V_2}$ e_2 [$_{V_2}$ geküßt e_2 *hat*]]]], [v_1 [$_{V_2}$ e_2 [$_{V_2}$ geküßt e_2 *hat*]]],
　　[$_{V_2}$ e_2 [$_{V_2}$ geküßt e_2 *hat*]], [$_{V_2}$ geküßt e_2 *hat*], [$_{V_2}$ geküßt]}

(80) a. [*daß* [$_{V_1}$ *ein* Junge [v_1 [$_{V_2}$ *das Buch* [$_{V_2}$ genommen e_2 *hat*]]]]]

　b. {[v_1 [$_{V_2}$ *das Buch* [$_{V_2}$ genommen e_2 *hat*]]], [$_{V_2}$ *das Buch* [$_{V_2}$ genommen e_2 *hat*]],
　　[$_{V_2}$ genommen e_2 *hat*], [$_{V_2}$ genommen], [$_{V_1}$ e]}

　c. {[v_1 [$_{V_2}$ *das Buch* [$_{V_2}$ genommen e_2 *hat*]]], [$_{V_2}$ *das Buch* [$_{V_2}$ genommen e_2 *hat*]],
　　[$_{V_2}$ genommen e_2 *hat*], [$_{V_2}$ genommen]}

The generalization that emerges from the proposed analysis is the following:

(81) If D_1 is a metrical sister of (an overtly or covertly) transitive lexical verb, then the verb may be ambiguously analyzed either as distinct from V_1 or as nondistinct from V_1 for the purpose of applying the revised NSR.

In effect, what distinguishes the examples in (48)–(49) and (75)–(77) (where the position of NS is ambiguous) from the examples in (43)–(46)

(where the position of NS is unambiguous) is this: In the former cases the subject and its metrical sister (i.e., the lexical verb) may or may not be analyzed as derivatively selectionally ordered. In the latter cases the projections of V_1 are necessarily metrically distinct from the projections of V_2 (see (72a–b)); therefore, V_1 and V_2 must be interpreted as metrically distinct as well. This analysis is further confirmed by examples such as (82) (cited by Prinzhorn (1994), who attributes it to Höhle (1981)).

(82) *Den* Húnd   *hat Karl*   geschlagen.
   the dog(ACC) has Karl(NOM) beaten
   'Karl beat the dog.'
   [What did Karl do?]

This example is particularly interesting because NS falls unambiguously on the direct object although the defocalized subject intervenes phonologically between the fronted object and the lexical verb. Indeed, NS on the verb in such examples would be interpreted as contrastive. This fact follows immediately from the analysis proposed here. The object and the verbal past participle are derivatively metrical sisters (given that the auxiliary and the defocalized subject are metrically invisible). And since the object is the nominal argument of the last V in the selectional chain of transitive verbs, the S-NSR assigns NS unambiguously to it.

To summarize: In the V-final structures examined above, the S-NSR takes precedence over the C-NSR in cases in which the verb and its metrical sister are selectionally ordered. In such cases the lowest metrically visible argument is assigned NS. If the verb and its metrical sister are not selectionally ordered, then the S-NSR fails to apply. In such a case the C-NSR applies, assigning main prominence to the verb, given that it is the lowest constituent in the c-command ordering. Other cases besides the ones examined above, in which the S-NSR fails to apply in V-final structures, allowing the C-NSR to apply instead, are those in which the metrical sister of the verb is an adjunct. This is the case in (50b), (51a), and (53), where the metrical sister of the verb is a locative, a manner, or a temporal adverbial.

I turn next to examples in which the verb is not in final position. To the extent that such structures are uniformly right-branching, the NSR will assign main prominence to the rightmost constituent. For example, consider (54a–b) and (55), repeated in (83) with a partial syntactic analysis (as usual, I omit the incorporated cognate object from the representation of structures with unergative verbs for the sake of simplicity). The verb in

Prosody and Focus in Germanic and Romance 63

second position (*arbeitet*) may be assumed to be a complex form $[V_1 + V_2]$, created via overt head movement V_1-to-V_2 on its way to C.

(83) a. [Hans₁ [arbeitet [*e₁* [*v₁* [an [*einem* Papier₂] [*v₂* [*e₂*]]]]]]]
 b. [Hans₁ [arbeitet [*e₁* [*v₁* [an [*einem* kleinen [Tisch]] [*v₂*]]]]]]
 c. [Hans₁ [arbeitet [*e₁* [*v₁* [an [*einem* Papier₂] [in [seinem [Zimmer]] [*v₂* [*e₂*]]]]]]]]

In these examples the subject *Hans* and the predicate [*arbeitet* XP] are metrical sisters, but not selectionally ordered. The head [*arbeitet*], but not [*arbeitet* XP], is part of the selectional chain, and they are metrically distinct. The C-NSR applies and assigns prominence to [*arbeitet* XP].[27] The NSR reapplies to the metrical sisters *arbeitet* and XP. If XP is an argument of *arbeitet*, as in (83a), XP is assigned NS by the S-NSR. If XP is not an argument of *arbeitet*, as in (83b) and (83c), XP is assigned NS via the C-NSR. The algorithm reapplies to the metrical constituents contained within XP, the end result being that the rightmost constituent is inexorably assigned NS, whether via the S-NSR or via the C-NSR (depending on the particular case at hand). The algorithm thus correctly predicts that in non-V-final structures the rightmost metrically visible word within the phrase is interpreted as rhythmically most prominent (i.e., *Papier*, *Tisch*, and *Zimmer* in (83a), (83b), and (83c), respectively).

The minimal contrast between (56a) and (56b) lends further support to the modular analysis of the NSR put forth here. The corresponding syntactic structures are given in (84) and (85), respectively.

(84) [das Taxi₁ [kommt [e₁ [*v* [e₁]]]]]

(85) [das Taxi₁ [kommt [spät [e₁ [*v* [e₁]]]]]]

The constituents [*das Taxi*] and [*kommt* [*e₁* [*v* [*e₁*]]]] in (84) are metrical sisters and also derivatively selectionally ordered, by virtue of the fact that the verbal phrase is metrically nondistinct from [*kommt*]. Since D_1 in (84) is lower in the selectional ordering than *kommt*, the S-NSR assigns NS to *Taxi*. By contrast, the metrical sisters [*das Taxi*] and [*kommt spät*] in (85) are not selectionally ordered (because the constituent [*kommt spät*] is metrically distinct from [*kommt*]). Since [*kommt spät*] is lower than [*das Taxi*] in the asymmetric c-command ordering, the C-NSR assigns NS to the predicate. The C-NSR reapplies within the predicate. The constituent *spät*, being lower than *kommt* in the asymmetric c-command ordering, receives NS. Thus, the algorithm correctly predicts that *Taxi* is the strongest constituent in (84), and *spät* is the strongest constituent in (85).

A contrast comparable to the one examined above is found between (86a) and (86b). Although the object and the verb constitute metrical sisters in (86a), giving rise to the application of the S-NSR, they do not in (86b). In the latter example the verb and the adjunct (*spät*) are metrical sisters. Since the adjunct is not part of the selectional chain, the S-NSR fails to apply. The C-NSR applies instead and assigns NS to the lowest constituent in the c-command ordering, namely, to the verb (*zurückgegeben*).

(86) a. Mein Búch   *hat Karl*   zurückgegeben.
         my   book(ACC) has Karl(NOM) returned
         [What did Karl do?]
     b. Mein Buch   *hat Karl*   spät zurückgegeben.
         my   book(ACC) has Karl(NOM) late returned
         [Why do you dislike Karl?]

As expected, if the adjunct that intervenes between the object and the verb is defocalized, then the S-NSR takes precedence over the C-NSR, assigning NS to the object. This is illustrated by the following contrasts:

(87) a. *Das* Taxi *ist* spät gekómmen.
         the taxi is late arrived
         [Out-of-the-blue context]
     b. *Das* Táxi *ist spät* gekommen.
         [Why are you late?]

(88) a. Hans *hat* seine Arbeit früh beéndet.
         Hans has his   work early finished
         [Out-of-the blue context]
     b. *Er hat* seine Árbeit *früh* beendet.
         he has his   work early finished
         [Why is Hans early?]

In (87a) and (88a) the adjuncts (*spät* and *früh*, respectively) are part of the focus and hence metrically visible. Therefore, the adjunct and the verb are metrical sisters; the C-NSR applies *in lieu of* of the S-NSR and assigns NS to the verb (*gekommen* and *beendet* in the respective examples). On the other hand, in (87b) and (88b) the adjuncts are defocalized and therefore metrically invisible. Consequently, the verb and the object are derivatively metrical sisters; the S-NSR applies and assigns NS to the object (*Taxi* and *Arbeit* in the respective examples).

Locative adjuncts in V-final structures give rise to some unexpected complications, in particular when such adjuncts intervene between the direct object and the verb in final position. The intuition seems to be that NS may fall either on the verb or on the object. This variability is unexpected. According to the analysis proposed here, NS should fall unambiguously on the verb. Indeed, the verb is metrically adjacent to the locative. Since the locative is not part of the selectional chain, the S-NSR fails to apply; the C-NSR applies instead and assigns NS to the verb (as in (89)). Surprisingly, though, according to my informants, NS may also fall on the object, and this does not seem to be contingent on the defocalization of the locative adjunct (see (90) and (91)). This would seem to indicate that locative adjuncts may optionally incorporate rightward into the adjacent verb. If the locative is incorporated into the verb, then the object is analyzed as a metrical sister of the verbal complex (loc+verb). The S-NSR then applies and assigns NS to the object (*Buch* and *Schnitzel* in the respective examples).[28] ((89) is an example from Abraham 1993.)

(89) Mutter wurde gebeten, ihren Sohn im Garten zu súchen.
Mother was asked   her son in-the garden to look-for

(90) Hans hat sein Búch im   Wohnzimmer verloren.
Hans has his book in-the living room   lost
[What happened?]

(91) *Er hat* sein Schnítzel im   Restaurant gegessen.
he has his schnitzel in-the restaurant eaten
[What did Hans do?]

The validity and details of the above proposal will have to await further research on incorporation in German, a task I cannot undertake here. Some of the questions that remain to be answered are these: Is this a case of syntactic incorporation or simply a case of metrical incorporation (i.e., a case in which an adjunct+verb is interpreted as metrically nondistinct from the verb)? What is the class of adjuncts that can "incorporate" and how can it be characterized?

Finally, let us examine sentences with generic subjects. In German, as in English (see section 3.2), generic subjects do not bear NS. This fact was noticed by Gussenhoven (1984) and is also discussed by Selkirk (1995). Thus, whereas NS falls on the existentially interpreted subject in (92a), it falls on the predicate in (92b).

(92) a. weil   Féuerwehrmänner verfügbar *sind*
         because the-firemen   available   are
     b. weil   Feuerwehrmänner altruístisch *sind*
         because firemen   altruistic are

The position of NS thus disambiguates the following sentences. In (93a) the subject of the passive verb is interpreted existentially; in (93b) it is interpreted generically.

(93) a. weil   in dieser Stadt Díebe verhaftet werden
         because in this   town thieves arrested become
         '...there are thieves that will be arrested in this town'
     b. weil in dieser Stadt Diebe verháftet werden
         '...if there are thieves in this town, they will be arrested'

A possible analysis of such contrasts is provided by the theory of indefinites and generics put forth by Diesing (1992a,b) (adopted by Selkirk (1995); see section 2.5). Diesing argues that the subject in (92a) is an argument of the eventive adjective *available* (raised into [Spec, I]), but the subject in (92b) is not an argument of the generic adjective *altruistic*. In the latter case the subject is an argument of the copula+adjective. Thus, (92a) is analyzed as a raising structure and (92b) as a control structure. The stress pattern then follows directly. In (92a) the subject is selectionally ordered with respect to the adjective; therefore, the S-NSR applies and assigns NS to the subject. In (92b) the subject is not an argument of the adjective; therefore, they are not members of the same selectional chain. Consequently, the S-NSR fails to apply; the C-NSR applies instead and assigns NS to the lowest constituent in the c-command ordering, namely, to the adjective.[29] The same analysis would extend to the contrast in (93).

Whether or not the analysis sketched above is viable depends crucially on the syntactic analysis of such sentences put forth by Diesing. There is an alternative analysis, independent of the particularities of the syntactic analysis of such constructions, which capitalizes on the fact that generics are bona fide sentence topics (as suggested by the fact that they license backward pronominalization; see section 1.1.2).[30] Suppose that generics in subject position are topics par excellence. Furthermore, if topics are never part of the focus by definition (see section 1.1.2),[31] then it follows that generic subjects cannot carry the NS within a phrase. In effect, if sentence topics are [−F], they are metrically invisible to the NSR.

To summarize: In this section I have provided an account for the interaction of NS and focus in German. The data are far from trivial. They go far beyond the generalization usually associated with German: NS falls on the complement immediately to the left of the verb in V-final structures and on the last constituent in V2 structures. When defocalized (or other metrically invisible) material is left-adjacent to the verb in V-final structures, the constituent that bears NS may be quite removed from the verb (e.g., (82)). I have also shown that there are cases in which the position of NS is ambiguous, although the focus structure remains the same. These are structures in which the complement is lacking or defocalized; NS then falls either on the subject or on the verb (e.g., (48), (49) and (75), (76), (77)). My working hypothesis has been that, in order to deal with this complex array of data, a modular NSR is needed—that is, an NSR that comprises two distinct parts: one sensitive to selectional ordering and one sensitive to constituent ordering. What is common to both is that NS falls on the last metrically visible constituent in the ordering (whether the domain is the selectional tree or the constituent structure tree). As I will show, there are ample crosslinguistic data to support such a modular view of the NSR.

2.3.2 English

Chomsky and Halle (1968) put forth the early version of the NSR on the basis of English data. Further research on the topic (see, e.g., Bolinger 1972, Schmerling 1976) showed that the facts concerning phrasal stress in English are more complex than initially thought and that the NSR (at least, in its original version) cannot account for the entire array of data.

Chomsky and Halle's NSR (in present terms, the C-NSR) correctly predicts the position of NS in the following cases, in which the VP contains a complement or an adjunct. In such cases NS falls on the rightmost constituent.

(94) a. Karl lost his bóok.
 b. Karl lost his book in the líving room.
 c. Karl worked in his óffice.
 d. Karl worked on his mánuscript.
 e. Karl worked on his manuscript in his óffice.

Schmerling (1976) made the important discovery that when the VP contains only the predicate, NS may fall on the subject in an out-of-the-blue context. Some examples are given in (95) and (96) (see Schmerling 1976 and Gussenhoven 1984 for many more).

(95) a. The báby's crying.
  b. The báby's laughing.
  c. The spíder jumps.
  d. Máry's dancing.
  e. Máry's reading.
  f. Máry voted.

(96) a. The sún came out.
  b. The máil has arrived.
  c. My bág has disappeared.

The stress pattern in (95) and (96) clearly shows that the S-NSR is also active in English. The question that arises at this point is whether (a) in English, as in German, the S-NSR has primacy over the C-NSR, or (b) *in English, unlike in German, the S-NSR and the C-NSR are on an equal footing, with either one applying at any given point in the computation.* This is not an easy question to answer, but if we take the entire array of data into consideration, it seems that the S-NSR does not have primacy over the C-NSR in English. Either one may apply, generating ambiguous prosodic patterns for a given focus structure in many cases. Which of the two patterns is actually used in a given discourse situation depends on extragrammatical considerations (such as the information that is considered to be most relevant and merits highlighting).

The examples in (95) may also be pronounced, in an out-of-the-blue context, with NS on the verb.

(97) a. The baby's crýing.
  b. The baby's láughing.
  c. The spider júmps.
  d. Mary's dáncing.
  e. Mary's réading.
  f. Mary vóted.

If the S-NSR applies, then NS is assigned to the subject (as in (95)); if the C-NSR applies, then NS falls on the predicate (as in (97)). Now, is this ambiguity due to the action of the auxiliary convention (74) (in conjunction with the Germanic version of the NSR), or to the fact that in English the S-NSR and the C-NSR are not ordered with respect to each other?[32] The relevant data to check would be structures with unaccusative and passive verbs. If NS falls unambiguously on the subject in such structures, then the facts (and therefore the analysis) would appear to be exactly like those of German. Most of the native speakers consulted in fact did not accept the examples in (96) with NS on the predicate in an out-of-the-blue context.[33] On the other hand, they did accept NS on the subject or on the verb in examples with *die*, also an unaccusative verb (cf. *Jóhn died* and *John díed*). But it is not clear that such an example is very compelling in light of the following well-known contrast, due to Schmerling (1976):

(98) a. Jóhnson died.
   b. Truman díed.

Schmerling comments:

The differences in stress contours seem to be correlated with differences in the contexts in which these two reports were uttered. Johnson's death came out of the blue; it was not news that we were waiting for.... When Truman died, on the other hand, his condition had been the subject of daily news reports for some time. Thus, a speaker uttering [(98b)] could assume that the audience was aware of the possibility that this report would in fact be given. (p. 90)

Given the discourse context attributed by Schmerling to the stress pattern in (98b), it is reasonable to assume that the subject in this example is a topic and therefore defocalized.[34]

Turning back to the examples in (96): It could very well be that the unavailability of a prosodic structure with NS on the predicate for such examples is due to the "pragmatic lightness" of the predicates involved. The subject being more noteworthy or relevant than the predicate, stress on the subject is preferred. (Note that the fact that pragmatically based notions such as "noteworthy" or "relevant" are difficult to define rigorously does not mean that they are not real.) If something of this sort is going on, then the grammar should allow both prosodic structures (with NS on the subject and with NS on the predicate) in an out-of-the-blue context for the examples in (96). Extragrammatical considerations (such as relevance or noteworthiness) will then force us to choose the pattern with NS on the subject. There are two reasons why this line of thought might in fact be correct.

First, the literature reveals at least one example with a passive verb, which is claimed to be prosodically ambiguous in an out-of-the-blue context.

(99) a. Tréspassers will be prosecuted.
   b. Trespassers will be prósecuted.

Selkirk (1995, 560), commenting on this example, claims that both patterns are possible with an eventive interpretation and a wide focus structure. Note that the fact that the subject is interpreted existentially in such examples renders the topic-based analysis (suggested by Schmerling for (98b)) impossible for (99b). Compare with the German example in (93a), which is prosodically unambiguous.

Second, English exhibits the following well-known contrasts, first discussed by Bolinger (1972):

(100) a. The end of the chapter is reserved for various problems to compúterize.
   b. The end of the chapter is reserved for various próblems to solve.

(101) a. I have a point to émphasize.
   b. I have a póint to make.

(102) a. I can't finish in an hour—there are simply too many topics to elúcidate.
   b. I can't finish in an hour—there are simply too many tópics to cover.

(103) a. I'm hot. I'm looking for something cool to drínk.
   b. Next month we may be out on the street. I'm looking for a hóuse to rent.

As Bolinger points out, both members of each pair are possible in an out-of-the-blue context. Whether NS falls on the relativized object (as predicted by the S-NSR) or on the predicate in the relative clause (as predicted by the C-NSR) depends on pragmatic factors. In effect, NS falls on the relativized object if the predicate is semantically light or highly predictable within that particular context (see example (b) in each pair). Otherwise, NS falls on the predicate (see example (a) in each pair).[35]

That fact that similar contrasts do not seem to exist in German is particularly informative. See for example the following pair (comparable to the English examples in (100)). In both cases NS falls on the relativized object (*Problem*).[36]

(104) a. Hans hat ein Problém zu lösen.
       Hans has a   problem to solve

b. Hans hat ein Problém zu digitalisieren.
   Hans has a problem to computerize

Finally, note that, as in German (see the contrast in (56)), the presence of an adjunct between the argument and the verb brings about a change in the position of NS. (The example is from Gussenhoven 1984, 27.)

(105) a. Our dóg's disappeared.
      b. Our dog's mysteriously disappéared.

The contrast receives the same explanation as in German. In (105a) the subject and the verb are derivatively metrical sisters; therefore, the S-NSR may apply and assign NS to the subject (i.e., the lowest constituent in the selectional ordering). On the other hand, in (105b) the subject and the verb are not metrical sisters. The adjunct and the verb are metrical sisters and, given that they are not selectionally ordered, only the C-NSR can apply, assigning NS to the verb (i.e., the lowest constituent in terms of asymmetric c-command).[37]

To conclude: It is unquestionable that the S-NSR is also active in English, alongside the C-NSR. Less obvious is whether, in English, the S-NSR has primacy over the C-NSR (as in German) or whether the S-NSR and the C-NSR are unordered. The prosodic ambiguity in (99) and Bolinger's examples (100)–(103) seem to point to the correctness of the latter analysis, especially in view of the absence of Bolinger's type of contrast in German.

2.3.3 Summary

On the basis of Germanic data, I have motivated the existence of a modular NSR (106) (=(66)), which consists of two parts: the S-NSR, defined in terms of selectional ordering, and the C-NSR, defined in terms of asymmetric c-command. The common property of the two parts of the NSR is that prominence is assigned to the *lowest* constituent in the relevant ordering. In German the S-NSR takes precedence over the C-NSR. Main phrasal prominence is then computed by rule (107) (=(10)) on the basis of the output of the NSR.

(106) *Revised NSR*
   Given two sister nodes C_i and C_j, (a) if C_i and C_j are selectionally ordered, in the sense of (57) (=(58)), the one lower in the selectional ordering is more prominent, (b) otherwise, the one lower in the asymmetric c-command ordering is more prominent.

(107) The terminal element dominated solely by prominent constituents within a phrase is designated as the rhythmically most prominent one within that phrase (see Liberman 1975).

The revised NSR is applied in accordance with the convention in (108) (=(19)), with the associated definitions in (109) (=(17)) and (110) (=(15)).

(108) *Convention for the application of the NSR*
Given two analyses of the syntactic tree $\ldots, C_i, \ldots, C_j, \ldots$ and $\ldots, K_i, \ldots, K_j, \ldots$ such that $\ldots, C_i, \ldots, C_j, \ldots$ and $\ldots, K_i, \ldots, K_j, \ldots$ are metrically nondistinct at (C_i, K_i) and at (C_j, K_j) and (C_i, C_j) meets some condition P of the structural description of the NSR in the standard sense, then (K_i, K_j) is taken to meet P as well.

(109) Two analyses $\ldots, C, \ldots$ and $\ldots, K, \ldots$ of the syntactic tree are *metrically nondistinct at* (C, K) $=_{def}$ the constituents C and K are metrically nondistinct.

(110) Constituents A and B are *metrically nondistinct* $=_{def}$ A and B dominate the same set of metrically visible heads.

A central subcase of the convention in (108) (=(19)) is the definition of metrical sisterhood in (111) (=(18)).

(111) Constituents X and Y are *metrical sisters* $=_{def}$ there exists an analysis of the syntactic tree $\ldots, Z, W, \ldots$ such that (a) Z and W are sisters and (b) the analysis $\ldots, Z, W, \ldots$ is metrically nondistinct from the analysis $\ldots, X, \ldots, Y, \ldots$ at (Z, X) and at (W, Y).

Metrically invisible constituents are characterized as in (112) (see (41) and (42)).

(112) The *metrically invisible* constituents for the NSR in English and German are defocalized constituents and anaphoric constituents, as well as empty categories (the latter are metrically invisible in all languages).

To account for ambiguities in cases in which the subject and (a covertly or overtly) transitive lexical verb are metrical sisters, I have appealed to the auxiliary convention in (113) (=(74)).

(113) *Auxiliary to convention (108) for application of the NSR (optional)*
If some projections of the verbal components V_i and V_j of the lexical verb are metrically nondistinct, then V_i and V_j are analyzed as metrically nondistinct for the purpose of applying the interpretive convention in (108) (= (19))

Finally, I have suggested that in English the S-NSR and the C-NSR have equal status: there is no ordering relation between them.

2.4 Romance

I turn now to Romance languages (in particular, to French and Spanish), which are fundamentally different from Germanic languages. Basically, the facts show that in Romance only the C-NSR is active; the S-NSR is not. Such crosslinguistic differences provide further support for a modularized version of the NSR. Furthermore, as we will see, there are interesting differences within the Romance languages. Whereas in French (as in English) defocalized and anaphoric materials are metrically invisible, in Spanish all phonological material is metrically visible. The consequence is that Spanish is even more rigid than French with respect to the positioning of NS.

Let us examine French first.[38] The availability of stress patterns like those in (114) and (115) in the contexts given in brackets indicates that defocalized material in this language is not metrically visible for the computation of the NSR. (As before, I mark the position of NS in Romance languages with underlining rather than with ´, since ´ is already used in these languages for other purposes. I continue to use italics to indicate metrical invisibility. Example (115) is from Ronat 1982, 37.)

(114) a. Jean *a   téléphoné.*
    Jean has phoned
        [Who phoned?]
   b. Marie *a   mangé le   gâteau.*
    Marie has eaten the cake
        [Who ate the cake?]

(115) *Pierre a   mis ton* livre *dans sa poche.*
    Pierre has put your book in   his pocket
        [What did Pierre put in his pocket?]

Given that the verb phrase in (114) and the prepositional phrase in (115) are metrically invisible for the computation of the NSR (more precisely, the C-NSR), the algorithm will compute the last metrically visible constituent as rhythmically most prominent: *Jean*, *Marie*, and *livre* in the respective examples. (Note that only the direct object is in fact metrically visible in (115).)

Ronat (1982) provides many examples in French comparable to Ladd's (1980) "default accent" cases, which I reanalyzed in section 2.2.2 in terms of anaphoricity (following insights in Williams 1997). In (116) and (117) the anaphoric constituent (*la télévision* and *les habits verts*, respectively) has been implicitly mentioned in the discourse. In effect, *la télévision* is "informally entailed" by the predicate *regarde les informations* and *les habits verts* is "informally entailed" by *Académie Française*; see note 4 in chapter 1 for discussion of the notions of formal and informal entailment. (Examples (116) and (117) are from Ronat 1982, 34–35.)[39]

(116) Paul regarde les informations tous les soirs; Marie est <u>jalouse</u>
Paul watches the news every evening Marie is jealous
de la télévision.
of the television

(117) A: Le professeur Dupont veut être élu à
Professor Dupont wants to-be elected to
l'Académie Française.
the Académie Française
B: Oui. Il aime <u>énormément</u> *les habits verts.*
yes he likes a-lot the suits green
'Yes. He likes green suits a lot.'

The statement in (41) can therefore by generalized to French.

(118) Defocalized and anaphoric constituents are *metrically invisible* for the NSR in English, in German, and in French.

Despite the prosodic similarities between French and English/German that are attributable to (118), there is a fundamental difference between the two. Unlike English and German, French does not allow NS on the subject in intransitive structures in an out-of-the-blue context. In effect, as (119) and (120) illustrate, the French counterparts of (95) and (96) are impossible in an out-of-the-blue context. In all cases NS falls on the predicate in an out-of-the-blue context.

(119) a. *Le bébé pleure. (vs. Le bébé pleure)
　　 b. *Le bébé rit. (vs. Le bébé rit)
　　 c. *L'araignée saute. (vs. L'araignée saute)
　　 d. *Marie dance. (vs. Marie dance)
　　 e. *Marie lit. (vs. Marie lit)
　　 f. *Marie a voté. (vs. Marie a voté)
　　　　 [Out-of-the-blue context]

(120) a. *Le soleil est sorti. (vs. Le soleil est sorti)
　　 b. *Le courrier est arrivé. (vs. Le courrier est arrivé)
　　 c. *Mon sac a disparu. (vs. Mon sac a disparu)
　　　　 [Out-of-the-blue context]

The object of a relative clause may not bear NS in French either, no matter how predictable the predicate in the relative clause might be. Thus, Bolinger's (1972) type of contrast does not exist in French.

(121) a. J'ai　un problème à　résoudre. (*un problème à résoudre)
　　　　 I have a　próblem　to solve
　　 b. J'ai　un problème à　digitaliser.
　　　　 I have a　problem　to compúterize

(122) a. J'ai　un travail à　faire. (*un travail à faire)
　　　　 I have a　jób　to do
　　 b. J'ai　un travail à　finir.
　　　　 I have a　job　to fínish

Such facts clearly show that in French the S-NSR is not active; the C-NSR applies in all cases.

Let us turn next to Spanish. As in French, the S-NSR is not active in this language. The C-NSR applies instead in all configurations. This is shown by the impossibility of stress patterns like the ones in (123) and (124) (the Spanish counterparts to the English examples in (95) and (96)). In fact, such examples are impossible with a narrow, noncontrastive focus interpretation in Standard Spanish as well (see below for further discussion).

(123) a. *El bebé llora. (vs. El bebé llora)
　　 b. *El bebé rie. (vs. El bebé rie)
　　 c. *La araña salta. (vs. La araña salta)
　　 d. *María baila. (vs. María baila)
　　 e. *María lee. (vs. María lee)
　　 f. *María votó. (vs. María votó)

(124) a. *El sol salió. (vs. El sol salió)
b. *El correo llegó. (vs. El correo llegó)
c. *Mi bolso desapareció. (vs. Mi bolso desapareció)

Nor does Bolinger's type of contrast exist in Spanish. The following are Spanish translations of the French examples in (121) and (122). Compare once more with the English pairs in (100)–(103).

(125) a. Tengo un problema que resolver. (*un problema que resolver)
b. Tengo un problema que computarizar.

(126) a. Tengo una tarea que hacer. (*una tarea que hacer)
b. Tengo una tarea que terminar.

I conclude then that in Spanish and French only the C-NSR part of the algorithm is active.

(127) *French and Spanish NSR*
Given two sister nodes C_i and C_j, the one lower in the asymmetric c-command ordering is more prominent.

On the other hand, Standard Spanish differs in an important way from French. In Spanish the statement in (128), rather than the statement in (118), applies.[40]

(128) All phonological material is metrically visible for the NSR in Spanish.

Consequently, Standard Spanish counterparts to the French examples in (114), with NS on the preverbal subject, do not exist. Sentences with main prominence on the preverbal subject can only have a contrastive (or emphatic) interpretation. In other words, they are appropriate in a situation in which the presupposition is explicitly negated, as indicated by the explicit or implicit presence of the negative tags in (129), but not as an answer to a *wh*-question. Recall that such prosodic patterns are generated by the Emphatic/Contrastive Stress Rule, rather than by the NSR (see section 2.1.2).

(129) a. JUAN llamó por teléfono (no Pedro).
Juan phoned (not Pedro)
b. MARÍA se comió el pastel (no Marta).
María ate the cake (not Marta)

Given (128), Standard Spanish also fails to treat anaphoric material as metrically invisible. Thus, the Standard Spanish counterpart to Ladd's

Prosody and Focus in Germanic and Romance 77

(1980, 81) example in (39) (repeated here as (130a)) has a contrastive (or emphatic) interpretation and is therefore inappropriate in the intended context (given that it is not unexpected that Republicans should denounce a bill proposed by a Democratic president).

(130) a. A bill was sent to Congress today by President Carter which would require peanut butter sandwiches to be served at all government functions. At a press conference today, a group of Senators led by Republican Barry Goldwater of Arizona [denóunced *the measure*]. Goldwater said ...
b. ...un grupo de senadores dirigido por el republicano Barry Goldwater de Arizona DENUNCIÓ *la medida*...

Similarly, the Spanish counterparts to the French examples in (116) and (117) would be interpreted emphatically.[41]

Because the position of NS in Standard Spanish is unambiguously at the end of the sentence (or phrase), cases in which the main prominence is in phrase-internal position never give rise to overlapping analyses, but instead are unambiguously interpreted as cases of contrastive focus. Therefore, in this language it is easy to assess the scope of the focus in sentences with contrastive stress. In section 2.1.2 I gave the following formulation of the Focus/Contrastive Stress Correspondence Principle.

(131) *Focus/Contrastive Stress Correspondence Principle*
A word with contrastive stress must be dominated by every F-marked constituent in the phrase.

Indeed, the sentences in (132) with contrastive stress on the adjective inside the subject are ambiguous with respect to the scope of the contrast, as indicated. Either the adjective or a constituent that exhaustively dominates the adjective may constitute the scope of the contrast. On the other hand, in (133), with contrastive stress on the noun, the scope of the contrast is limited to the noun. In effect, the DP subject that contains the contrastively stressed noun cannot be interpreted as focused, because if the DP is marked [F], so is the PP that it dominates, but the contrastively stressed noun does not dominate the PP (as required by (131)). In effect, a constituent marked [+F] may only dominate [+F] constituents; see note 7 in chapter 1 as well as the appendix to this chapter.

(132) a. El gato de sombrero {ROJO} escribió un libro sobre
the cat of hat   red   wrote   a book about
ratones (no el   de sombrero AZUL).
rats   not the-one of hat   blue

'The cat with a red hat wrote a book about rats (not the one with a blue hat).'

 b. {El gato de sombrero ROJO} escribió un libro sobre
   the cat of hat   red wrote a book about
   ratones (no el perro de chaqueta VERDE).
   rats not the dog of jacket green
   'The cat with a red hat wrote a book about rats (not the dog with a green jacket).'

(133) a. El {GATO} de sombrero rojo escribió un libro sobre ratones (no el PERRO de sombrero rojo).
   'The cat with a red hat wrote a book about rats (not the dog with a red hat).'

 b. *El {GATO de sombrero rojo} escribió un libro sobre ratones (no el PERRO de chaqueta verde).

To summarize: We have seen that Romance languages (such as French and Spanish) differ in a fundamental way from Germanic languages (such as English and German) with respect to the positioning of NS. Although in Germanic languages NS is sensitive to the selectional properties of predicates in certain structural environments, this is never the case in Romance. In Romance NS is always assigned to the last (metrically visible) constituent. In other words, in these languages only constituent structure is relevant in computing the position of NS. The modular formulation of the NSR put forth here allows the differences between Germanic and Romance to be characterized correctly. In Germanic both the S-NSR and the C-NSR are active; in Romance only the C-NSR applies.

2.5 Alternative Analyses

2.5.1 Schmerling 1976, Selkirk 1984, 1995, Gussenhoven 1984

As mentioned earlier, it was Schmerling (1976) who first uncovered the relevance of selectional relations in the computation of phrasal stress in English, on the basis of which she proposed the following set of rules (pp. 76, 82):

(134) *Principle 1*
   Those portions of a sentence receive reduced stress which contain material presupposed by the speaker to be true and to be known to the addressee(s).[42]

(135) *Principle 2*
 The verb receives lower stress than the subject and the direct object, if there is one; in other words, predicates receive lower stress than their arguments, irrespective of their linear position in surface structure.

The fact that the last constituent in non-V-final structures is systematically the most prominent, whether the last constituent is an argument or an adjunct (as in the examples in (94)), is attributed to a late rhythmic rule, first suggested by Newman (1946).

(136) *Principle 3*
 Given a sequence of stresses which are equal and greater than other stresses within the intonational unit, the last such stress will be more prominent than the others.

As pointed out by Selkirk (1984), the empirical problem with the formulation of Schmerling's Principle 2 is that verbs may be stressed in English; see the intransitive examples in (97). In none of these examples does the subject need to be interpreted as presupposed or defocalized. See also Bolinger's (1972) examples in (100)–(103) and Gussenhoven's (1984) example in (105b). This is also true in German; see the unergative structures in (48a) and (49a) and the transitive structures with a defocalized object in (75b), (76b), and (77b), among others.

The proposals made by Selkirk (1984, 1995) and Gussenhoven (1984) incorporate the basic insights of Schmerling's work: it is the predicate-argument relations, not constituent structure, that is relevant in determining phrasal stress assignment. But both Selkirk's and Gussenhoven's analyses depart from Schmerling's in assuming that the relation between stress (in their terms, pitch accent) assignment and predicate-argument relations is mediated by focus projection rules (or focus-domain formation rules). Selkirk (1984, 1995) proposes the set of rules in (137). Rule (137a) establishes a relation between pitch accent and focus (focus may only "project" from accented words). Rule (137b) dictates that the focus may be "projected" from a head or its internal argument. (The formulation in (137) is from Selkirk 1995, 555, 561).

(137) a. *Basic Focus Rule*
 An accented word is F-marked.
 b. *Focus Projection Rules*
  i. F-marking of the head of a phrase licenses the F-marking of the phrase.

ii. F-marking of an internal argument of a head licenses the F-marking of the head.
iii. F-marking of the antecedent of a trace left by NP- or *wh*-movement licenses the F-marking of the trace.

It is assumed that F-marking is intimately related to the informational structure of the sentence. More precisely:

(138) a. The Focus of a sentence (FOC) is defined as an F-marked constituent not dominated by any other F-marked constituent.
b. F-marked constituents which are not a Focus are interpreted as new in the discourse, while a constituent without F-marking is interpreted as given. A Focus constituent, on the other hand, may be interpreted as either given or new in the discourse.

((138a) and (138b) are quoted from Selkirk 1995, 555 and 556, respectively.) As in Schmerling's system, late rhythmic rules ensure that the last accented word receives main prominence, but they play no role in determining the possible F-Structure of the sentence. (The rules in (139) are quoted from Selkirk 1995, 562–563.)

(139) a. *Pitch Accent Prominence Rule (PAPR)*
A syllable associated to a pitch accent has greater stress prominence than a syllable which is not associated to a pitch accent.
b. *Nuclear Stress Rule*
The most prominent syllable of the rightmost constituent in a phrase P is the most prominent syllable of P.

To ilustrate very briefly: Consider the wide focus interpretation of the examples in (140), where deaccented constituents are marked with italics and the rhythmically most prominent syllable is marked as usual.

(140) a. $_{FOC}[[_{F_1}$ The $[_{F_2}$ báby's]]$_i$ $[_{F_3}[_{F_4}$ e]$_i$ $[_{F_5}$ *crying*]]]$_{FOC}$.
b. $_{FOC}[[_{F_1}$ The *baby's*]$_i$ $[_{F_2}[_{F_3}$ e]$_i$ $[_{F_4}$ crýing]]]$_{FOC}$.

The interpretation of (140a) is accounted for by the rules in (137) in the following way. The argument's nominal head is pitch-accented and therefore F-marked by rule (137a); this F-marking is inherited by the nominal projection by virtue of rule (137bi). The F-marking of the argument is inherited by its trace by virtue of rule (137biii) and the F-marked trace then licenses the F-marking of the verbal head by rule (137bii). This captures the fact that although the verb is deaccented, it is part of the focus.

The wide focus interpretation of (140b) is accounted for as follows: both the head of the NP argument and the head of the VP predicate are pitch-accented and therefore F-marked (rule (137a)); their projections are then F-marked by rule (137bi). The location of main prominence is determined by rule (139b): the last pitch-accented word is the most prominent (namely, *baby* in (140a) and *crying* in (140b)).

Although the trace of the subject of an intransitive verb (as in (140)) is intended to qualify as an internal argument (where *internal argument* is understood as "sister argument to the verb"; see Selkirk 1995, 556—no distinction is made between unergatives and unaccusatives in this respect), the trace of the subject of a transitive verb does not qualify as an internal argument. Therefore, in the case of (141) (where italics indicate the "deaccented" material), the trace of the subject cannot license the F-marking of the verb, which in turn would have licensed the F-marking of the VP. Therefore, such an example may have narrow focus only on the subject.

(141) $_{FOC}[[_F$ Máry$]]_{FOC}$ *bought a book about rats.*

Although Selkirk's system correctly accounts for the English facts discussed above,[43] it fails to account for the most basic fact of German. As we have seen, in V-final transitive structures, a non-defocalized direct object obligatorily carries NS; see (43)–(44), (104), and (82), repeated here.[44] In Selkirk's terms, in these cases the verb in final position must be "deaccented," but why this should be so remains a mystery.

(142) a. Hans hat ein Búch gelesen.
Hans has a   book read
b. Karl hat ein Búch gekauft.
Karl has a   book bought
[Out-of-the-blue context]

(143) a. Hans hat ein Problém zu lösen.
Hans has a   problem to solve
b. Hans hat ein Problém zu digitalisieren.
Hans has a   problem to computerize
[Out-of-the-blue context]

(144) Den Húnd   *hat Karl*   *geschlagen.*
the   dog(ACC) has Karl(NOM) beaten
[What did Karl do?]

Similarly, we have seen that if the verb selects an object and a PP (directional) complement, NS falls obligatorily on the PP directional complement (if it is not defocalized); see (45)–(46), repeated here. Again the reason why the verb in such cases must be "deaccented" remains unaccounted for.

(145) a. Karl hat ein Buch ins Regál gestellt.
Karl has a book on-the shelf put
b. Karl hat die Milch in den Kühlschrank gestellt.
Karl has the milk in the refrigerator put
[Out-of-the-blue context]

Not only does Selkirk's system fail to account for the above-mentioned facts in German, it also fails to account for the differences between Germanic and Romance. In effect, we have seen that in Romance, information concerning selectional relations is irrelevant in the computation of rhythmic prominence. It is hard to see how the focus projection rules in (137) can be modularized to account for such crosslinguistic differences.

The system put forth by Gussenhoven (1984) is very close in spirit to Selkirk's (1984, 1995) (although developed independently). It assumes that the relation between pitch accent assignment and predicate-argument relations is mediated by focus domain formation rules, the main component of which is the *Sentence Accent Assignment Rules (SAAR)*; see (146). Gussenhoven (1984, 28) comments:

... SAAR operates over focus domains. A focus domain can be defined as one or more constituents whose [+focus] status can be signalled by a single accent. We will therfore formulate SAAR in terms of (1) a domain assignment rule, and (2) a rule assigning an accent to every domain formed. In [(146)], A, P and C stand for Argument, Predicate and Condition, respectively, while X and Y stand for any of these. Underlining symbolises [+focus], absence of underlining [−focus]. Square brackets are used to mark off focus domains, and the asterisk indicates a sentence accent.

As in Schmerling's and Selkirk's system, the NSR is also assumed to be a late rhythmic rule that asigns main prominence to the last pitch-accented word.

(146) *Sentence Accent Assignment Rules*
    a. Domain assignment
        $\underline{P}(X)\underline{A} \to [P(X)A]$
        $\underline{A}(X)\underline{P} \to [A(X)P]$
        $\underline{Y} \to [Y]$

b. Accent assignment
  [ ] → [*]. In AP/PA, accent A.

In the spirit of Schmerling's (1976) Principle 2, Gussenhoven's accent assignment rule says explicitly that if a predicate and an argument are part of the same focus domain, the argument must be accented. But, unlike Schmerling's Principle 2, Gussenhoven's accent assignment rule does not preclude in principle that in such contexts a predicate may be assigned an accent as well. Therefore, it leaves open two possibilities: (a) a predicate may not be assigned an accent if it is part of the same focus domain as its argument, and (b) a predicate may (optionally) be assigned an accent if it is part of the same focus domain as its argument. If we assume (a), then the SAAR face the same type of empirical shortcomings as Schmerling's system, given that in both English and German there are numerous cases in which the predicate is accented in such contexts (see discussion of Schmerling's system). If we assume (b), then the SAAR face the same empirical shortcomings as Selkirk's system. In effect, there are cases in German in which the verb must be analyzed as deaccented since NS falls obligatorily on the object and not on the verb (see discussion of Selkirk's system). One could perhaps refine Gussenhoven's assumptions concerning lexicosyntactic structures (along the lines suggested in section 2.3.1) and revise his rules accordingly in order to make them empirically adequate for Germanic, an exercise that I will not attempt her. On the other hand, it is hard to see how the SAAR can be modularized to account for the differences between Germanic and Romance.

The only way to deal with the Romance languages within the Schmerling-Selkirk-Gussenhoven approach is to assume that an intonational constraint is active in such languages. In effect, I have made such a proposal elsewhere (Zubizarreta 1995b, 1996), suggesting that Romance (unlike Germanic) is subject to the following constraint:

(147) Within an intonational phrase, the rhythmically most prominent word must be right-adjacent to the intonational phrase boundary.

The problem with such a constraint is that it can be violated in certain cases. First consider Standard Spanish, in which the exceptional cases can perhaps be accommodated via a refinement of the constraint. In this language, although phrasal main prominence must be right-adjacent to the intonational phrase in cases of noncontrastive focus, it need not be right-adjacent to the intonational phrase in cases of contrastive focus or emphasis. See for instance the discussion with respect to the examples in

(129).[45] In order to deal with such facts, I suggested in Zubizarreta 1995b, 1996 that the two cases of rhythmic prominence could be distinguished in terms of their intonational properties. The pitch accent associated with contrastive focus or emphasis is marked with the diacritic Ex-H (for extra-High).[46] The constraint in (147) can therefore be reformulated for Standard Spanish as in (148).

(148) Within an intonational phrase, the rhythmically most prominent word must be right-adjacent to the intonational phrase boundary, unless it is associated with an Ex-H pitch accent.

Although the facts of Standard Spanish can be handled in this manner, the facts of French and of Brazilian Portuguese (a language comparable to French with respect to the pertinent issue) are not amenable to the same analysis.[47] In these languages the word bearing main prominence may be nonadjacent to the intonational phrase boundary in cases of noncontrastive focus (see (114) and (115)), as well as in cases involving anaphoric constituents (see (116) and (117)). On the other hand, there are basic differences between these languages and Germanic with respect to the placement of NS; see (119)/(120) and (121)/(122). This state of affairs suggests that it is incorrect to define the differences between Romance and Germanic with respect to the placement of NS in terms of an intonational constraint. As shown in section 2.4, the differences between the two types of languages are better captured in terms of a modularized NSR, in conjunction with a parameter that establishes whether or not a language may analyze certain phonologically overt elements as metrically invisible.[48]

Finally, it is worthwhile to point out another insufficiency in Selkirk's and Gussenhoven's systems, in which [+F] and [−F] domains are defined in terms of presence versus absence of pitch accent within such domains. Recall that the defocalized phrase, which in Selkirk's and Gussenhoven's terms is defined as "deaccented," actually does contain an audible miniature accent (cf. (32a) and (33a), repeated here as (149a) and (150a)); I have referred to such miniature accents as echo accents because their location is determined by the context question (given in (149b) and (150b)).

(149) a. [F The cat in the blue hát] *has written a book about râts.*
b. (I would like to know) who has written a book about ráts.
  (NS on *rats*)

(150) a. [_F The cat with the blue hát] *has written a bôok about rats.*
b. (I would like to know) who has written a Book about rats.
(contrastive stress on *book*)

The same remark can be made with respect to German. In the following examples, in which the VP is defocalized, a miniature accent is present on the complement in (151a) and on the verb in (151b). If the location of the miniature accent is displaced within the defocalized VP, the focus/presupposition structure is affected. In effect, displacement of the miniature accent in such examples would require a context question with a different prosodic structure and a distinct focus/presupposition structure.

(151) a. Háns *hat an seinem Papîer gearbeitet.*
Hans has on his paper worked
[Who has worked on his paper?]
b. Háns *hat in seinem Büro geârbeitet.*
Hans has in his office worked
[Who has worked in his office?]

The conclusion is, then, that although in certain cases defocalized constituents are pronounced with a reduced pitch accent, they cannot be said to be deaccented. Such domains contain miniature pitch accents, which are focus-relevant. The notion of "absence of pitch accent" in the phonological description of intonation assumed by Selkirk and Gussenhoven needs to be refined.

2.5.2 Cinque 1993

Cinque's (1993) proposal was designed to account for what he understood to be a basic generalization regarding NS.

(152) NS falls on the most embedded element on the recursive side of the tree.

This generalization was meant to capture the fact that NS falls on the verbal or prepositional object in transitive and ditransitive structures, respectively, regardless of whether the structure is head initial or head final. In effect, Cinque's proposal is prior to Kayne's (1994). It assumes that languages are parameterized into right-branching and left-branching, German being of the former type and English of the latter.

In order to ensure that NS is not attracted by the subject or other specifiers when these are more complex than the predicate (e.g., [[*the cat* *that chased the ràt's] hát*] vs. *[[*The cat that chased the ràt's] hàt*]), a distinction is made between "major" and "minor" paths of embedding (see (153)), and the convention in (154) is adopted.

(153) a. The *major path of embedding* is constituted by nodes on the X-bar axis (X, X′, XP) and the nodes on the recursive side of the tree.
b. The *minor path of embedding* is constituted by nodes on the nonrecursive side of the tree.

(154) *Convention*
When the minor path joins the major path, the minor cycle is visible in the form of one asterisk.

As Truckenbrodt (1993) notes, the distinction between major path and minor path formulated in terms of "recursive versus nonrecursive side" of the tree gives the wrong result for a language like German. Here, the recursive side of the VP is to the left (the VP is head final). Adjuncts are also on the left. Still, they do not attract main stress (see (50b), (51a), and (53a–c). As Truckenbrodt points out, adjuncts do not attract NS even when they have a complex structure (i.e., a structure with a greater depth of embedding). This is illustrated by the examples in (155). The difficulty with such examples is that because they are phonologically heavy, there is a strong tendency to divide them into smaller intonational units. But to the extent that they can be pronounced as one intonational unit (although this is not the preferred choice), the stress pattern does not change.[49]

(155) a. *Manner*
Maria kann [auf eine bezaubernde Art [die sie wohl
Maria can in a charming way which she presumably
von ihrer Schwester gelernt hat]] flírten.
from her sister learned has flirt
'Maria can flirt in a charming way which she has presumably learned from her sister.'
b. *Time*
Peter ist [an dem Tag [an dem seine Frau Geburtstag
Peter is on the day on which his wife birthday
hatte]] wéggefahren.
had driven-away
'Peter drove away on the day of his wife's birthday.'

c. *Place*
[in den Bergen [wo Peters Verwandten wohnen]]
in the mountains where Peter's relatives live
skífahren
ski
'to ski in the mountains where Peter's relatives live'

As suggested in Zubizarreta 1995b, 1996, we could attempt to remedy the problem noted by Truckenbrodt by reformulating the distinction between major path and minor path of embedding in terms of the notions of *complement node* and *noncomplement node*.

(156) a. The *major path of embedding* is constituted by nodes on the X-bar axis (X, X', XP) and the nodes dominated solely by the complement node, where the complement node is defined as the sister of a head X^0.
b. The *minor path of embedding* is constituted by nodes dominated by a noncomplement node.

If we encode the modifier/complement distinction structurally in terms of adjunction versus sisterhood relations (as in the standard theory), then Cinque's revised NSR and convention (with the notions of major and minor path of embedding revised as in (156)) can correctly capture the facts. The main stress falls on the most deeply embedded *accessible* node in the structure. The complement attracts main stress in the above examples, irrespective of the length of the adjunct, because only the internal structure of material dominated uniquely by complement nodes is accessible to the computation of metrical structure.[50]

Although the distinction between adjuncts and arguments may be accommodated within Cinque's system as indicated above, there are other basic facts about Germanic that it fails to account for. In effect, although Cinque's attempt to formulate the NSR purely in terms of constituent structure captures an important insight, it inherits most of the empirical shortcomings of the *SPE* version of the rule. First, it fails to account for the ambiguity in the position of NS in the case of intransitives in English, and more specifically in the case of unergatives in German. Because Cinque's version of the NSR (like the *SPE* version) is rigidly formulated in terms of constituent structure, there is no auxiliary hypothesis comparable to (81) that can be added to his system in a natural way. (Note that it would be insufficient to refine Cinque's algorithm by appealing to the relevance of VP-internal traces to deal with cases in which NS falls on the subject, given contrasts like *The dóg disappeared* versus *The dog mysteriously disappéared.*) Second, Cinque explicitly assumes that his version of the NSR is meant to account for focus-neutral structures, attributing the prosodic properties of nonneutral focus structure to some unspecified discourse rule. This, I believe, is also a serious shortcoming, given that nonneutral focus structures are subject to the same generalizations as neutral focus structures. The fact that NS falls unambiguously on the object in the example with nonneutral focus in (144) is to be related to the fact that NS falls unambiguously on the object in the examples with neutral focus in (142) and (143). Similarly, the fact that the position of NS is ambiguous in transitive structures with a defocalized object is to be related to the fact that in intransitive structures the position of NS is ambiguous in the same way. Compare (75)–(77) and (48)–(49).

2.6 The Nature of the Focus Prosody Correspondence Principle

Consider the FPCP in (2), repeated in (157), and the rule in (34), repeated in (158), which I will call the *Echo/Nonecho Relative Prominence Principle (ERPR)*.

(157) *FPCP*
 The F-marked constituent of a phrase must contain the rhythmically most prominent word in that phrase.

(158) *ERPP*
 A word that bears an echo stress within a phrase is rhythmically subordinate to the word that bears a nonecho stress within the same phrase.

The FPCP and the ERPP have something in common. The FPCP says that the focused phrase must contain the word that bears main phrasal prominence. The ERPP says that the stress contained within the defocalized phrase (i.e., the echo stress) must be less prominent than the stress contained within the focused phrase (i.e., the nonecho stress). Postulating both the FPCP and the ERPP is redundant. I therefore propose to collapse the two in the form of a rule, which I will call the *Focus Prominence Rule (FPR)*.

(159) *FPR*
 Given two sister nodes C_i (marked [+F]) and C_j (marked [−F]), C_i is more prominent than C_j.

An interesting consequence follows from the interaction of the NSR and the FPR. Strictly speaking, the application of the NSR and the application of the FPR could conflict. In effect, suppose the NSR applies to two sister nodes C_i and C_j and assigns prominence to C_j, where C_j is [−F] and C_i is [+F]; the output of the NSR will then conflict with the FPCP, which requires main prominence on C_i. See the following example:

(160) [[$_F$ The cat in the blue hat] [$_{-F}$ wrote a book about rats]].
    a. The NSR applies to the sister nodes (DP, VP) and assigns main prominence to the VP (which will materialize on *rats*, by virtue of the reapplication of the NSR within the VP).
    b. The FPR applies to the sister nodes (DP, VP) and assigns main prominence to the DP subject (which will materialize on *hat*, by virtue of the application of the NSR within the DP subject).

Languages have ways of resolving or avoiding such a conflict. As we have seen, languages like English and German analyze a [−F] constituent as metrically invisible for the NSR, thus voiding the context of application of this rule. Recall the convention in (12), repeated here.

(161) Relative prominence between two constituents is established by the NSR iff they are both metrically visible (i.e., iff they each dominate at least one metrically visible head).

Thus, in (160) the NSR fails to apply to the sister nodes (DP, VP). The FPR then applies without giving rise to any conflict. In effect, it applies to the sister nodes (DP, VP) and assigns main prominence to the [+F] DP subject. The application of the NSR within the DP subject then places main prominence on *hat*, as shown in (162). Recall that the stress within the VP (marked with the diacritic ˆ) is an echo accent (i.e., a copy of the NS in the context question (*Who wrote a book about ráts?*)), which, owing to the FPR, is less prominent than the stress on the subject (as indicated above).

(162) [[$_F$ The cat in the blue hát] [$_{-F}$ wrote a book about râts]].

In chapter 3 I will discuss how languages like Spanish and Italian, in which all phonologically specified material is metrically visible, resolve such a conflict. Basically, they do so via movement of the [−F] constituent. Such movement operations can be seen as the syntactic counterpart of metrical invisibility.

2.7 Summary and Concluding Remarks

In this chapter I have argued against a monolithic view of the NSR and in favor of a modular view. The modularized NSR that I proposed integrates insights from previous works. It incorporates, and elaborates on, Schmerling's (1976) hypothesis that selectional properties are relevant in computing prominence in Germanic. It also incorporates insights of Cinque's (1993) proposal that the "lowest" element in the constituent structure has a privileged status. The relevance of selectional information is captured by the S-NSR part of the rule (which assigns prominence to the constituent that is *lowest* in the selectional chain), and the relevance of constituent structure is captured by the C-NSR (which assigns prominence to the constituent that is *lowest* in the c-command ordering). Note that the two parts of the rule have something essential in common: each assigns prominence to the lowest constituent in its domain. Where the two parts differ is in their domain of application. The modular NSR has been shown to correctly characterize differences between German and English, and between Germanic and Romance.

Where does the NSR apply: in the PF component or in the syntactic component of the grammar? Although there are PF rules that are sensitive to certain aspects of the syntactic structure (e.g., French liaison and other sandhi rules; see Elordieta 1997 for a comprehensive review and assessment of the literature), I know of no PF rule that is sensitive to selectional relations. Given that the NSR is sensitive not only to constituent structure (i.e., asymmetric c-command) but also to selectional relations, I conclude that the NSR applies in the syntax. More precisely, its natural place of application is prior to Spell-Out and after the feature-checking-driven syntactic derivation (see section 1.3.3).

Cases such as (163) can be readily attributed to a PF restructuring of the metrically interpreted syntactic tree. In effect, if the metrically interpreted syntactic tree is broken into small intonational phrases, the syntactic tree will be concomitantly broken up into smaller trees that correspond to the intonational phrases; see (164). This is so because each intonational phrase is associated with one intonational nucleus, which in the languages under discussion is identified via NS.

(163) (This is the cát) (that chased the rát) . . .

(164) [$_S$ This [$_S$ is [$_S$ the [$_S$ cat [$_S$ that [$_S$ chased [$_S$ the [$_S$ rat]]]]]]]] . . .
    a. [$_S$ This [$_S$ is [$_S$ the [$_S$ cat]]]]
    b. [$_S$ that [$_S$ chased [$_S$ the [$_S$ rat]]]]

My attempt to revise the NSR in order to make it compatible with recalcitrant data in Germanic was not guided simply by an interest in empirical adequacy. Attaining a descriptively adequate formulation of the NSR is of utmost importance here to the extent that I have adopted Chomsky's (1971) and Jackendoff's (1972) hypothesis that NS is relevant in identifying the focus constituent in Germanic and Romance languages (recall the FPCP reformulated as the FPR in section 2.6). I thus diverge from proposals like those of Selkirk (1984, 1995) and Gussenhoven (1984), where what is relevant in determining the scope of the focus is the distribution of accents within the phrase and not the relative rhythmic prominence between accents. As I will show in chapter 3, the Romance languages, especially Spanish and Italian, provide indirect evidence for the FPR. These languages employ sentence-level scrambling operations that ensure that sentence-internal focused constituents end up at the rightmost edge of a phrase (i.e., in the lowest position in the c-command ordering). This is exactly the position to which the C-NSR assigns main prominence. It is not obvious how this generalization can be captured within a theory that denies the relevance of NS in the phonological identification of focus.

Finally, although I have argued in favor of the revised NSR for languages like Germanic and Romance, in which the intonational peak is identified with the rhythmically most prominent syllable in the phrase, I do not want to give the impression that this rule is universal. In a language such as Bengali, described by Hayes and Lahiri (1991), the intonational peak is identified in terms of the intonational phrasing. The intonational nucleus is associated with the leftmost syllable of a nonclitic word within an intonational unit smaller than the intonational phrase— that is, the intermediary phrase in the terms of Beckman and Pierrehumbert (1986), which Hayes and Lahiri argue to be equivalent to the phonological phrase (or p-phrase) of prosodic phonology (Selkirk 1980, Nespor and Vogel 1986, Inkelas and Zec 1990). In focus-neutral structures, the intonational nucleus is on the rightmost p-phrase. In structures that are not focus neutral, the focus must obligatorily form an independent p-phrase and the intonational nucleus is found in this p-phrase. Bengali thus differs from Germanic and Spanish in this respect. In these languages the focus does not form an independent intonational unit (see Beckman and Pierrehumbert 1986 and the appendix to chapter 3). It is furthermore interesting to note that "stress in Bengali is usually quite weak phonetically, sometimes to the point of being almost inaudible"

(Hayes and Lahiri 1991, 56–57). This suggests that Bengali and Germanic/Romance are typologically different; the two types of languages differ with respect to the mechanisms they employ to determine the position of the intonational nucleus. (See Truckenbrodt 1995 for discussion of other languages in the same typological class as Bengali.)

Appendix: Wh-Phrases, the Nuclear Stress Rule, and the Focus Prominence Rule

In this appendix I will briefly discuss the position of NS in simple and multiple questions. I suggest that the FPR does not apply to a *wh*-phrase in C, but does apply to a *wh*-in-situ. Having recognized the relevance of the FPR for *wh*-in-situ, I suggest that superiority effects in questions involving multiple *wh*-phrases can be partially attributed to prosodic considerations.

A.1   *Wh*-Phrase in C and the Focus Prominence Rule

If focus is defined as the nonpresupposed part of the sentence (see section 1.1.1), then the focus of a question is the *wh*-phrase, by definition. I therefore assume that *wh*-phrases are [+F] phrases (see, e.g., Rochemont 1986, Horvath 1986, Tuller 1992). It is then remarkable that the fronted *wh*-phrase in a question such as (165) does not, and may not, bear NS.

(165) a.   (I wonder) what did John réad?
      b. *(I wonder) whát did John read?

Such cases are the mirror image of statements. Whereas in statements NS is contained within the focused constituent, in (165) NS is contained within the presupposed part of the sentence. It must be the case, then, that a fronted *wh*-phrase is licensed by some alternative grammatical mechanism. As indicated at the start of this chapter, there are multiple ways of identifying or licensing the focus of a sentence: by means of prosody, morphology, or a syntactically specified position. In Germanic and Romance the focus is prosodically licensed in statements, but syntactically licensed in questions such as (165). More precisely:

(166)   A fronted *wh*-phrase is licensed by virtue of occupying the specifier position of a functional category with the feature [+wh] (i.e., via the feature-checking mechanism; see section 1.3.1).

On the other hand, note that the *wh*-in-situ in (167) bears NS. This in-

Prosody and Focus in Germanic and Romance 93

dicates that a *wh*-in-situ is licensed prosodically (rather than in terms of feature checking).

(167) (I wonder) who ate whát?

Therefore, let us make the following assumption:[51]

(168) In the languages under discussion, a *wh*-phrase is licensed either syntactically or prosodically, but not both.[52]

The generalizations in (166) and (168) can be formally instantiated within the system developed in this chapter by reformulating the FPR in (159) (repeated in (169)) as in (170).

(169) *FPR*
Given two sister categories C_i (marked [+F]) and C_j (marked [−F]), C_i is more prominent than C_j.

(170) *FPR (revised)*
Given two sister categories C_i (marked [+F]) and C_j (marked [−F]), C_i is more prominent than C_j, unless C_i is a *wh*-phrase and is syntactically licensed by the *wh*-head of C_j.

Recall furthermore that a defocalized constituent is analyzed as metrically invisible for the NSR in cases where the NSR and the FPR conflict. When no such conflict arises, it is unnecessary to treat a defocalized constituent as metrically invisible. Therefore, let us assume that a [−F] constituent is analyzed as metrically invisible iff the FPR applies to it.

(171) Given two sister categories C_i (marked [+F]) and C_j (marked [−F]), C_j is metrically invisible iff the FPR applies to the sister categories C_i and C_j.

We are now ready to examine how the NSR applies to (165). The FPR (formulated as in (170)) does not apply to the sister nodes C [*what*] and C′ [*did John read*]. Consequently, the C′ constituent, although marked [−F], is interpreted as metrically visible (see (171)), and the C-NSR assigns main prominence to it. The C-NSR reapplies to the metrical sister nodes [*John*] and [*read*] and assigns main prominence to *read* (the lower constituent in the asymmetric c-command ordering).[53]

A.2 *Wh*-in-Situ, Superiority Effects, and the Focus Prominence Rule
Let us turn next to questions with multiple *wh*-phrases. As is well known, such questions give rise obligatorily to a paired-reading interpretation.

This suggests that there can be at most one focus per sentence, and in the case of multiple *wh*-phrases, the focus is the pair of variables, as indicated by the absorption structure in (172b) (see section 1.1.1).

(172) a. Who ate whát?
b. there is an (x, y), such that x ate y

It is therefore reasonable to assume that main phrasal prominence on any of the linked *wh*-phrases may serve to identify the pair, which constitutes the focus of such sentences. The question is, on which *wh*-phrase does main prominence fall?

Before we examine in detail how the NSR applies to multiple *wh*-questions, we need to refine the F-marking rules. Until now we have been using the F-marking rules in (173a–b) and a simplified notation whereby [F] stood for [+F] and no marking at all stood for [−F]. But, as pointed out in note 7 of chapter 1, we must also recognize the existence of constituents that are unmarked for the feature [F]; this case arises when a constituent dominates both [+F] and [−F] material. See (173c). We now have a tripartite distinction: [+F], [−F], and unmarked for [F].

(173) a. A constituent C is marked [+F] iff C is focused or part of the focus.
b. A constituent C is marked [−F] iff C is presupposed or part of the presupposition.
c. A constituent C is unmarked for the feature [F] if it dominates both [+F] and [−F] constituents.

We will see the real significance of (173c) when we examine examples with multiple instances of *wh*-in-situ. But let us begin by examining how the algorithm works for (172), which has the F-marking in (174).

(174) [$_{F/wh}$ Who [[$_{-F}$ ate] [$_{+F}$ whát]]]?

Note that [*ate what*] is unmarked for the feature [F] because it dominates both a constituent marked [−F] (*ate*) and a constituent marked [+F] (*what*). Therefore, the FPR does not apply to the sister constituents [$_{F/wh}$ *who*] and [*ate what*]; in effect, the FPR applies only when one of the sister nodes is [+F] and the other one is [−F]. The NSR applies and assigns main prominence to [*ate what*]. The rule reapplies to [$_{-F}$ *ate*] and [$_F$ *what*]; it assigns NS to *what*, an output compatible with the FPR. The *wh*-in-situ is thus correctly assigned main phrasal prominence.[54]

Given the analysis outlined above, it is reasonable to explore the hypothesis that superiority effects in multiple *wh*-questions can be reduced, at least partly, to prosodic considerations. Consider (175). In effect, the ill-formedness of (175) can be attributed in part to the fact that the C-NSR has assigned main prominence to the verb in violation of the FPR (which requires *who* to be more prominent than the verb).[55,56]

(175) *[[_F What] [[_F who] [_-F bóught]]]?

The plausibility of this explanation is suggested by the well-formedness of (176) (from Lasnik and Saito 1992). In this case the FPR has applied to the sister categories [_F who] and [_-F bought] and has assigned main prominence to *who*. Concomitantly, the verb is analyzed as metrically invisible (see (171)), rendering the output of the FPR compatible with the NSR (i.e., the NSR does not apply at all in this case; recall that it only applies when both sisters dominate at least one metrically visible constituent).[57,58]

(176) Who knows what whó bought?
   cf. *Who know what who bóught?

It is equally relevant to note that in the Spanish counterpart to (175), in which the subject is postverbal, superiority effects are considerably attenuated; see Jaeggli 1982.[59] Although direct questions begin with a High pitch in Spanish, main prominence falls at the end of the phrase in such cases, as in declaratives (see Sosa 1991).

(177) a. ?Qué compró quién?
    what bought who
    'Who bought what?'
   b. ?Qué bebida trajo quién?
    which drink brought who
    'Who brought which drink?'

As expected, the acceptability status of such examples is degraded if a phrase follows the *wh*-subject *quién* within the same intonational phrase. See the examples in (178), where NS is assigned to the benefactive *a María* and to the locative *a la fiesta*.

(178) a. *Qué le compró quién a María?
    what DAT.CL bought who to María
    'Who bought what for María?'
   b. *Qué bebida trajo quién a la fiesta?
    what drink brought who to the party
    'Who brought which drink to the party?'

On the other hand, if the PP complement is right-dislocated, in which case it constitutes a distinct intonational phrase (see the appendix to chapter 3), then NS falls on the postverbal *wh*-subject and the resulting sentences are considerably improved.

(179) a. ?Qué le compró quién # a María?
(cf. (178a))
b. ?Qué bebida trajo quién # a la fiesta?
(cf. (178b))

In the French stylistic inversion construction (in which the subject is postverbal), superiority effects are also attenuated. Compare (180a) with (180b).

(180) a. *Je me demande à qui   qui a parlé.
I wonder   to whom who spoke
(cf. Je me demande à qui Pierre a parlé)
b. ?Je me demande à qui   a parlé qui.
I wonder   to whom spoke who
(cf. Je me demande à qui a parlé Pierre)

The importance of phrasal prominence on the in-situ *wh*-phrase is further confirmed by the contrast in (181). The in-situ *wh*-subject in (181b) violates the FPR (which dictates that *qui* should be stronger than its metrical sister *demain*).

(181) a. Je me demande où   va parler Pierre   demain.
I wonder   where will speak Pierre(S) tomorrow
b. *Je me demande où   va parler qui   demain.
I wonder   where will speak who(S) tomorrow

On the basis of the above discussion, I conclude that unlike fronted *wh*-phrases, in-situ *wh*-phrases are in many cases subject to the FPR; for example, they may—and in many cases they must—bear main prominence.

Next consider cases that contain more than one in-situ *wh*-phrase, such as (182) and (183).

(182) Who bought [_F what [whére]]?

(183) a. ?What did [[_F who] [[_-F buy] [_F whére]]]?
b. *What did [[_F who] [_-F buy thére]]?

The case in (182) is less remarkable, given that the two *wh*-phrases form an F-marked constituent. The contrast in (183), due to Kayne (1983), is more interesting. Although (183a) is far from perfect, it is certainly better than (183b). I attribute this to the fact that although the former violates the "Shortest Movement" Condition (on which, see section 1.3.2), it is prosodically well formed. The NSR applies to the metrical sister nodes [*who*] and [*buy where*] and assigns main prominence to [*buy where*]; this output does not contradict the FPR because the FPR fails to apply to these sister nodes. (Recall that the FPR applies to two sister nodes when one is marked [+F] and the other is marked [−F]. The constituent [*buy where*] is unmarked for the feature [F] because it dominates both [+F] material (*where*) and [−F] material (*buy*).) The NSR reapplies to the metrical sister nodes [*buy*] and [*where*] and assigns prominence to *where*. Next consider (183b). This example is syntactically ill formed because it violates "Shortest Movement." It is also prosodically ill formed. In effect, NS is predicted to fall on *who* and not on *there*. Since [*buy there*] is [−F], it must be analyzed as metrically invisible for the NSR; therefore, the NSR fails to apply to it and its metrical sister. The FPR can then assign main prominence to *who*, without conflicting with the NSR. The prediction is then that *(I wonder) what whó bought there* (with main prominence on *who* and the predicate *bought there* destressed) should be closer in acceptability to (183a) than to (183b). Similarly, *Who knows what whó bought there?* should be better than *Who knows what who bought thére?* I leave the task of verifying these judgments to the reader.[60]

Chapter 3
Clausal Structure, the Position of Subjects, and a Case of Prosodically Motivated Movement in Romance

In chapter 2 I showed that phrasal rhythmic prominence, as determined by the NSR and by the Emphatic/Contrastive Stress Rule, plays a crucial role in licensing focus in the Germanic and Romance languages (cf. the FPR). I also showed that in cases where the output of the NSR and the output of the FPR clash, certain languages (German, English, and French) resolve the conflict by rendering the defocalized constituent metrically invisible. And I showed that there are languages like Spanish (and Italian) in which phonologically specified material cannot be analyzed as metrically invisible. In this chapter I examine how such languages resolve cases of conflict between the NSR and the FPR. More precisely, I argue that they are resolved by deleting and copying (i.e., moving) the defocalized constituent, an operation I refer to as *p-movement* (for prosodically motivated movement). I begin by examining some properties of the preverbal field in Spanish (section 3.1) and in Italian (section 3.2). With this as background, I embark on a detailed discussion of the descriptive properties of p-movement in Spanish (section 3.3) and in Italian (section 3.4). I suggest that certain differences in the output of p-movement in the two languages are to be traced back to differences in the structure of their preverbal field. I then consider how p-movement should be formalized and where it applies (section 3.5). Finally, I investigate whether languages that can resolve conflicts between the NSR and the FPR in terms of metrical invisibility can also resolve them in terms of movement (section 3.6).

3.1 The Preverbal Field in Modern Standard Spanish

In this section I examine some basic clausal properties of Modern Standard Spanish (MS).[1] I argue that the specifier of the functional category that contains the tensed verb in MS can contain phrases other than the subject, and that such phrases may be either focused, emphatic, or topic phrases. I suggest that this functional category is the T(ense)P. This analysis for MS was first put forth in Zubizarreta 1992b, 1994, and an analysis along similar lines has been argued to exist for Old Spanish (OS) in Fontana 1993. If this analysis is correct, Spanish to some extent resembles some of the Germanic languages—specifically, Yiddish and Icelandic (as analyzed in Diesing 1990, Santorini 1989, Thráinsson 1985, Rögnvaldsson and Thráinsson 1990; see also Iatridou and Kroch 1991 for relevant discussion). I will refer to it as the *generalized TP analysis*. Within a view of syntactic structure in which heads consist of features that need to be checked against other heads, languages with a generalized TP may be said to allow a certain amount of feature syncretism. More precisely, in these languages a discourse-based functional feature, such as "topic," "focus," or "emphasis," may combine with the feature T(ense), giving rise to the syncretic categories T/"topic," T/"focus," T/"emphasis."[2] (On the notion of syncretic category, see Giorgi and Pianesi 1996). A topic, focused, or emphatic phrase may therefore be moved to [Spec, T] for feature-checking purposes (on feature checking, see sections 1.3.1 and 1.3.2).[3] This of course is possible only to the extent that the nominative subject can be licensed in these languages in some way other than via specifier-head agreement with T.

3.1.1 Tense as a Syncretic Category in Modern Standard Spanish: The Structure of VSO Order

Although it might very well be that the use of VSO order in Spanish is declining (a matter that can only be resolved with some serious statistical production data), it is part of native speakers' intuition that the examples in (1) and (2) are possible sentences of the language. The same sentences can be embedded under predicates of propositional attitude such as *parecer* 'to seem', *creer* 'to believe', *estar segura* 'to be sure', verbs of saying such as *decir* 'to say', negative verbs such as *dudar* 'to doubt', and factive verbs such as *lamentar* 'regret'; the last two classes of verbs require that the complement be in the subjunctive.[4]

(1) a. Todos los días compra Juan el diario.
    every day   buys   Juan the newspaper
    'Juan buys the newspaper every day.'

b. El primer día de escuela deberá acompañar cada madre a
   the first day of school must accompany each mother ACC
   su hijo.
   her child
   'Each mother must accompany her child the first day of school.'
c. Ayer presentó María su renuncia.
   yesterday handed-in María her resignation
   'María handed in her resignation yesterday.'
d. En este bar escribió Max su primera novela.
   in this bar wrote Max his first novel
   'Max wrote his first novel in this bar.'
e. A María le regaló su abuelo un caballo de pura raza.
   to María DAT.CL gave her grandfather a horse of pure breed
   'Her grandfather gave María a purebred horse.'
f. Debajo de esta cama suelen guardar los niños sus juguetes
   under this bed usually keep the children their toys
   preferidos.
   favorite
   'The children usually keep their favorite toys under this bed.'

(2) a. Me devolvió María el libro que le presté.
       DAT.CL returned María the book that to-her (I) lent
       'María returned to me the book that I lent her.'
    b. Se comieron los niños todo el pastel.
       BENEF.CL ate the boys all the cake
       'The boys ate up all the cake.'

The sentences in (1) are topic-comment sentences, in which the topic may be an adverb (such as a temporal or a locative) or an argument (dative or locative). The sentences in (2) are also amenable to a topic-comment analysis, if the topic is analyzed as a silent pronominal linked to the indirect object or benefactive dative clitic. As suggested in Zubizarreta 1992b, 1994, all such sentences can be analyzed as having a structure in which the verb has been raised to T and a phrase other than the subject occupies [Spec, T]. Indeed, to the extent that the subject is licensed in a position other than [Spec, T] in these sentences, [Spec, T] is a position that is readily available for other kinds of phrases; no further structure needs to be postulated to accommodate the XP in the XPVSO structures.[5] If we assume that an analysis with the most minimal structure is to be preferred (see Chomsky 1995), then we are also warranted in assuming that the above examples are unambiguously associated with an analysis in which the fronted topic (whether phonologically overt or not) occupies [Spec, T]. To the extent that there may be more than one topic per sentence, it is reasonable to assume that there may be more than one "topic" feature that participates in the feature-checking algorithm. Thus, besides the "topic" feature on T, there may be a "topic" feature on a functional category above TP, as in the following examples:

(3) a. Todos los días, Juan compra el diario.
     every day   Juan buys   the newspaper
   b. El primer día de escuela, cada madre deberá acompañar a
      the first day of school each mother must accompany ACC
      su hijo.
      her child
   c. Ayer,   María presentó su renuncia.
      yesterday María handed-in her resignation
   d. En este bar, Max escribió su primera novela.
      in this bar Max wrote   his first   novel
   e. A María,   su abuelo   le   regaló un caballo de pura
      to María her grandfather DAT.CL gave a horse of pure
      raza.
      breed
   f. Debajo de esta cama, los niños suelen guardar sus
      under   this bed   the children usually keep their
      juguetes preferidos.
      toys   favorite

The XP in an XPVSO structure may be something other than a topic (see Hernanz and Brucart 1987, Torrego 1984). In particular, it may be an emphatic element, such as the bare negative phrases *nadie/nada* 'nobody/no one' or bare indefinites *algo/alguien* 'something/someone'; see (4). Note that these are purely emphatic in nature in that they negate or reassert part of the hearer's presupposition but, unlike contrastive focused phrases, they do not introduce a variable with an associated value. Alternatively, the XP may be a case of contrastive focus; see (5). Here, it is the case both that the hearer's presupposition is negated (as indicated by the tag) and that a variable and its associated value are introduced. (On the distinction between emphasis and contrastive focus, see section 1.1.1). Like the sentences in (1) and (2), those in (4) and (5) can be embedded under predicates of propositional attitude, verbs of saying, negative verbs, and factive verbs; the last two classes of verbs require that the complement be in the subjunctive.[6]

(4) a. A NADIE le devolvió María su manuscrito.
   to nobody DAT.CL returned María his manuscript
   'María returned his manuscript to nobody.'
   b. Con NADIE compartió María su secreto.
   with nobody shared María her secret
   'María shared her secret with nobody.'
   c. ALGO debe haberte dicho María para que te hayas
   something must have-DAT.CL said María for (you) to be
   enojado tanto.
   angry so-much
   'María must have said something for you to be so angry.'
   d. Con ALGUIEN debe haber hablado Pedro acerca de ésto.
   with someone must have spoken Pedro about this
   'Pedro must have spoken about this with someone.'

(5) a. Las ESPINACAS destesta Pedro (y no las papas).
   the spinach hates Pedro (not the potatoes)
   'Pedro hates the spinach (not the potatoes).'
   b. Con MARÍA habló Pedro (y no con Marta).
   with María spoke Pedro (and not with Marta)
   'Pedro spoke with María (and not with Marta).'

Though a sentence may have more than one topic, it may have at most one focus; see section 1.1.1.[7] I suggest that, for this reason, there may be at most one functional "focus" feature per sentence for feature-checking purposes. It therefore follows that at most one F-marked constituent may be fronted. In Spanish the functional "focus" feature (when present in the structure) obligatorily constitutes a syncretic category with T. This accounts for the ungrammaticality of (6a–b) (where the focus precedes the topic); compare with (7a–b) (where the topic precedes the focus).

(6) a. *Las ESPINACAS, Pedro trajo (y no las papas).
   the spinach Pedro brought (and not the potatoes)
   b. *Con MARÍA, Pedro habló (y no con Marta).
   with María Pedro spoke (and not with Marta)

(7) a. (Estoy segura que) Pedro, las ESPINACAS trajo (y no
   ((I) am sure that) Pedro the spinach brought (and not
   las papas).
   the potatoes)

b. (Estoy segura que) Pedro, con MARÍA habló (y no con
   ((I) am sure that) Pedro with María spoke (and not with
   Marta).
   Marta)

The same remarks hold with respect to emphatics. There is at most one functional feature "emphasis" per sentence, and it obligatorily constitutes a syncretic category with T. This accounts for the ungrammaticality of (8a–d), where the emphatic phrase precedes the topic. Compare (8a–d) with (9a–f), where the topic precedes the emphatic phrase.

(8) a. ?*A NADIE, María le devolvió su manuscrito.
      to nobody María DAT.CL returned his manuscript
   b. ?*Con NADIE, María compartió su secreto.
      with nobody María shared her secret
   c. ?*ALGO, María te habrá dicho para que te hayas
      something María to-you must-have said for (you) to be
      enojado tanto.
      angry so-much
   d. ?*A VARIOS amigos, Pedro invitó a la fiesta.
      ACC several friends Pedro invited to the party

(9) a. (Estoy segura que) su manuscrito, a NADIE se lo
                                              DAT.CL ACC.CL
      devolvió María. (cf. (8a))
   b. (Estoy segura que) María, su manuscrito, a NADIE se
                                                    DAT.CL
      lo devolvió. (cf. (8a))
      ACC.CL
   c. (Estoy segura que) su secreto, con NADIE lo
                                             ACC.CL
      compartió María. (cf. (8b))
   d. (Estoy segura que) María, su secreto, con NADIE lo
                                                      ACC.CL
      compartió. (cf. (8b))
   e. (Estoy segura que) María, ALGO te habrá dicho para que te
      hayas enojado tanto. (cf. 8c))
   f. (Estoy segura que) Pedro, a VARIOS amigos invitó a la fiesta.
      (cf. (8d))

The alternative to the view I have just outlined (based on feature syncretism) would be to assume that the features "topic," "focus," and "emphasis" give rise to their own independent functional projection, located above TP, and that the ill-formedness of the examples in (6) and (8) should be attributed to a universal constraint that the topic must precede the Focus or Emphasis projection, in conjunction with the hypothesis that the verb must move obligatorily to the head of the Focus/Emphasis projection. Comparing Spanish with Italian suggests that this is not the right solution (see section 3.2).[8]

Goodall (1991) has argued that fronted *wh*-arguments in Standard Spanish questions occupy [Spec, T] ([Spec, I], in his terms). See also Solà 1992, Arnaiz 1992, Fontana 1993, and references cited therein. As is well known, in Standard Spanish, fronted *wh*-complements must be adjacent to the verb in both matrix and subordinate clauses. In effect, the subject may not intervene between the two. This constraint does not hold in the case of sentential *wh*-adverbs such as *porqué* 'why' and *como* 'how come' (see Torrego 1984). Compare (10)/(11) with (12)/(13).[9]

(10) a. *(No sé)   qué cosa María comió.
         ((I) don't know) what   María ate
     b. No sé qué cosa comió María.

(11) a. *(No sé)   a quién María invitó.
         ((I) don't know) whom   María invited
     b. (No sé) a quién invitó María.

(12) a. (No sé)   porqué María no vino.
         ((I) don't know) why   María not come
         'I don't know why María didn't come.'
     b. (No sé) porqué no vino María.

(13) a. (No sé)   como   María se atreve a decir eso.
         ((I) don't know) how-come María dares + say   such-things
     b. (No sé) como se atreve María a decir eso.

Nor may a topic intervene between a fronted *wh*-complement and the verb (14a), although one may intervene between a sentential *wh*-adverb such as *porqué* and the verb (14b).

(14) a *Me pregunto qué cosa a María le   regalaron.
        (I) wonder   what   to María DAT.CL (they) gave
        'I wonder what they gave a María.'
     b. Me pregunto porqué a María le   regalaron eso.
        (I) wonder   why   to María DAT.CL (they) gave that
        'I wonder why they gave that to María.'

If fronted *wh*-complements occupy [Spec, T], then an emphatic phrase should not be able to cooccur with a fronted *wh*-complement. And indeed, the prediction is borne out. Topics typically precede *wh*-phrases in root clauses (15), but a bare (emphatic) Q may neither precede nor immediately follow a fronted *wh*-complement (16).

(15) A María, cuando la invitarás?
 ACC María when ACC.CL (you) will-invite
 'When will you invite María?'

(16) a. *ALGO, donde encontraste?
  something where (you) found
  'Where did you find something?'
 b. *A NADIE, cuando invitarás?
  ACC nobody when (you) will-invite
  'When will you not invite anybody?'

Although a bare (emphatic) Q following a fronted *wh*-adverb is somewhat stilted, there is certainly a contrast between forms involving a *wh*-adverb and forms involving a *wh*-complement. Compare (17) with (18).

(17) a. ?Porqué a NADIE quieres invitar?
  why ACC nobody (you) want to-invite
  'Why don't you want to invite anybody?'
 b. ?Porqué ALGO no me compras?
  why something not for-me (you) buy
  'Why don't you buy me something?'

(18) a. *Donde ALGO encontraste?
  where something (you) found
  'Where did you find something?'
 b. *Cuando a NADIE invitarás?
  when ACC nobody (you) will-invite
  'When will you not invite anybody?'

The same observation holds for contrastive focused phrases.

(19) a. A MARÍA quieres invitar (y no a Marta)?
  ACC María (you) want to-invite (and not ACC Marta)
  'Do you want to invite María (and not Marta)?'

b. ?Porqué a   MARÍA quieres   invitar (y   no a
   why   ACC María   (you) want to-invite (and not ACC
   Marta)?
   Marta)
   'Why do you want to invite María (and not Marta)?'
c. *A donde a   MARÍA quieres   invitar (y   no a
   to where ACC María   (you) want to-invite (and not ACC
   Marta)?
   Marta)
   'Where do you want to invite María (and not Marta)?'

To summarize: The data discussed above lead to the plausible hypothesis that in Standard Spanish, [Spec, T] is not restricted to subjects. Different types of constituents may occupy [Spec, T] in this language: topics, emphatics, focused phrases (including *wh*-phrases). This suggests that in this language T and "topic," T and "emphasis," and T and "focus" (which may or may not be further specified as *wh*) may constitute a syncretic category. Such a syncretic category would then attract a topic, focused, or emphatic phrase to its specifier for feature-checking purposes.[10] Although there may be more than one "topic" feature per sentence, there is at most one "focus" feature and one "emphasis" feature per sentence, and these obligatorily constitute a syncretic category with T.[11]

Given the hypothesis that [Spec, T] may be occupied by phrases other than the subject, three questions arise. First, must [Spec, T] be obligatorily filled in MS?[12] Although the most common examples of VSO are cases in which it can be readily argued that an XP occupies [Spec, T], less obvious cases of V2 are purely eventive sentences such as (20a–b) and sentences with a contrastive focus such as (21a–b) (see section 3.3 for further discussion of the latter type of example). It could perhaps be argued that in such cases [Spec, T] is occupied by a covert anaphoric temporal adverb. In (20) the anaphoric temporal adverb is controlled by the time of speech, and in (21) it is controlled by the discourse. This is not an implausible hypothesis since it is known that certain temporal adverbs can function as anaphoric elements and as such they are analyzed as metrically invisible for the NSR in languages like English (see chapter 2, note 13).

(20) a. Acaba de   ganar   España el mundial   de
       RECENT PAST(3RD PERS) win(INF) Spain   the World Cup of
       football.
       soccer
       'Spain just won the soccer World Cup.'
   b. Acaba de   romper   el niño una copa de
       RECENT PAST(3RD PERS) broke(INF) the boy a   glass of
       cristal.
       crystal
       'The boy just broke a crystal glass.'

(21) a. Lavó   NINA los platos (no María).
        washed Nina the dishes (not María)
   b. Lavé   YO los platos (no María).
        washed I the dishes (not María)

Second, how does the nominative Case on the postverbal subject, which occupies the specifier of (the highest) VP, get checked? I will discuss this point briefly in section 3.1.2.

Third, as I will show in section 3.1.3, an object that has been fronted to [Spec, T] needs to be clitic-doubled in MS. In effect, in MS, objects in [Spec, T] behave like left-dislocated objects in this respect (where by "left-dislocated object" I mean an object in the specifier of a Topic projection above TP). This was not the case in OS. How can we account for this difference between MS and OS?

3.1.2 Nominative Case Checking

It is assumed in much current work that T plays a crucial role in licensing nominative Case. In SVO structures, where the subject occupies [Spec, T], nominative Case is assumed to be checked via specifier-head agreement with T. If, in the VSO structures illustrated above, V occupies T and the subject has remained in its VP-internal position, how is nominative Case checked in such structures?[13]

If we were to assume a theory in which covert movement has properties comparable to those of overt movement (such as the one proposed in Chomsky 1993, prior to the covert-feature-movement theory proposed in Chomsky 1995), a logical possibility would be that the postverbal DP subject may move to [Spec, T] covertly (i.e., at LF in the standard framework) in order to bear the appropriate structural relation to T and thus check its Case. Such an analysis would of course undermine the hypothesis that [Spec, T] may be occupied by phrases other than the subject in VSO structures. This prediction is not easy to check empirically in Spanish, but two subject/object asymmetries that have been explained in terms of LF conditions suggest that the postverbal surface subject is not preposed at LF.

The first asymmetry is found in the distribution of bare plurals (see Suñer 1982, Contreras 1986, Lois 1989). Unlike bare plurals in English, bare plurals in Spanish are unambiguously existential (unless they are in topic position), and their distribution is restricted. In particular, they may appear in postverbal but not in preverbal subject position, as illustrated in (22). To the extent that this distribution can be accounted for in terms of LF conditions,[14] such contrasts argue against covert LF movement of the postverbal subject.

(22) a. A menudo juegan niños en este parque.
    often play children in this park
    'Children often play in this park.'
   b. i. *Niños juegan a menudo en este parque.
      ii. *A menudo, niños juegan en este parque.

The second asymmetry involves Condition C effects. For example, the adnominal genitive *Juan* may be coreferential with the accusative clitic *lo* when it is contained in a preverbal subject position (23a), but not when it is contained in a postverbal subject position (23b).[15] (As we will see in the next section, such preverbal/postverbal asymmetries cannot be attributed to a difference in Assertion Structure.)

(23) a. Esta mañana, la madre de Juan lo castigó.
    this morning the mother of Juan ACC.CL punished
    'This morning, Juan's mother punished him.'
    [Coreference: OK]
   b. Esta mañana lo castigó la madre de Juan.
    [Coreference: *]

If the postverbal subject moved covertly to [Spec, T], we would not expect to find such contrasts between structures with a postverbal subject and structures with a preverbal subject. At LF the two structures would be indistinguishable.[16]

Chomsky's (1995) theory of feature movement provides a solution compatible with the structural analysis put forth above for the word order (XP)VSO. Within this theory, features of constituents (rather than constituents themselves) enter into formal licensing relations; Move X(P) is therefore replaced by Move f; see section 1.3.2. Whereas "overt" feature movement pied-pipes the constituent that contains it, "covert" movement does not. Thus, in this feature-checking theory it is the D-feature, rather than the DP, that must enter into a particular relation with T. Nominative Case is checked by virtue of the D-feature moving to [Spec, T] "overtly" (in which case the entire DP moves along with the D-feature) or by virtue of the feature D adjoining to T "covertly." In the latter case [Spec, T] is free to be occupied by material other than the DP subject.[17]

3.1.3 Modern Standard Spanish versus Old Spanish

On the basis of 12th- to 15th-century texts, Fontana (1993) argues that in OS [Spec, T] could be occupied by different types of constituents.[18] I have argued that this is still a grammatical possibility in MS, although such constructions are perhaps less productive in MS than they were in OS (perhaps reflecting a process of language change).[19] But there is an important difference between the OVS structures of OS and MS. Accusatives and datives in [Spec, T] are obligatorily clitic-doubled in MS (see (24a), (25a), (26a)), just as they are in left-dislocated constructions (see (24b), (25b), (26b)).

(24) a. Esta ciudad$_i$ *(la$_i$) destruyeron los bárbaros.
      this city   (ACC.CL) destroyed the barbarians
      'The barbarians destroyed this city.'
   b. Esta ciudad$_i$, los bárbaros *(la$_i$) destruyeron.

(25) a. Este libro$_i$ se   *(lo$_i$)   regaló María a su madre.
      this book DAT.CL (ACC.CL) gave   María to her mother
      'María gave this book to her mother.'
   b. Este libro$_i$, María se *(lo$_i$) regaló a su madre.

(26) a. A su madre$_i$ *(le$_i$)   regaló María un libro.
      to her mother (DAT.CL) gave María a book
      'María gave a book to her mother.'
   b. A su madre$_i$, María *(le$_i$) regaló un libro.

In OS an object in [Spec, T] was not clitic-doubled (see (27)), in contrast with left-dislocated phrases, which were doubled either by a tonic pronoun or by a clitic (see (28)).

Clausal Structure

(27) a. Este logar mostro dios a abraam.
this place showed God to Abraham
'God showed Abraham this place.'
(cited in Fontana 1993, 64)

b. A micer May, que era enbaxador en Roma, hizo S.M.
ACC Micer May who was ambassador in Rome made H.M.
Vicechanciller.
vice-chancellor
'His Majesty made Micer May, who was ambassador in Rome, vice-chancellor.'
(cited in Fontana 1993, 64)

c. Esto-t lidiare aquí antel Rey don alfonso.
this-you challenge(1SG) here before-the king Don Alfonso
'I will challenge you on this in front of King Alfonso.'
(cited in Fontana 1993, 53)

(28) a. Tovieron que iudos$_i$, esa falsa mesnada, ellos$_i$ avian la
(they) thought that Jews that false crowd they had the
carne de don Christo furtada.
flesh of Lord Christ stolen
'They thought that the Jews, that false crowd, they had stolen Christ's body.'
(cited in Rivero 1986, 792)

b. E estas pazes$_i$ traxo-las$_i$ marutas Obispo de
and these peaces brought ACC.CL (3PL) Marutas bishop of
mesopotamia.
Mesopotamia
'And Marutas, bishop of Mesopotamia, brought this peace.'
(cited in Fontana 1993, 185–186)

c. & esto$_i$ prouaua-lo$_i$ por la sandalia dell
& this proved(3SG) ACC.CL(3SG) by the sandal of-the
apostoligo que traye.
apostolic that brought(3SG)
'And this he proved by the sandal belonging to the pope which he brought with him.'
(cited in Fontana 1993, 185–186)

The above-mentioned difference between MS and OS can be attributed to the status of the clitics in the respective languages. The most salient property of clitics in OS, as in many other Old Romance languages, is that they were not verbal clitics. On the basis of their distribution, Rivero (1986) and Fontana (1993) have argued that in OS, nontonic pronouns (like tonic pronouns) were maximal projections, which undergo cliticization at PF.[20] More specifically, Fontana argues that nontonic pronouns in OS fronted to TP-initial position, and from there underwent PF encliticization. They could encliticize onto an adjacent complementizer, a *wh*-phrase, a negation, a verb, or a noun (as indicated by the underlines in (29)).[21] ((29a–f) are cited in Rivero 1986).

(29) a. bronnuelos con manteca, que le   el grand sennor enbia
       doughnuts with lard   that to-him the great lord   sends
       'doughnuts with lard that the great lord sends him'
    b. quien te algo   prometiere ...
       who you something would-promise
       'the one who would promise something to you ...'
    c. Fara   bien d'ello a quantos se   a el
       (he) will-make well of it to all themselves to him
       ayuntaren.
       will-come-close
       'It will be profitable to whoever comes close to him.'
    d. No-l   querades.
       not to-him (you) want
       'Do not want it/him.'
    e. et el padre firio-l   et maltrexo lo
       and the father hurt him and mistreated him
    f. Por   la montanya se-n   metio.
       through the mountain herself in-it (she) put
       'She went into the mountains.'

On the other hand, MS clitics have a much more restricted distribution; they are always attached to the tensed verb or auxiliary (whether finite or nonfinite). Clitics in MS can be analyzed as heads of functional projections (as argued in Sportiche 1992, Franco 1993). The clitic has a D-feature to be checked, and this is achieved by covert adjunction of the object's D-feature to the clitic. More precisely, an accusative Cl will attract an accusative D and a dative Cl will attract a dative D. (On the details of covert feature movement, see section 1.3.1. In the structures below, I indicate covert movement with italics and mark the trace of the moved feature with parentheses.)[22]

(30) $[_{\text{ClP}}[_{\text{Cl}} D [_{\text{Cl}}]] [\ldots (D) \ldots]]$

Clausal Structure

There is evidence based on binding that the accusative Cl is located between TP and VP_1 (the highest verbal phrase), and the dative Cl is located below VP_1, as suggested by Demonte (1993). I assume, as in chapter 2, that transitives are composed of two distinct predicates and ditransitives are composed of three distinct predicates; in other words, one predicate per argument. (As shown in (31), before adjoining to Cl, D adjoins to V to check accusative Case on the V or it adjoins to P to check dative Case on the P.)

(31) a. $[_{TP}$ T $[_{ClP}$ $[D$ [acc Cl]] $[_{VP}\ldots V_1$ $[_{VP}[(D)$ $[V_2]]$ $(D)\ldots$
  b. $[_{TP}$ T $[_{VP}\ldots V_1$ $[_{ClP}[D$ [dat Cl]] $[_{VP}\ldots V_2$ $[_{PP}[(D)$ $[P_3]]$ $(D)\ldots$

One piece of evidence is provided by the contrast in (23) (repeated in (32)) and the lack of contrast in (33). In effect, if the accusative Cl is above the VP that contains the subject (that is, above VP_1), the ill-formedness of (32b) can be explained in terms of Condition C: the name *Juan*, contained within the VP-internal subject position, is coindexed with the c-commanding accusative Cl. See the structure in (34) (prior to cliticization). On the other hand, coreference between the dative Cl and the name contained within the postverbal subject is possible; see (33b), with the structure in (35) (prior to cliticization). The intended antecedent *Juan* (contained within the postverbal subject) is coindexed with the dative Cl, which is below the subject; therefore, Condition C is not violated. Note that the absence of contrast in (33) is particularly informative because it shows that the contrast in (32) cannot be attributed to a difference in assertion structure between clauses with preverbal and postverbal subjects, such as the fact that a preverbal, but not a postverbal, subject can function as a topic (see note 25 in chapter 1). In effect, the examples in (32a) and (33a) have exactly the same set of potential assertion structures, and so do the examples in (32b) and (33b).

(32) a. Esta mañana, la madre de Juan$_i$ lo$_i$ castigó.
    this morning the mother of Juan ACC.CL punished
    'This morning, Juan's mother punished him.'
  b. *Esta mañana lo$_i$ castigó la madre de Juan$_i$.

(33) a. El mes pasado, la madre de Juan$_i$ le$_i$ envió varias
    last month the mother of Juan DAT.CL sent several
    cartas.
    letters
    'Last month, Juan's mother sent him several letters.'
  b. El mes pasado le$_i$ envió la madre de Juan$_i$ varias cartas.

(34) [TP castigó [CIP[D [lo]]i [VP la madre de [Juani] V1 [VP(D) [V2 (D) ...

(35) [TP envió [VP V1 [VP[la madre de [Juani] V1 [CIP[D [le]]i [VP varias cartasj [V2 ej [(D) [P (D) ...

If clitics are analyzed as heads of a functional projection in MS (rather than as phrasal arguments), [Spec, ClP] is an available position, in particular for DP topics. Thus, (24a) and (26a) can be assigned the structures in (36a) and (36b), respectively. (25a) would have a structure comparable to (36a).[23]

(36) a. [TP esta ciudadj [destruyeron [CIP ei [D [la]]i [VP los bárbaros [V1 [VP[(D) [V2]] (D)]]]]]]

b. [TP a su madrei [regalo [VP María [V1 [CIP ei [D [le]i [VP un libro [V [PP[(D) [P]] (D)]]]]]]]]]

Pronominal binding provides evidence that, in languages with a Cl projection, a fronted topic indeed originates in [Spec, Cl], thus providing further evidence for a Cl projection in MS. The data, first reported in Zubizarreta 1993, are as follows.[24] A matrix subject, whether preverbal or postverbal, may bind a pronoun contained within a fronted accusative object that originates in the embedded clause, as shown in (37a–c).

(37) a. A   *sui* hijo, *ninguna madrei* desea   que se
       ACC her son no   mother desires that INDEF.SUBJ.CL
       lo   regañe.
       ACC.CL scold
       'No mother desires that someone scold her son.'

   b. A   *sui* hijo, no desea *ninguna madrei* que se
       ACC her son not desires no   mother that INDEF.SUBJ.CL
       lo   regañe.
       ACC.CL scold
       'No mother desires that someone scold her son.'

   c. No desea *ninguna madrei* que a *sui* hijo se lo regañe.

On the other hand, there is a preverbal/postverbal subject asymmetry in cases where the fronted accusative topic (which contains the intended bindee) and the subject (which contains the intended binder) originate in the same clause.[25] Compare (38a) and (38b), as well as (39a) and (39b).

(38) a.   A   *sui* hijo, cada madrei deberá acompañarloi   el
           ACC her child each mother must   accompany ACC.CL the
           primer día de escuela.
           first   day of school

'Each mother must accompany her child on the first day of school.'
b. ?*El primer día de escuela, a su$_i$ hijo deberá acompañarlo$_i$ cada madre$_i$.

(39) a. A su$_i$ propio hijo, ningún padre$_i$ lo$_i$ quiere castigar.
ACC his own child no father ACC.CL wants to-punish
'No father wants to punish his own child.'
b. ?*A su$_i$ propio hijo no lo$_i$ quiere castigar ningún padre$_i$.
ACC his own child not ACC.CL wants to-punish no father
'No father wants to punish his own child.'

The contrast between (38a) and (38b) and between (39a) and (39b) can be attributed to the fact that the fronted accusative object can be "reconstructed" to the [Spec, acc Cl], but not to the argument position within VP, as shown in (40). The ill-formedness of (40b) can then be attributed to the fact that the QP does not c-command the intended bindee at LF.[26]

(40) a. [$_{TP}$ QP$_i$ T[$_{ClP}$[su$_i$ N] [[D [Cl]]$_i$ [$_{VP}$ e$_i$ [V$_1$ [$_{VP}$(D) [V$_2$...
b. *[$_{TP}$ T [$_{ClP}$[su$_i$ N] [[D [Cl]]$_i$ [$_{VP}$ QP$_i$ [V$_1$ [$_{VP}$(D) [V$_2$...

Consider next the case of the dative. Since the dative Cl projection is below VP$_1$, it is predicted that a postverbal subject must be able to bind a pronoun contained within a fronted object. In effect, the bound reading is available in (41a) (where the binder is a preverbal subject), as well as in (41b) (where the binder is a postverbal subject). See their respective structures in (42a) and (42b). The contrast between (40b) and (41b) provides further evidence that the accusative Cl projection is located above VP$_1$ and the dative Cl projection is located below VP$_1$.

(41) a. A su$_i$ editor, cada autor$_i$ le envió un manuscrito.
to his editor each writer DAT.CL sent a manuscript
b. A su$_i$ editor le envió cada autor$_i$ un manuscrito.

(42) a. [$_{TP}$ QP$_i$ T [$_{VP}$ e$_i$ [V$_1$ [$_{ClP}$[su$_i$ N] [[D [Cl]]$_i$ [$_{VP}$(D) [V$_2$...
b. *[$_{TP}$ T [$_{VP}$ QP$_i$ [V$_1$ [$_{ClP}$[su$_i$ N] [[D [Cl]]$_i$ [$_{VP}$(D) [V$_2$...

Interestingly, fronted PP topics do not cooccur with a clitic (there are no PP clitics in MS).[27] We may assume that such phrases originate in argument position (like the fronted objects in [Spec, T] in OS). The prediction is then that a pronoun contained within a fronted PP topic can be bound by a postverbal subject. In effect, if the fronted PP originates in an argument position within VP, it must be able to "reconstruct" to this position (as shown in (45)). The prediction is borne out; see (43b) and (44b).

(43) a. Sobre su$_i$ silla, cada niño$_i$ puso un libro.
 on his chair each child put a book
 'Each child put a book on his chair.'
 b. Sobre su$_i$ silla puso cada niño$_i$ un libro.

(44) a. De su$_i$ madre, nadie$_i$ nos habló.
 about his mother nobody to-us talked
 'Nobody talked to us about his mother.'
 b. De su$_i$ madre no nos habló nadie$_i$.
 about his mother not to-us talked nobody
 'Nobody talked to us about his mother.'

(45) [$_{TP}$ T [$_{VP}$ QP$_i$ [V [$_{PP}$ P [su_i N]]]]]

We can now return to our original question: why must an object topic in [Spec, T] or in a dislocated position cooccur obligatorily with a clitic in MS? The answer is to be found in the empirical generalization in (46).

(46) In languages with a Cl projection, a DP marked [+topic] must be inserted in [Spec, ClP].

Clitics in MS are functional projections, and there is empirical evidence that a DP marked [+topic] must be generated directly in [Spec, Cl] in languages in which the clitic has the status of a functional projection. In effect, as shown above, in Spanish and other languages (see note 25) a fronted DP topic may "reconstruct" to [Spec, Cl] but not lower, and this follows immediately from the empirical generalization in (46).[28] Following work by Iatridou (1990b), we may furthermore assume that the clitic in MS and similar languages functions as a predicate-variable, which converts the clause into an open predicate. The DP topic in [Spec, Cl] functions as the subject of this predicate.[29] The generalization in (46) did not hold in OS, in which clitics were syntactically phrases rather than functional projections. Fronted topics that coexisted with a clitic in OS must be analyzed in the same way as the left-dislocation construction in English (as suggested in Rivero 1986): the topic is base-generated in its surface position and is related to the pronominal phrasal clitic via coreference.

3.1.4 Summary and Concluding Remarks

In this section I have explored an analysis for MS in which [Spec, T] is not restricted to subjects; that is, phrases other than those Case-marked nominative may appear in [Spec, T]. These may be topics, emphatics, or focused phrases. I have suggested that this is so because in MS the feature T may constitute a syncretic category with discourse-based features that belong to the outer layer of the clausal structure; these are the features "topic," "emphasis," and "focus" (which may be further specified as *wh*). If we make the assumption in (47), then it follows that the feature syncretism discussed above is possible only to the extent that a nominative D may check its Case in some way other than via the specifier-head relation with T; that is, in MS nominative may be checked via covert adjunction of D to T.

(47) A phrase may not check more than one type of feature in a given specifier-head configuration. In other words, a phrase may not simultaneously check an intrinsically grammatical feature such as Case and a discourse-based feature such as "topic," "emphasis," or "focus."[30]

The two properties that underlie the generalized TP analysis are stated in (48).[31,32] Note that, given the assumption in (47), the property in (48b) is a necessary condition for the existence of the property in (48a) in the grammar of a language.

(48) a. In MS the feature T may constitute a syncretic category with other discourse-based features, such as "topic," "focus," or "emphasis." (In such cases the verb is overtly adjoined to the syncretic categories T/"topic," T/"focus," T/"emphasis.")
   b. In MS nominative Case may be checked either overtly in [Spec, T] or via covert adjunction of D to T.

It is less obvious whether the property in (48b) is a sufficient condition for the existence of the property in (48a). If we assume a minimalist approach to syntactic structure (see (49)), following Chomsky (1995), then a grammar should tend toward feature syncretism in cases like the one discussed above.

(49) Minimize structure whenever possible in a given derivation.

Given the principle in (49), if the initial array of a given derivation contains both a functional feature T and a functional feature "focus" or "emphasis," these will be unambiguously analyzed as forming a syncretic category (T/"focus" or T/"emphasis"). Similarly, if the initial array of a derivation contains both a functional feature "topic" and a functional feature T, these will be analyzed as a syncretic category (T/"topic"), unless other considerations impose the alternative analysis, in which the feature "topic" is analyzed as an independent projection (for example, if [Spec, T] is occupied by a nontopic phrase).

The analysis outlined above relates the following two distribution facts:

(50) a. In MS the word order (XP)VSO is still a grammatical option, where the subject is in [Spec, V] and where XP may be any type of phrase (a topic, focused, or emphatic phrase) and it may be either an argument or an adjunct.
 b. In MS the following orders are not an option: *Emphatic-XP-V ..., *Focus-XP-V ... Only the orders Emphatic-V ... and Focus-V ... are possible (in structures involving fronting of focused or emphatic phrases).

3.2 The Preverbal Field in Italian: Some Comparative Remarks

Italian differs from MS precisely with respect to the two properties in (50). As Belletti and Shlonsky (1995, 510) note, Italian does not allow (XP)VSO order.[33]

(51) *Ieri   ha dato Gianni un libro a Maria.
     yesterday gave   Gianni a   book to Maria

All the Italian speakers I consulted found the Italian counterparts of the MS examples in (1) and (2) unacceptable.

Pinto (1994) and Adger (1996) claim that postverbal subjects with intransitive verbs are also restricted in Italian. Pinto suggests that cases of VS with focus-neutral interpretation in Italian must be analyzed as covert or overt locative constructions. Pinto reports that the locative may remain implicit only if it can be understood deictically with respect to the speaker (an observation due initially to Paola Benincà). Thus, whereas the location of arrival and the location of the call are understood as unspecified in (52a–b), they are identified with the speaker's location in (53a–b). This suggests that the latter examples are cases of covert locative constructions, where the implicit locative is interpreted deictically with respect to the speaker's location. The analysis of (53a–b) is therefore comparable to the analysis of overt locative constructions such as (54).[34] (Note that presentational constructions, such as *Sono arrivati molti ragazzi* 'There arrived many children', should probably be analyzed as a subcase of the locative construction, as Pinto also remarks.)[35]

(52) a. Gigi è   arrivato.
     Gigi has arrived
   b. Gigi ha   telefonato.
     Gigi has called

(53) a. E arrivato Gigi.
   b. Ha telefonato Gigi.

(54) In questo albergo hanno lavorato molte donne   straniere.
     in this   hotel   have   worked many women foreign
     'Many foreign women have worked in this hotel.'
     (Pinto 1994, 177–178)

Pinto and Adger point out the ungrammaticality of (55b) and (56b) with a wide focus interpretation. These sentences are well formed only if the subject is focused. However as I will show in section 3.4, the cases with narrow focus on the subject have a distinct analysis, comparable to the analysis of VOS, a word order in which the subject is also unambiguously focused. I put such cases aside for the time being. At this point what is relevant to note is the contrast between (55a–b)/(56a–b) and their MS counterparts, where both SV and VS are perfectly well formed with a wide focus interpretation: *Juan (se) rió/(Se) rió Juan*; *Tres leones han estornudado/Han estornudado tres leones*.[36]

(55) a. Gigi ha   riso.
       Gigi has laughed
   b. *Ha riso Gigi.
       [What happened?]
     (Pinto 1994, 178)

(56) a. Tre   leoni hanno starnutito.
       three lions have   sneezed
   b. *Hanno starnutito tre leoni.
       [What happened?]
     (Adger 1996, 118)

On the basis of the contrasts in (55) and (56), Pinto suggests that not all predicates (because of their intrinsic meaning) are compatible with a locative argument. Actually, whether or not a predicate is compatible with the locative might depend more on the tense/aspect property of the construction than on the intrinsic meaning of the predicate (see Borer 1994).

Like those in Italian, locative constructions in French are restricted to intransitive verbs. See the contrast between (57) and (58). The impossibility of VSO order in the locative construction of both languages may be attributed to the same constraint, whatever this might be. (Note though that in French, but not in Italian, there is a definiteness constraint in locative constructions, a difference that must be attributed to an independent parameter.)

(57) a. Il   a dormi beaucoup de rois   dans ce   lit.
         there slept   many   kings in this bed
     b. Il   a mangé beaucoup de gens   dans ce   restaurant.
         there ate   many   people in this restaurant

(58) a. *Il   a mangé beaucoup de gens   de la choucroute dans ce
         there ate   many   people sauerkraut   in   this
         restaurant.
         restaurant
     b. *Il   a écrit beaucoup d'enfants   des longues lettres
         there wrote many   children long letters
         á leurs parents dans cette classe.
         to their parents in this class

As in Italian (see (55b)/(56b)), in French there are restrictions on the locative construction. It is generally the case that the intransitive predicates that can appear in this construction are those in which the predicate can readily be interpreted as a property of the locative; and this seems to be contingent on the aspectual properties of the construction, as shown by the following contrast:[37]

(59) a. *Il   a péroré   un politicien dans cet amphithéâtre
         there declaimed a politician in   this lecture-hall
         la semaine dernière.
         last week
     b. Il   a péroré   beaucoup de politiciens dans cet
         there declaimed many   politicians in   this
         amphithéâtre sous   la   deuxième République.
         lecture-hall   during the Second   Republic

Clausal Structure   121

We may conclude, then, that putting aside locative constructions, nominative Case must be checked overtly in [Spec, T] in Italian. In other words, Italian lacks VS(O) because it checks nominative Case overtly in [Spec, T] (with the exception of the locative construction). If we accept this conclusion, the problem that immediately comes to mind is the status of postverbal subjects in Italian. In Italian interrogatives, postverbal subjects appear in final position; see the contrasts in (60) and (61). (Note that the Spanish counterpart to (61c) is perfectly well formed: *Cuando ha comido Juan una manzana?*)

(60) a. Cosa ha fatto Gianni?
         what has done Gianni
         'What has Gianni done?'
     b. *Cosa ha Gianni fatto?

(61) a. Quando ha mangiato una mela Gianni?
         when   has eaten   an apple Gianni
         'When has Gianni eaten an apple?'
     b. *Quando ha Gianni mangiato una mela?
     c. *Quando ha mangiato Gianni una mela?

We may assume, following Antinucci and Cinque (1977) and Calabrese (1990), that postverbal subjects in interrogatives are "emarginated" (i.e., right-dislocated). If right-dislocation is derived from left-dislocation via leftward adjunction (in the spirit of Kayne 1994), then (60a) is derived from (62a), as shown in (62b), and (61a) is derived from (63a), as shown in (63b).

(62) a. Gianni, cosa ha fatto?
     b. [[cosa ha fatto]$_i$ [Gianni [e$_i$]]]

(63) a. Gianni, quando ha mangiato una mela?
     b. [[quando ha mangiato una mela]$_i$ [Gianni [e$_i$]]]

This analysis merits closer scrutiny than is possible here, but a fact cited by Guasti (1996, 176) suggests that it may have some plausibility. Guasti notes that whereas (64a) is ambiguous between a *molti-non* reading ('many students are such that they have not read something') and a *non-molti* reading ('few students have read something'), (64b) is unambiguous, having only the *molti-non* reading. Interestingly, *molti-non* is the only reading available in (64c) as well. These facts follow immediately if the postverbal subject in the interrogative construction in Italian is dislocated.

(64) a. Non l'hanno letto molti studenti.
    not it have read many students
  b. Cosa non hanno letto molti studenti?
    what not have read many students
  c. Molti studenti, cosa non hanno letto?
    many students what not have read

On the other hand, in Spanish both (65a) and (65b) (the counterparts of the Italian (64a) and (64b)) are ambiguous, whereas (65c) (like its Italian counterpart (64c)) is unambiguous. The contrast between (64b) and (65b) immediately follows if in Italian, but not in Spanish, the postverbal subject in the interrogative construction is dislocated.

(65) a. No lo han leido muchos estudiantes.
  b. Qué no han leido muchos estudiantes?
  c. Muchos estudiantes, qué no han leido?

Interestingly, Italian differs from Spanish not only with respect to the property in (50a) but also with respect to the property in (50b). In effect, there is reason to believe that fronted focused phrases and emphatics in Italian are left-dislocated (that is, they occupy a position above TP). They differ from their Spanish counterparts in two respects. On the one hand, Calabrese (1990, n. 7) remarks that in Italian "focus may also be assigned to a preverbal constituent, [in which case] it forms an intonational group by itself ..." On the other hand, the preverbal focused or emphatic constituent need not be adjacent to the verb, as shown by (66a–b). If the subject is postverbal, as in (67a), it is "emarginated," as in the case of interrogatives. (67a) is then derived from (66b), via leftward movement, as shown in (67c).[38]

(66) a. QUESTO Gianni ti dira (non quello che pensavi).
    this Gianni to-you will-say (not what (you) thought)
    (Rizzi 1995, 48)
  b. QUALCOSA, di sicuro, io farò.
    something surely I will-do
    (Cinque 1990, 15)

(67) a. QUESTO ti dira, Gianni.
    (Guglielmo Cinque, personal communication)
  b. Gianni, QUESTO ti dira.
  c. [[QUESTO ti dira]$_i$ [Gianni [e$_i$]]]

Clausal Structure 123

The above facts suggest that Italian has a Focus or Emphasis projection located between CP and TP (cf. Rizzi 1995). In effect, in Italian nominative Case must be checked overtly (with the exception of locative constructions); this implies overt movement of the nominative DP to [Spec, T]. This property of Italian, in conjunction with the assumption in (47), entails that the functional feature T cannot constitute a syncretic category with the functional feature "topic," "focus," or "emphasis" (as it does in Spanish). If present in the clausal structure, these features must be realized as independent functional projections in this language.[39]

To summarize: I have noted two relevant facts of Standard Italian:

(68) a. Italian lacks the order (XP)VSO.
b. Italian allows the order Focus-XP-V and Emphatic-XP-V.

I have attributed generalization (68a) to the property in (69a). Given this property and the assumption in (47), it follows that in Italian the feature T cannot constitute a syncretic category with the feature "topic," "focus," or "emphasis." These features must therefore be realized as independent functional categories in this language; see the property in (69b), from which generalization (68b) immediately follows.

(69) a. In Italian nominative Case must be checked overtly in [Spec, T] (with the exception of locative constructions).
b. Italian has an optional Focus or Emphasis projection, as well as an optional (recursive) Topic projection, located between CP and TP (cf. Rizzi 1995).

I will show in section 3.4 that Italian, like Spanish, has a VOS word order in which the subject is focused. I will argue that the position of the focused subject in this case is not the same in both languages. In Spanish, VOS is derived from VSO (where S is in its initial position within the VP) via leftward movement of the object; see section 3.3. But no such source exists in Italian; in this language VOS (as well as VS in cases other than the locative construction) is derived from SVO (with the subject in the specifier of the F(ocus) Phrase located above TP).[40]

3.3 P-Movement in Spanish

I have shown in chapter 2 (see in particular section 2.6) that cases of potential contradiction between the NSR and the FPR in Germanic are resolved by analyzing the defocalized constituent as metrically invisible.

(These rules are repeated in (70) and (71).) In effect, if a constituent marked [−F] is metrically invisible, then the NSR will never assign it main prominence, an outcome compatible with the FPR.

(70) a. *NSR (German)*
Given two sister nodes C_i and C_j, (a) if C_i and C_j are selectionally ordered, the one lower in the selectional ordering is more prominent (the S-NSR); (b) otherwise, the one lower in the asymmetric c-command ordering is more prominent (the C-NSR).
b. *NSR (English)*
Given two sister nodes C_i and C_j, either (a) if C_i and C_j are selectionally ordered, the one lower in the selectional ordering is more prominent (the S-NSR), or (b) the one lower in the asymmetric c-command ordering is more prominent (the C-NSR).

(71) *FPR*
Given two sister nodes C_i (marked [+F]) and C_j (marked [−F]), C_i is more prominent than C_j.

In Spanish, unlike in Germanic, all phonologically specified material is metrically visible. Therefore, Spanish must have recourse to a different mechanism to resolve cases of conflict between the FPR and the NSR (more precisely, the C-NSR, which is the only part of the NSR that is active in Romance).

(72) *NSR (Romance)*
Given two sister nodes C_i and C_j, the one lower in the asymmetric c-command ordering is more prominent (the C-NSR).

The purpose of this section is to demonstrate that in cases where the NSR and the FPR conflict, Spanish has recourse to movement (i.e., copying and deletion) or the [−F] constituent. I refer to the strategy employed by Spanish as *p-movement* (for *prosodically motivated movement*). The purpose of this movement operation is not feature checking; rather, it is to ensure that the focalized constituent is in a position to receive prominence via the C-NSR, thus ensuring that the output is compatible with the FPR. As I will show, p-movement obeys Last Resort (see section 1.3.2). Here, as well as in section 3.4 on Italian, my discussion of p-movement will be informal. A precise formulation of the rule and a general discussion of its properties are to be found in section 3.5.

3.3.1 VOS Order in Spanish

Both the VSO and SVO structures of MS are compatible with a focus-neutral interpretation, in which case NS falls on the last constituent, as illustrated by (73a–b).

(73) a. María me   regaló la botella de <u>vino</u>.
       María to-me gave   the bottle of wine
   b. Me regaló María botella de <u>vino</u>.

If the intonational nucleus is on the subject rather than on the object, then a contrastive focus interpretation is obtained.

(74) a. MARÍA me regaló la botella de vino (no Juan).
                                          (not Juan)
   b. Me regaló MARÍA la botella de vino (no Juan).

This follows immediately from the analysis of NS put forth in chapter 2. Recall that in Spanish all material is metrically visible, including defocalized constituents, and that only the C-NSR is active in Spanish (as well as in other Romance languages). This rule places NS on the lowest constituent in the c-command ordering (i.e., on the rightmost constituent). Cases of main prominence that are not generated by the NSR are generated by the Emphatic/Contrastive Stress Rule. Recall that the prominence generated by this rule gives rise to an interpretation in which (part of) the presupposition is reasserted or denied (see section 2.1.2). This is indeed the case in (74). Such sentences attribute to the listener a presupposition that is denied by the speaker. As indicated by the tag, the presupposition attributed to the listener is *Juan me regaló la botella de vino* 'Juan gave to me (as a present) the bottle of wine'. Speakers therefore generally do not accept such a sentence as an answer to the question in (75). (The same remarks hold for (5) and (21).)

(75) Quién te   regaló la botella de vino?
     who   to-you gave   the bottle of wine

Besides the SVO and VSO orders, there is another possible rearrangement of constituents in Spanish—namely, VOS, in which the subject is not right-dislocated (see (76)).[41] But this order has a peculiarity: it is not compatible with a focus-neutral interpretation. It is only compatible with narrow focus on the subject (as indicated by the braces). Furthermore, (76) differs from (74) in that its interpretation is not necessarily contrastive. In fact, (76) is the only possible way of answering the question in (75) with a full sentence.⁴² This observation leads me to believe that main stress on the focused subject in (76) is generated by the NSR and not by the Emphatic/Contrastive Stress Rule.

(76) Me regaló la botella de vino {María}.

It is also to be noted that the position of phrasal stress in VOS structures (where the subject is not right-dislocated) is unambiguous. In effect, main phrasal stress on the object is not possible with VOS (whether contrastive or not), unless S is right-dislocated (i.e., with an intonational hiatus between the subject and the material that precedes it).

(77) a. *Me regaló la BOTELLA de vino María.
     b. *Me regaló la botella de VINO María.

Note that the type of object scrambling discussed above is not constrained to specific DPs (unlike the type of scrambling in Germanic languages discussed by Diesing (1992a,b) and the clitic left-dislocation construction discussed in section 3.1.3). The negative polarity item *nada* in (78a) is clearly an indefinite, as is the DP *una secretaria* in (78b). Specific direct object DPs are preceded by the preposition *a* in Spanish, and *a* is absent in (78b) (cf. (78c)).

(78) a. No trajo   nada   {Juan}.
        not brought anything Juan
        'Juan didn't bring anything.'
     b. Está buscando   una secretaria {el jefe de fábrica}.
        is   looking-for a   secretary the factory's foreman
        'The factory's foreman is looking for a secretary.'
     c. Está buscando   a   una secretaria {el jefe de fábrica}.
        is   looking-for ACC a   secretary the factory's foreman
        'The factory's foreman is looking for a certain secretary.'

To summarize, the VOS order has two salient properties: the subject bears unambiguously nuclear stress and the subject is focused. On the basis of this observation, it is reasonable to hypothesize that the underlying structure of VOS is either SVO or VSO, and the motivation for reordering is to put the focused subject in a position to receive NS via the C-NSR (see (72)), an output compatible with the FPR (see (71)). If the C-NSR is sensitive to syntactic c-command as I argued in chapter 2, it follows that the reordering does not simply affect linear ordering but in fact also affects c-command relations between the reordered constituents.

Clausal Structure

To conclude, VOS is derived from either the SVO or the VSO structure via movement. I have thus isolated a case of movement, the purpose of which is not formal feature checking; the motivation for such movement is prosodic in nature.

Let us take a closer look at the source of VSO order in Spanish. As noted, there are two a priori possibilities. The first is that the source is SVO, in which case VOS is derived by leftward adjunction of T' to TP, as illustrated in (79).

(79) $[[_{T'}$ me regaló $[e_j$ $[V_1$ [la botella de vino$_k$ $[V_2$ $e_k]]]]]_i$ $[_{TP}$ María$_j$ $[e_i]]]$

But recall that X' nodes cannot undergo movement (i.e., only maximal projections and heads are visible to the syntactic computation); see section 1.3.1. It follows then that SVO, where S is in [Spec, T], cannot be a source for VOS in MS. Indeed, T' cannot be subject to any syntactic operation. The second possibility is that the source is VSO, in which case VOS is derived by leftward adjunction of O to VP_1 (see (80a)), or by leftward adjunction of VP_2 to VP_1, if movement of the object triggers pied-piping of the VP that immediately contains it (see (80b)).[43]

(80) a. $[_{TP}$ me regaló $[_{VP_1}[_{DP}$ la botella de vino$]_k$ $[_{VP_1}$ María $[_{VP_2}$ V_1 $[e_k$ $[V_2$ $e_k]]]]]]$
  b. $[_{TP}$ me regaló $[_{VP_1}[_{VP_2}$ la botella de vino$_k$ $[e_k$ $[V_2$ $e_k]]]]_i$ $[_{VP_1}$ María $[V_1$ $[e_i]]]]]$

I will show in section 3.5.1 that formulating p-movement in terms of Last Resort entails the analysis in (80b). In what follows I will therefore accept this conclusion, stated in (81).

(81) In MS, VOS order is derived from VSO order via leftward adjunction of VP_2 to VP_1.

3.3.2 Related Cases

The properties just isolated for VOS order (phrasal stress falls unambiguously on the subject, and the subject is unambiguously interpreted as focused) are also found in the orders VPPS and V[OPP]S. Consider first the source structures VSPP in (82b), (83b), and (84b) and VSOPP in (85b) and (86b). These sentences, with NS on the rightmost constituent (as dictated by the C-NSR), are compatible with a wide focus interpretation (i.e., a focus-neutral interpretation).

(82) a. El sindicato(S) habló(V) contra el gobierno(PP).
    the union   talked   against the government

b. Ayer habló(V) el sindicato(S) contra el gobierno(PP).
yesterday talked the union against the government

(83) a. Los alumnos(S) se enfrentaron(V) con la policía(PP).
the students themselves confronted with the police
b. Ayer se enfrentaron(V) los alumnos(S)
yesterday themselves confronted the students
con la policía(PP).
with the police

(84) a. Los congresistas(S) discutieron(V) sobre el problema(PP).
the congressmen talked about the problem
b. Ayer discutieron(V) los congresistas(S)
yesterday talked the congressmen
sobre el problema(PP).
about the problem

(85) a. La camarera del hotel(S) puso(V) la valija(O)
the hotel's attendant put the suitcase
sobre la cama(PP).
on the bed
b. Ayer puso(V) la camarera del hotel(S) la valija(O)
yesterday put the hotel's attendant the suitcase
sobre la cama(PP).
on the bed

(86) a. Ayer los alumnos de la primaria(S) colgaron(V)
yesterday the elementary students hung
la bandera(O) en el mástil(PP).
the flag on the pole
b. Ayer colgaron(V) los alumnos de la primaria(S)
yesterday hung the elementary students
la bandera(O) en el mástil(PP).
the flag on the pole

On the other hand, the derived structures VPPS in (87) and V[OPP]S in (88) are not compatible with a focus-neutral interpretation. Although NS is on the rightmost constituent, such sentences are compatible only with an interpretation in which the subject has narrow focus (as indicated by the braces). In fact, the sentences in (87) and (88) are the only way to answer the questions in (89) with a full sentence in MS.

Clausal Structure 129

(87) a. Ayer habló(V) contra el gobierno(PP) {el <u>sindicato</u>}(S).
  b. Se enfrentaron(V) con la policía(PP) {los <u>alumnos</u>}(S).
  c. Ayer discutieron(V) sobre el problema(PP) {los <u>congresistas</u>}(S).

(88) a. Puso(V) la valija(O) sobre la cama(PP) {la camarera del <u>hotel</u>}(S).
  b. Ayer colgaron(V) la bandera(O) en el mástil(PP) {los alumnos de la <u>primaria</u>}(S).

(89) a. Who spoke yesterday against the government?
  b. Who confronted the police?
  c. Who discussed the problem yesterday?
  d. Who put the suitcase on the bed?
  e. Who hung the flag on the pole yesterday?

Note furthermore, as shown in (90), that the Emphatic/Contrastive Stress Rule can apply in place of the NSR in (82)–(86) and assign main prominence to some constituent other than the rightmost one.

(90) a. EL SINDICATO habló contra el gobierno
    the union   spoke against the government
    (y no el partido).
    (and not the party)
  b. Ayer   se enfrentaron   los ALUMNOS con la policía
    yesterday themselves confronted the students   with the police
    (y no los profesores).
    (and not the professors)
  c. La camarera del hotel puso la VALIJA sobre la cama
    the hotel's attendant   put   the suitcase on the bed
    (y no el maletín).
    (and not the briefcase)
  d. Ayer   colgaron los alumnos de la PRIMARIA la bandera
    yesterday hung   the elementary students   the flag
    en el mástil (y no los alumnos de la secundaria).
    on the pole (and not the secondary students)

On the other hand, in the case of (87) and (88), the intonational nucleus cannot be anywhere else than on the subject. Thus, the following examples are ill formed, unless the constituent with main prominence is followed by an intonational hiatus, indicating that the material on its right is right-dislocated. (On the prosodic properties of right-dislocation, see the appendix to this chapter.)

(91) a. *Habló contra el GOBIERNO el sindicato
spoke against the government the union
(no contra el partido).
(not against the party)
 b. *Ayer   colgaron la bandera FRANCESA en el mástil
yesterday hung   the French flag   on the pole
los alumnos de la primaria (no la bandera americana).
the elementary students   (not the American flag)

On the basis of such observations, I conclude that the orders VPPS/ V[OPP]S are also generated by p-movement: a defocalized constituent moves leftward of the focused subject in order to put the subject in a position to receive main prominence via the NSR. More precisely, p-movement left-adjoins VP_2 to VP_1. This is illustrated in (92).

(92) a. [$_{TP}$ ayer [habló [$_{VP_1}$ [$_{VP_2}$ V_2 contra el gobierno]$_i$ [$_{VP_1}$ el sindicato [V_1 [e_i]]]]]]
(cf. (87a))
 b. [$_{TP}$ puso [$_{VP_1}$ [$_{VP_2}$ la valija$_k$ [V_2 [e_k [$_{PP}$ sobre la cama]]]]$_j$ [$_{VP_1}$ la camarera del hotel [V_1 [e_j]]]]]
(cf. (88a))

P-movement is triggered not only by a focused subject, but also by a focused complement, as illustrated by (93a), where the object is unambiguously interpreted as focused. In effect, (93a) is the only way of answering question (93b) with a full sentence in MS.

(93) a. Ana(S) escondió(V) debajo de la cama(PP) {la muñeca}(O).
Ana   hid   under the bed   the doll
 b. What did Ana hide under the bed?

(93a) is derived via p-movement by left-adjoining the PP to VP_2.

(94) [$_{TP}$ Ana$_j$ [escondió [$_{VP_1}$ e_j [V_1 [$_{VP_2}$ [$_{PP}$ debajo de la cama]$_i$ [$_{VP_2}$ la muñeca [V_2 [e_i]]]]]]]]

Like all structures derived via p-movement, (94) is prosodically unambiguous. Main prominence must be on the object, as shown by the ill-formedness of (95a–b). Note that these sentences cannot be saved by analyzing the object as right-dislocated, even if an intonational break is inserted after the prepositional object, given that dislocated objects obligatorily cooccur with a clitic in MS. (See the appendix to this chapter.)

(95) a. *Ana escondió debajo de la CAMA la muñeca
Ana hid under the bed the doll
(y no debajo de la comoda).
(and not under the dresser)
b. *ANA escondió debajo de la cama la muñeca
Ana hid under the bed the doll
(y no Victoria).
(and not Victoria)

In the appendix to chapter 2, I argued that a *wh*-in-situ is subject to the FPR. If this is the case, then it is to be expected that a *wh*-in-situ will be affected by the type of scrambling that I have called p-movement. The prediction is borne out, as illustrated by the contrasts in (96) and (97). In these examples the object is p-moved, thus allowing the *wh*-subject in (96b) and the *wh*-prepositional complement in (97b) to be assigned main prominence by the NSR, without conflicting with the FPR.

(96) a. *Dime: donde compró(V) quién(S) el libro(O)?
tell me: where bought who the book
b. Dime: donde compró(V) el libro(O) quién(S)?
tell me: where bought the book who

(97) a. *Quién puso(V) qué cosa(O) sobre la mesa(PP)?
who put what on the table
b. Quién puso(V) sobre la mesa(PP) qué cosa(O)?
who put on the table what

On the other hand, a *wh*-phrase itself cannot be p-moved; see (98b).[44] This immediately follows from the fact that p-movement only affects defocalized constituents; that is, p-movement applies in order to resolve the conflict between the NSR and the FPR, but no such conflict exists in (98a).

(98) a. Quién compró(V) un libro(O) para quién(PP)?
who bought a book for whom
b. *Quién compró(V) para quién(PP) un libro(O)?
who bought for whom a book

Finally, p-movement is strictly local. In effect, a defocalized constituent moves immediately above the focused constituent. Thus, compare (80b) (repeated in (99a)) with (99b), where the object was moved not only across the focused subject but also across the verb, giving rise to OVS.

(99) a. $[_{TP}$ me regaló $[_{VP_1} [_{VP_2}$ la botella de vino$_k$ $[e_k [V_2 \ e_k]]]_i [_{VP_1}$ María $[V_1 [_{VP_2} e_i]]]]]$
b. *$[_{TP}[_{VP_2}$ la botella de vino$_k$ $[e_k [V_2 \ e_k]]]_i [_{TP}$ me regaló $[_{VP_1}$ María $[V_1 [VP_2 \ e_i]]]]]$

The local nature of p-movement is further illustrated by the examples that follow. In the case of VSOPP, where the subject is focused, the constituent [OPP] must move immediately above S, giving rise to the order VOPPS; see (88), repeated in (100). The constituent [OPP] cannot move above V, giving rise to the order OPPVS, as shown in (101).

(100) a. Puso(V) la valija(O) sobre la cama(PP)
put   the suitcase on the bed
{la camarera del <u>hotel</u>}(S).
the hotel's attendant
b. Ayer   colgaron(V) la bandera(O) en el mástil(PP)
yesterday hung   the flag   on the pole
{los alumnos de la <u>primaria</u>}(S).
the elementary students

(101) a. ?*La valija(O) sobre la cama(PP) puso(V) {la camarera del <u>hotel</u>}(S).
b. ?*La bandera(O) en el mástil(PP) colgaron(V) {los alumnos de la <u>primaria</u>}(S).

In the case of VS{O}PP/SV{O}PP, where the object is focused, the PP must move immediately above the O; it may not move above S. Compare (102a) and (102b).

(102) a. Ayer   escondió(V) Ana(S) debajo de la cama(PP)
yesterday hid   Ana   under the bed
{un <u>libro</u>}(O).
a book
b. *Ayer escondió(V) debajo de la cama(PP) Ana(S) {un <u>libro</u>}(O).

Note that (103b) is well formed, as is (103a), but the fronting of the PP in (103b) is a case of left-dislocation and not a case of p-movement. This is shown by the fact that the word order in (103b) does not impose a narrow focus interpretation on the object; compare (103b) with (103a).

(103) a. Ana(S) escondió(V) debajo de la cama(PP) {un <u>libro</u>}(O).
    [What did Ana hide under the bed?]
    [*What did Ana do under the bed?]

Clausal Structure   133

   b. Debajo de la cama(PP) Ana(S) escondió(V) un <u>libro</u>(O).
      [What did Ana hide under the bed?]
      [What did Ana do under the bed?]

3.3.3 Summary

In this section I have uncovered a type of scrambling in the grammar of MS with particular properties: it gives rise to structures that are prosodically unambiguous and that are associated with a narrow focus interpretation. On the basis of these observations, I have suggested that this case of scrambling is prosodically motivated. A defocalized constituent is moved immediately above the focused constituent in order to ensure that the focused constituent is in a position to be assigned main prominence by the C-NSR; the output structure is thus compatible with the FRP. More precisely, I am suggesting that p-movement in Spanish plays exactly the same role as metrical invisibility in other languages. As noted in section 2.6 and at the outset of this section, the fact that [−F] constituents are metrically invisible for the NSR in certain languages (such as English and German) ensures that the output of the NSR is compatible with the FPR. In effect, there are multiple cases in which the NSR would assign main prominence to a defocalized constituent if it were not analyzed as metrically invisible, giving rise to a contradictory situation between the NSR and FPR. In Spanish all phonologically specified material is metrically visible for the NSR. Therefore, in cases in which the NSR would assign main prominence to a [−F] constituent (generating an output that contradicts the FPR), this language has recourse to an alternative strategy, namely, movement. I have shown furthermore that p-movement is strictly local in nature. I will argue in section 3.5.1 that this property follows from the formulation of the rule itself.

So far I have examined cases where p-movement affects the relative ordering of major argument constituents of the sentence (i.e., where it affects the subject, the object, or the PP complement of a verbal predicate), but there is no reason why p-movement cannot affect the relative ordering of constituents contained within theses major constituents. I illustrate such cases in (104). As indicated by the context questions, (104b) has narrow focus on the genitive complement of the verb's direct object. More precisely, in this example p-movement has occurred within the direct object: the *por*-phrase has p-moved around the focused genitive complement of the object's head noun.

(104) a. El pueblo denunció la invasión del Canal de Panamá por
the people denounced the invasion of Panama by
los americanos.
the Americans
[What happened?]
b. El pueblo denunció la invasión por los americanos {del Canal de Panamá}.
[Which place did the people denounce the invasion of by the Americans?]
[*What happened?]

P-movement can also affect the relative order of an adverb and an argument, as shown in (105). In (105b) the locative adverb *en el jardín* has p-moved around the focused object.

(105) a. Juan plantó un rosal en el jardín.
Juan planted a rose-bush in the garden
[What did Juan do?]
[*What did Juan plant in the garden?]
b. Juan plantó en el jardín un rosal.
[*What did Juan do?]
[What did Juan plant in the garden?]

By extension, p-movement may also apply in the context of an emphatic constituent. The same logic applies here as with focused constituents. Suppose that the subject in the VSO structure is emphatic and receives main prominence via the Emphatic/Contrastive Stress Rule. If the NSR does not apply, the forms in (106a) and (107a) result. On the other hand, if the NSR also applies and assigns main prominence to O, a prosodically contradictory situation arises. This contradiction is resolved via p-movement of O across S, giving rise to the forms in (106b) and (107b).

(106) a. No probó NADIE la tarta.
not tasted nobody the pie
'Nobody tasted the pie.'
b. No probó la tarta nadie.

(107) a. No puse ningún LIBRO sobre la mesa.
not (I) put no book on the table
'I didn't put any book on the table.'
b. No puse sobre la mesa ningún libro.

3.4 P-Movement in Italian: Some Comparative Remarks

Like Spanish VOS order, Italian VOS order has unambiguously narrow focus on the subject.

(108) ?Ha mangiato la mela Gianni.
       has eaten the apple Gianni
       [*What happened?]
       [*What did Gianni do?]
       [Who ate the apple?]

VOS order in Italian is sensitive to a certain "relative heaviness" constraint, as shown by the less than perfect status of (108). On the other hand, the Spanish counterpart to (108) is perfect.

(109) Ha comido la manzana Juan.

The "relative heaviness" effect disappears if the object is removed—for example, by cliticization. Compare (110) with (108).

(110) La mela, l'ha mangiata Gianni.
       the apple ACC.CL has eaten Gianni

Further minimal contrasts are given in (111) and (112) (from Rizzi 1991, 19).

(111) a. ?Ha risolto il problema Gianni.
         has solved the problem Gianni
    b. ?Ha vinto la corsa Gianni.
         has won the race Gianni
    c. ??Ha parlato con Maria Gianni.
         has spoken with Maria Gianni

(112) a. Lo ha risolto Gianni.
         ACC.CL has solved Gianni
    b. L'ha vinta Gianni.
         ACC.CL has won Gianni
    c. Le ha parlato Gianni.
         DAT.CL has spoken Gianni

Note that whereas the Spanish example in (113) is perfectly compatible with an interpretation in which the scope of the focus includes either just the subject or both the verb and the subject, the Italian example in (110) has unambiguously narrow focus on the subject. Compare the context questions in (113) and (114). The same comment holds for the Italian examples in (112).

(113) La manzana la   comió Juan.
 the apple   ACC.CL ate   Juan
 [What happened to the apple?]
 [Who ate the apple?]

(114) La mela, l'ha   mangiata Gianni.
 the apple ACC.CL has eaten   Gianni
 [*What happened to the apple?]
 [Who ate the apple?]

The above observation follows directly from the fact that the Spanish example has a VSO structure as its source (and recall that VSO is compatible with a wide focus interpretation). (113) thus has the structure in (115). (On clitic left-dislocation, see section 3.1.3.)

(115) [$_{TP}$ la manzana$_i$ la comió [$_{ClP}$ e$_i$ [D [Cl]]$_i$ [$_{VP}$ Juan V$_1$ [$_{VP}$[(D)] [V$_2$]] (D)]]]]

Italian, on the other hand, lacks VSO order (see section 3.2). The Italian example is therefore unambiguously related to the VOS structure, which is associated with a narrow focus interpretation on the subject. What, then, is the source of VOS in Italian? Given the analysis of Italian put forth in section 3.2, the source of VOS in Italian must be SVO, where S is in the specifier of a Focus projection above TP. Leftward p-movement adjoins the TP to the F(ocus)P, thus ensuring that no conflict arises between the NSR and the FPR. (Recall that VOS cannot be derived from a SVO structure in which the subject is in [Spec, T] by left-adjoining T' to TP; only maximal categories and heads may undergo movement.)

(116) In Modern Standard Italian VOS is derived from SVO via leftward adjunction of TP to FP.

Therefore, (108) has the structure in (117).

(117) [$_{FP}$[$_{TP}$ e$_i$ [ha mangiato la mela]]$_j$ [$_{FP}$ Gianni$_i$ [$_{TP}$ e$_j$]]]

The same analysis applies to (114), where the object has been left-dislocated; see (118). (For simplicity's sake, I ignore the complex verbal structure that underlies transitive verbs.)

(118) [$_{TopP}$ la mela$_k$ [$_{FP}$[$_{TP}$ e$_i$ l'ha [$_{ClP}$ e$_k$ [D [Cl]]$_k$ [mangiata (D)]]]$_j$ [$_{FP}$ Gianni$_i$ [$_{TP}$ e$_j$]]]]

To summarize: I conclude that VOS in Italian and VOS in Spanish have different sources. VOS in Spanish has as its source a VSO structure; VP_2 (which contains O) is p-moved around VP_1 (which contains S). On the other hand, VOS in Italian has as its source a SVO structure; TP (which contains VO) is p-moved around FP (which contains S). It is to this difference in analysis that I attribute the contrast between the status of the Italian example in (108) and the status of the Spanish example in (109). More precisely, I suggest that p-movement is sensitive to the *Relative Weight Constraint*.

(119) *The Relative Weight Constraint*
P-movement of constituent A across constituent B is degraded if A is "metrically heavier" than B.

Although the notion of metrical heaviness is still poorly understood (but see Guasti and Nespor 1996 for relevant discussion), it seems that the following generalization holds:

(120) A is "metrically heavier" than B if A is branching and B is not (where only metrically visible material counts for computing "branchingness"), unless B has heavier pitch than A.

Let us assume that light functional categories such as bare determiners in Italian (and in Spanish) are metrically invisible, a hypothesis that is independently supported by the data discussed in note 46. It is then the case that in (121a) (as well as in (108) and (111)), the TP is metrically branching but the subject is not. In effect, TP dominates two metrically visible constituents (*letto* and *discorso*), and the DP subject dominates a single metrically visible constituent (*Gianni* or *ragazzo*). The marginality of such examples disappears if the subject carries a heavy pitch accent or if the subject is metrically branching, as illustrated in (121b) and (121c), respectively. The same analysis applies to the contrast in (122).[45]

(121) a. ?[[$_{TP}$ Ha letto il discorso] [$_{FP}$ Gianni/il ragazzo]].
          has read the lecture   Gianni/the boy
   b. [$_{TP}$ Ha letto il discorso [$_{FP}$ GIANNI/il RAGAZZO]].
   c. [$_{TP}$ Ha letto il discorso [$_{FP}$ solo Gianni/il ragazzo]].

(122) a. ?[$_{TP}$ Ha parlato bene [Gianni]].
         has spoken well Gianni
   b. [$_{TP}$ Ha parlato bene [GIANNI]].
         has spoken well Gianni

c. [$_{TP}$ Ha parlato bene [solo Gianni]].
 has spoken well only Gianni
 (Belletti and Shlonsky 1995, 522, n. 28)

On the other hand, in Spanish VOS the relative heaviness of [VO] with respect to S is irrelevant, since [VO] does not move around S. In Spanish O moves around S, and if anything, it is the relative heaviness of O and S that is relevant (e.g., *?Ha leido el discurso del director Juan/Ha leido el discurso del director JUAN*).

Italian, like Spanish, also has SVPPO structures, where the O is interpreted as focused. Such cases are derived by p-moving the PP immediately above the O, as in Spanish. See (123). As expected, no heaviness effects are attested in this case.[46,47]

(123) a. Maria ha messo il libro sul tavolo.
 Maria has put the book on-the table
 [What happened?]
 b. Maria ha messo sul tavolo il libro.
 [*What happened?]
 [What did Maria put on the table?]

To summarize: In this section I have argued that Italian VOS has a source distinct from that of Spanish VOS. Italian lacks VSO. Consequently, the only possible source for VOS in this language is SVO, where the focused subject occupies the specifier of a functional projection above TP, namely, the specifier of a Focus projection. P-movement left-adjoins the TP, which contains [VO], to the FP, which contains the focused S. In support for this analysis of Italian VOS, I have brought to bear two facts: (a) the nonambiguity of examples such as those in (108) and in (111) with respect to the scope of the focus, and (b) the Relative Weight Constraint to which the VOS order in Italian is sensitive.[48]

3.5 The Nature of P-Movement and Where It Applies

In chapter 2 I demonstrated that in German and in English, when there is a conflict between the NSR and the FPR, it is resolved by rendering the [−F] constituent metrically invisible. In effect, given two metrical sister nodes (C_i, C_j), where C_i is [+F] and C_j is [−F], if the NSR assigns main prominence to C_j and the FPR assigns main prominence to C_i, this conflict is resolved in these languages by analyzing C_j as metrically invisible

Clausal Structure

for the purpose of the application of the NSR. I also showed that there are languages, such as Spanish and Italian, that do not allow a node that dominates phonological material to be interpreted as metrically invisible (with the exception of "light" functional categories; see section 3.4). In sections 3.3 and 3.4 I suggested that these languages resolve cases of conflict between the NSR and the FPR via movement. More precisely, given two metrical sister nodes (C_i, C_j), where C_i is [+F] and C_j is [−F], if the NSR assigns main prominence to C_j and the FPR assigns main prominence to C_i, this conflict is resolved in Spanish and in Italian by moving C_j. The informal discussion of p-movement to this point might lead one to suspect that this rule is global in nature, but this proves not to be the case. I turn to this issue in section 3.5.1, and to the issue of where p-movement applies in section 3.5.2.

3.5.1 The Formulation of P-Movement

Let us return to the logic behind p-movement. I have argued that the type of movement described in sections 3.3 and 3.4 is not a case of feature checking, formulated in terms of Attract in the Minimalist Program (see section 1.3.2). Rather, such movement applies in cases where two nodes α and β have prosodically contradictory properties. Such a case arises in a well-defined situation. The nodes α and β are analyzed as having prosodically contradictory properties iff two conditions are met: (a) α and β are sisters and (b) the FPR assigns main prominence to one node (say, to α) and the NSR assigns main prominence to the other node (say, to β). Recall that the notion of prominence encoded by the FPR and the NSR is strictly local. In effect, *it is part of the definition of these rules that they define prominence relations among (metrical) sister nodes* (see chapter 2). If indeed the FPR and the NSR define prominence relations only between (metrical) sister nodes, then it follows that nodes α and β may be understood as having contradictory prosodic properties iff they are (metrical) sisters. Such a contradictory situation arises if the FPR assigns main prominence to one node (say, to α) and the NSR assigns main prominence to the other node (say, to β) because prominence is a relative notion: if α is strong with respect to β, then β is weak with respect to α (and vice versa). If we mark this derivative notion of strength with the diacritic [ph*] (where *ph* stands for *phonological content*), we may define a prosodically contradictory structure as follows:

(124) ... [$_\delta$[$_\alpha$ ph*] ... [$_\beta$ ph*]], where α and β are metrical sisters.

The prosodic structure in (124) is uninterpretable, and the purpose of p-movement is to undo it. P-movement may be formulated in the most general possible terms as shown in (125).

(125) Affect the nodes α and β iff these nodes have contradictory prosodic properties, where the notion of prosodic contradiction is to be understood as in (124).

The term *affect* can be interpreted in the most general syntactic terms—that is, as changing the c-command relation between α and β. This can be achieved via copying, deletion, or both. Clearly, copying one of the nodes without deleting the phonological content of the initial copy will give rise to a nonconvergent derivation that will crash at PF. Deletion without copying is also excluded by the condition on recoverability of deletion. Therefore, both copy and deletion must apply, and copying plus deletion equals movement. In a structure like (124), β can move above α, but not vice versa, because it is a general property of movement that it is always leftward; there is no rightward movement (see Kayne 1994). The only option is then that β adjoins to δ, as shown in (126). After p-movement applies, the NSR and the FPR can reapply without yielding a prosodically contradictory output.[49]

(126) ... $[_\delta [_\beta \text{ ph*}] [_\delta [_\alpha \text{ ph*}] \ldots [_\beta \quad]]]$

Consider the structure in (127a). β cannot move higher than δ (i.e., it cannot adjoin to χ), giving rise to (127b). Such an operation will also affect the c-command relation between β and γ, but these nodes are not defined as prosodically contradictory (cf. (124)) and p-movement only affects two nodes that are defined as having contradictory prosodic properties.

(127) a. $[_\chi \gamma [_\delta [_\alpha \text{ ph*}] \ldots [_\beta \text{ ph*}]]$, where α and β are metrical sisters.
    b. $[_\chi [_\beta \text{ ph*}] [_\chi \gamma [_\delta [_\alpha \text{ ph*}] \ldots [_\beta \quad]$

To recapitulate: I have proposed a formulation of p-movement that has Last Resort built into it, just as Attract has Last Resort built into it. This is achieved via the "iff" condition. The local property of p-movement—namely, that it can only affect two metrical sister nodes—follows from the nature of the rule itself. I conclude that p-movement as formulated in (125) is a perfectly plausible rule of grammar to the extent that it is local in nature, with no risk of giving rise to the computational explosion typical of global rules.

3.5.2 Where Does P-Movement Apply?

According to the analysis presented above, p-movement feeds the NSR. Therefore, its point of application depends on where the NSR applies. In chapter 2 I proposed a formulation of the NSR that makes crucial reference to syntactic notions such as asymmetric c-command and selectional ordering; under this proposal, it is natural to place the NSR in the syntax. More precisely, I suggested that the NSR applies at the end of the syntactic derivation. This implies that p-movement (of the type identified in sections 3.3 and 3.4) must also apply in the syntax. The question then arises whether there is empirical evidence for or against this conclusion. To answer this question, we need to examine how the type of scrambling that I have analyzed in terms of p-movement interacts with LF or post-LF phenomena. In effect, given the architecture of the grammar assumed here (see section 1.3.3), if p-movement applies after Spell-Out (i.e., at PF), then we would expect that it should have no effect with respect to LF (or post-LF) phenomena. Because of they very local nature of the scrambling that is under discussion, the type of LF (or post-LF) phenomenon that we could look at is practically limited to the one that pertains to the theory of (anaphora) binding. If we find that p-movement bleeds binding or creates new binding possibilities, we could take this behavior as evidence that p-movement applies prior to Spell-Out. On the other hand, if we find that p-movement does not affect binding, nothing can be inferred with respect to the locus of application of p-movement. It could be argued that p-movement fails to affect binding either because of "reconstruction" of the p-moved material or because the structures generated by p-movement are nonneutral with respect to focus and focus may, in certain cases, have an impact on binding irrespective of syntactic structure (see section 1.1.4). As the data examined below demonstrate, p-movement (of the sort described in sections 3.3 and 3.4) has no effect whatsoever on anaphora binding. It does not give rise to new binding possibilities, nor does it bleed binding relations that were available prior to its application. I conclude, then, that binding is absolutely neutral with respect to the question of where p-movement applies.

I show below that VO{S} has the same array of quantifier binding possibilities as V{S}O, where both have the same focus structure, as indicated by the braces. The importance of controlling for focus structure is of course dictated by the fact that focus may have an effect on quantifier binding (see section 1.1.4). Since VOS requires narrow focus on the subject obligatorily, then the comparison requires VSO to have narrow focus on the subject as well. This means that in examining the data, it is very important to control for intonation: in both structures main prominence must be on the subject. Although the focus is necessarily contrastive in V{S}O, this is not the case in VO{S}. The comparison is therefore less than perfect, but a more complete view of the parallelism will be obtained when we examine French in section 3.6.1. Given that the prosody of French is less constrained than that of Spanish, as shown in chapter 2, a perfect comparison can be obtained in French between binding in structures with sentence-internal noncontrastive focus (which involves no p-movement) and binding in structures with a rightmost noncontrastive focused constituent (derived via p-movement).

First, let us examine quantifier binding in V{S}O structures, in which the binder is the object and the bindee is contained within the subject. The QP object *cada N* 'each N' may readily bind the subject in (128a). The intended binding relation is marginal when the object is the partitive negative polarity item *ninguno de esos N* 'none of those N'; see (128b). On the other hand, if the object is the indefinite negative polarity item *nadie* 'nobody' or *ningún N* 'no N', the intended binding relation is impossible; see (128c).[50] (Recall that main prominence assigned by the Emphatic/Contrastive Stress Rule (capitals) may only be associated with a contrastive interpretation, whereas main prominence assigned by the NSR (underlining) may be associated with a contrastive or a noncontrastive interpretation.)

(128) a. El primer día de escuela acompañará   su MADRE a
         the first   day of school will-accompany his mother   ACC
         cada niño (y   no su padre).
         every child (and not his father)
         [Binding: OK]
    b. El primer día de escuela no acompañará   su MADRE
         the first   day of school not will-accompany his mother
         a   ninguno de estos niños   (sino su padre).
         ACC none   of those children (but his father)
         [Binding: ?]
    c. El primer día de escuela no acompañará   su MADRE
         the first   day of school not will-accompany his mother
         a   nadie/   a   ningún niño (sino su padre).
         ACC nobody/ACC no   child (but his father)
         [Binding: *]

Clausal Structure   143

The same array of quantifier binding relations is found in VO{S}, where the binder is the object and the bindee is contained within the subject.[51]

(129) a. El primer día de escuela acompañará a cada niño su <u>madre</u> (y no su padre).
[Binding: OK]
b. El primer día de escuela no acompañará a ninguno de estos niños su <u>madre</u> (sino su padre).
[Binding: ?]
c. El primer día de escuela no acompañará a nadie/a ningún niño su <u>madre</u> (sino su padre).
[Binding: *]

(130) Q: Quisiera   saber   quién acompañará   a   cada naño
I-would-like to-know who   will-accompany ACC each child
el   primer día de escuela.
the first   day of school
A: El primer día de escuela accompañará   a   cada niño(O)
the first   day of school will-accompany ACC each child
su <u>madre</u>(S).
his mother
[Binding: OK]

Next, let us examine cases in which the binder is the subject and the bindee is contained within the object. Again, there is no contrast between the V{S}O and the VO{S} structures with respect to quantifier binding.

(131) a. El primer día de escuela acompañará   cada MADRE a
the first   day of school will-accompany each mother   ACC
su hijo.
her child
[Binding: OK]
b. El primer día de escuela acompañará a su hijo cada <u>madre</u>.
[Binding: OK]

The fact that V{S}O and VO{S} give rise to the same array of quantifier-binding possibilities is unsurprising. In effect, as shown in section 1.1.4, {S}VO has exactly the same array of quantifier-binding possibilities as V{S}O and VO{S}. Compare (132) with (128) and (129).

(132) a. El primer día de escuela, su MADRE deberá acompañar
                                               must   accompany
   a cada niño.
   [Binding: OK]
   b. El primer día de escuela, su MADRE no deberá acompañar
                                           not must   accompany
   a ninguno de estos niños.
   [Binding: ?]
   c. El primer día de escuela, su MADRE no deberá acompañar a nadie/a ningún niño.
   [Binding: *]

For the sake of completeness, let us examine quantifier binding in V{O}PP and VPP{O} structures. Again, they exhibit comparable binding relations. Compare (133a) with (133b–c) and (134a) with (134b).[52]

(133) a. Fotografiaron   su mejor MONUMENTO en cada
   (they) photographed its best monument   in each
   ciudad (y   no a   sus habitantes).
   city   (and not ACC its inhabitants)
   [Binding: OK]
   b. Fotografiaron en cada ciudad su mejor <u>monumento</u> (y no a sus habitantes).
   [Binding: OK]
   c. Fotografiaron   en cada ciudad su mejor <u>monumento</u>.
   (they) photographed in each city   its best   monument
   [Binding: OK]
   [What did they photograph in each city?]
(134) a. No fotografiaron   su CATEDRAL en ninguna ciudad
   not (they) photographed its cathedral in no   city
   (sino su museo).
   (but its museum)
   [Binding: *]
   b. No fotografiaron en ninguna ciudad su <u>catedral</u> (sino su museo).
   [Binding: *]

To recapitulate: We have seen that p-movement does not affect quantifier-binding possibilities. This is unsurprising to the extent that the structures derived via p-movement are nonneutral with respect to focus, and focus has an effect on quantifier binding independently of syntactic structure. Whatever the account for the above-mentioned paradigm might be (see section 1.1.4 for a proposal), nothing can be concluded on the basis of such facts about where p-movement applies. Finally, p-movement does not affect binding of lexical anaphora either; this fact can readily be attributed to "reconstruction" of the p-moved object.

(135) a. Vendió [el pintor FRANCES]$_i$ varios retratos de
sold   the painter French   several portraits of
[sí mismo]$_i$ (no el pintor inglés).
himself   not the painter English
'The French painter sold several portraits of himself, not the English painter.'
b. Vendió varios retratos de [sí mismo]$_i$ [el pintor <u>francés</u>]$_i$.

3.5.3 Summary

We have seen in this section that p-movement does not affect binding, but this fact is empirically neutral with respect to the question of where p-movement applies. P-movement of the sort described in this chapter applies in structures where the NSR and the FPR give rise to a prosodically contradictory output. P-movement undoes such structures, after which the NSR and the FPR may apply again, this time giving a felicitous result. If, as suggested in chapter 2, the NSR and the FPR apply in the syntax (more precisely, at the end of the syntactic derivation, when the syntactic structure is fully formed), then p-movement must apply in the syntax as well (i.e., before Spell-Out).

Some evidence for this conclusion is provided by the Italian contrast in (136).

(136) a. Nessuno ha mangiato la mela.
          nobody has eaten   the apple
b. *(Non) ha mangiato la mela nessuno.
          not   has eaten   the apple nobody

I argued in section 3.4 that VOS in Italian is derived from SVO via p-movement of the TP across the subject, which is located in the specifier of a functional projection above TP (in [Spec, Emphasis] in the case of (136)). As mentioned in note 31, in Romance a negative phrase in postverbal position, unlike a negative phrase in preverbal position, must be licensed by an overt negative morpheme. Compare (137a) with (137b).

(137) a. Nessuno è   arrivato.
         nobody   has arrived
      b. Non è   arrivato nessuno.
         not has arrived nobody

The paradigm in (136) shows that a negative polarity item subject in VOS must also be licensed by the negative morpheme, unlike a negative polarity item subject in SVO.[53] If p-movement feeds negative polarity item licensing and this licensing is to be stated at LF (as is standardly assumed), it must be that p-movement feeds LF.

3.6 Is There P-Movement in French and in English?

Recall that both French and English may resolve a situation where the output of the NSR and the output of the FPR conflict by analyzing defocalized material as metrically invisible; see sections 2.3.2 and 2.4. If p-movement (like Move f) is a last resort grammatical mechanism, then we would expect that neither French nor English would use p-movement to resolve a clash between the NSR and the FPR. Although this seems to be the case in English, in French metrical invisibility and p-movement alternate freely. Rather than giving up last resort as a property of movement in general, I suggest that French has two coexisting grammars: one that uses metrical invisibility and another that uses p-movement, perhaps as a reflex of the fact that French is in a transitional stage of language change with respect to certain aspects of its prosodic properties (see Kroch 1989 for arguments in favor of the existence of dual grammars in transitional stages of language change).[54]

3.6.1 French

The examples in (138) (VOPP, with NS on the PP) are compatible with a wide focus interpretation, but they are not compatible with an interpretation in which the object has narrow focus. The VPPO examples in (139) (generated via p-movement of PP across O and with NS on O) are compatible only with a narrow focus interpretation on the object.

(138) a. Nous avons rendu   son livre à <u>Marie</u>.
         we   have returned his book to Marie
         [What did you do?]
         [*What did you return to Marie?]

b. Nous avons mis trois livres sur la table.
   we have put three books on the table
   [What did you do?]
   [*What did you put on the table?]

(139) a. Nous avons rendu à Marie son livre.
      [*What did you do?]
      [What did you return to Marie?]
   b. Nous avons mis sur la table trois livres.
      [*What did you do?]
      [What did you put on the table?]

On the other hand, note that the examples in (140) (VOPP, with NS on O an PP "destressed") are also compatible with an interpretation in which the object is a noncontrastive focus, as indicated by the fact that they can function as answers to the specified context questions. Hence, the examples in (139) and (140) show that metrical invisibility and p-movement are in free complementary distribution in French.

(140) a. Nous avons rendu son livre *à Marie.*
      [What did you return to Marie?]
   b. Nous avons mis trois livres *sur la table.*
      [What did you put on the table?]

The following pair of examples shows that p-movement does not affect quantifier binding in French either, a fact that I have attributed to the focus structure of such examples (see section 1.1.4).[55]

(141) a. On a rendu son livre *à chaque enfant.*
      we returned his book to each child
      [Binding: OK]
   b. On a rendu à chaque enfant son livre.
      [Binding: OK]
      [What did you return to each child?]

(142) a. On a déposé son avis de mission *chez chaque fonctionnaire.*
      we delivered his assignment at each civil servant's place
      [Binding: OK]
   b. On a déposé chez chaque fonctionnaire son avis de mission.
      [Binding: OK]
      [What did you deliver at each civil servant's place?]

Unlike p-movement in Spanish and Italian, p-movement in French affects complements but not the subject. In effect, French lacks VO{S}. Furthermore, French differs from Italian in that it lacks the source structure for VO{S}, namely, a structure with a functional focus projection above TP; see (143).

(143) *(Je crois que) le VERRE Rafael a   cassé, non pas la
       I believe that the glass Rafael has broken not   the
       tasse.
       cup

But even if French had such a structure, the educated guess is that the output would be impossible because French, unlike Italian, is not a pro-drop language. Let us assume that a language must be able to retrieve grammatical relations both from its PF and from its LF representations. Let us furthermore assume that either morphological information (provided by overt verbal agreement or Case morphemes) or structural information (such as that provided by traces) may be used to retrieve grammatical relations from the PF representation. Now consider the Italian structure in (144a) and its French counterpart in (144b).

(144) a. $[[_{TP}\ e_i\ \text{ha mangiato una mela}]_j\ [_{FP}\ \text{Maria}_i\ [e_j]]]$
          has eaten   an apple   Maria
       b. $[[_{TP}\ e_i\ \text{a mangé une pomme}]_j\ [_{FP}\ \text{Marie}_i\ [e_j]]]$

In (144a), although the DP in [Spec, F] does not properly bind its trace in [Spec, T] at PF, the DP is interpreted as the subject at PF because this language has a sufficiently rich subject agreement morphology on the verb. In other words, Italian may use morphology rather than structural information to interpret a DP as a subject at PF. On the other hand, because of its poor subject agreement morphology, French may use only structural information to interpret a DP as the subject of its sentence at PF. I suggest that this is not possible in (144b) because of lack of proper binding of the trace in [Spec, T] at PF.

3.6.2 English
The prime candidate for an analysis in terms of p-movement in English is the construction that Larson (1988a) describes in terms of light predicate raising, the so-called heavy NP shift (HNPS) construction.[56]

(145) (Max put in his cár) (all the boxes of home fúrnishings).

(146) (I talked about Bíll) (to MARY).
    (cf. *(I talked about Bíll) (to Máry))

Larson argues that these sentences should be derived via V'-reanalysis and V-raising, as shown in (147) and (148).

(147) a. ...[$_{VP}$ Max [$_{V'}$ V [$_{VP}$ all the boxes of home furnishings [$_{V'}$ put in his car]]]]
     b. ...[$_{VP}$ Max [$_{V'}$[$_{V_j}$ put in his car] [$_{VP}$ all the boxes of home furnishings [V$_j$]]]]

(148) a. ...[$_{VP}$ I [$_{V'}$ V [$_{VP}$ to Mary [$_{V'}$ talked about Bill]]]]
     b. ...[$_{VP}$ I [$_{V'}$[$_{V_j}$ talked about Bill] [$_{VP}$ to Mary [$_{V'}$ V$_j$]]]]

Is raising of the reanalyzed V' a case of prosodically motivated movement? It may very well be, but here p-movement does not apply in order to resolve a conflict between the NSR and the FPR. This is shown by the fact that (145) is compatible with a wide focus interpretation; that is, it can be a response to the question *What is Max doing?* Although (146) is compatible only with a narrow focus interpretation on *Mary*, this limitation is due solely to the obligatory heavy accent that *Mary* bears. I therefore conclude that English resolves contradictions between the NSR and the FPR in terms of metrical invisibility only, never in terms of movement.

Despite this conclusion, the question still remains: is raising of the reanalyzed V' a case of prosodically motivated movement? I believe it is, because of its prosodic properties. It applies only when the rightmost constituent is analyzed as metrically "heavy," owing to its syntactically complex structure (as in (145)) or to the heavy accent that it carries (as in (146)). Notice furthermore that the heavy constituent is preceded by an intonational boundary. It is possible that "heavy" constituents define a domain of their own for NS. This can be achieved by restructuring the syntactic tree and inserting an intonational boundary before and after the heavy constituent, yielding the following structures:

(149) a. (Max pút) (all the boxes of home fúrnishings) (in his cár).
     b. (I tálked) (to MARY) (about Bíll).

Because they are unbalanced, such intonational phrasings sound awkward. On the other hand, raising of a reanalyzed V' yields a more natural intonational parsing, made up of two intonational phrases; see (145) and (146). It remains to be seen how this analysis can be formalized, a task I will not attempt here.

3.7 Summary and Concluding Remarks

In this chapter I have argued that languages like Spanish and Italian use movement instead of metrical invisibility to resolve conflicts between the NSR and the FPR ((72) and (71), repeated here).

(150) *NSR (Romance)*
Given two sister nodes C_i and C_j, the one lower in the asymmetric c-command ordering is more prominent (the C-NSR).

(151) *FPR*
Given two sister nodes C_i (marked [+F]) and C_j (marked [−F]), C_i is more prominent than C_j.

Such conflicts arise when a defocalized constituent C_j is lower in the asymmetric c-command ordering than its focused metrical sister C_i. In such a configuration, the NSR assigns main prominence to C_j and the FPR assigns main prominence to C_i. To resolve the contradiction that arises with respect to prominence, the grammar of such a language resorts to deletion plus copying (i.e., movement) of C_j.

I showed that p-movement can be formulated in terms of the general operation Affect constrained by the "iff" condition (i.e., Last Resort). ((152) and (153) repeat (125) and (124), respectively.)

(152) Affect the nodes α and β iff these nodes have contradictory prosodic properties, where the notion of prosodic contradiction is to be understood as in (153).

(153) ...$[_\delta [_\alpha \text{ ph}^*] [_\beta \text{ ph}^*]]$, where [ph*] stands for a phonologically specified category interpreted as "strong" relative to its metrical sister.

The type of p-movement described above generates a variety of word orders, in which the focused constituent is rightmost (i.e., the lowest in the asymmetric c-command ordering). Among the word orders generated by p-movement is Spanish and in Italian is VOS, in which the subject is unambiguously focused and bears main phrasal prominence. There is an interesting difference between the VOS orders in the two languages. Italian, but not Spanish, exhibits a "heaviness effect." If the subject is "light," VOS order in Italian is less than perfect. I attribute this difference to the conjunction of the Relative Weight Constraint and the fact that the sources of VOS in the two languages differ. ((154) and (155) repeat (119) and (120).)

Clausal Structure

(154) *The Relative Weight Constraint*
P-movement of constituent A across constituent B is degraded if A is "metrically heavier" than B.

(155) A is "metrically heavier" than B if A is branching and B is not (where only metrically visible material counts for computing "branchingness"), unless B has heavier pitch than A.

The source of VOS in Spanish is VSO; VOS in Spanish is derived from VSO by moving VP_2 around S (more precisely, by adjoining VP_2 to VP_1, which contains S). VP_2 contains only O because V_2 is empty—hence, the relative heaviness of [VO] with respect to S is irrelevant in this language. Italian, on the other hand, lacks VSO. I have argued that the source of VOS in this language is SVO, where S is in [Spec, F] above TP. VOS in Italian is derived by moving TP (which contains [VO]) around S. Consequently, the relative heaviness of [VO] with respect to S is relevant in this language.

I showed that the type of p-movement discussed above does not affect binding relations, but concluded that this fact is empirically neutral with respect to the question of where it applies (namely, before or after Spell-Out). On the other hand, data in Italian show that p-movement affects the licensing of negative polarity items. To the extent that such items are licensed at LF, we must conclude that p-movement applies prior to Spell-Out. This is as expected if the function of p-movement is to reconcile conflicts between the NSR and the FPR. In effect, if, as suggested in chapter 2, these prominence-assigning rules apply in the syntax (more precisely, at the point in the derivation where the sentence is associated with a single phrase marker) and if p-movement feeds these rules, then p-movement must apply in the syntax as well (i.e., prior to Spell-Out). In section 1.3.3, where I discussed the architecture of the grammar, I in fact proposed that there is a stretch at the end of the syntactic derivation where the prosody-related rules (the NSR, the FPR, and p-movement) apply, the output of which feeds both PF and LF.

Appendix: Intonational, Syntactic, and Interpretive Properties of Right-Dislocation in Modern Standard Spanish

In an attempt to determine the intonational phrasing of right-dislocated objects in Spanish, I compared the fundamental frequency (F_0) of sentences containing such objects with the F_0 of sentences containing a clause-internal focused constituent, following Beckman and Pierrehumbert's (B&P) 1986 study of right-dislocated tags in English.[57] I begin by briefly presenting their results.

Pierrehumbert (1980) (following Liberman (1975)) recognizes a *boundary tone*, obligatory at the end (and optional at the beginning) of an Intonational Phrase (IntP). B&P (1986) recognize an intermediate prosodic phrase below the IntP; the terminal tone of the intermediate prosodic phrase is the *phrase accent*. B&P (p. 288) describe the phonetic transition between the nuclear pitch accent and the phrase accent as follows: "there is a relatively abrupt transition from the last target level specified by the pitch accent to the target level for the phrase accent, which is then maintained over the remainder of the phrase." They argue that certain lists, sequences of modifiers, and tags in English should be characterized in such terms. The case of right-dislocated tags is particularly interesting because it provides the basis for constructing minimal pairs with sentences that contain a focused constituent in clause-internal position.

Tags are prosodically in closer construction with the main clause than a separate intonational phrase would be in that it is unnatural to insert a pause between the clause and the tag. On the other hand, the F_0 properties of such constructions indicate that they are not part of the same prosodic phrasing. B&P suggest that this can best be illustrated by comparing tags with focused structures. Consider figures 3.1a and 3.1b (from B&P 1986, 293). B&P (p. 294) comment as follows:

In the first utterance [figure 3.1a], the verb *win* in under focus and its object *Manny* is deaccented because it is in postnuclear position in the same phrase. In the second utterance [figure 3.1b], *win* is intransitive and *Manny* is interpreted as a vocative tag. Note that in the second utterance, the F_0 fall is complete by the end of *win*, so that the F_0 level on the [m] of *Manny* is low and level. In the first utterance, on the other hand, the F_0 fall only begins on *win*, and it continues through the [m] of *Manny* and into the following vowel. A related observation is that the syllable *win* is much longer in the utterance with the vocative tag. These differences may be summarized by saying that in the utterance with the vocation tag, *win* has a duration and F_0 pattern which is typical of a phrase-final nuclear stressed syllable. In the utterance with a deaccented object, *win* has the typical phonetics of a syllable which has nuclear stress but is not phrase-final.

Furthermore, the pitch range may vary from phrase to phrase (Liberman and Pierrehumbert 1984). The tag is assumed to have a pitch range that is subordinate to the pitch range of the main clause. Consequently, its strongest syllable is not intonationally as prominent as the strongest syllable of the main clause. This would account for the fact that, although the tag

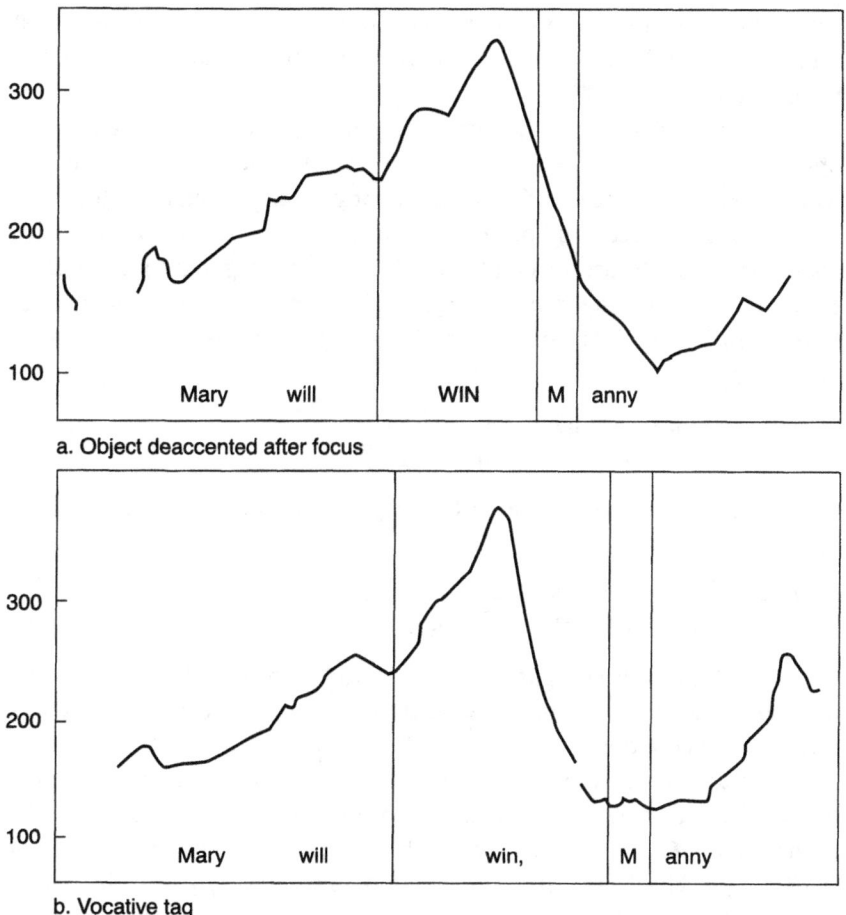

Figure 3.1
F_0 contours for two segmentally matched utterances *Mary will win Manny*. In version (a) *Manny* is the object of the transitive verb *win*. In version (b) *Manny* is a vocative tag following the intransitive verb. (From Beckman and Pierrehumbert 1986, 293; used by permission.)

constitutes a distinct prosodic phrase from the main clause, its most prominent syllable is perceived as rhythmically subordinate to that of the main clause.

In order to determine the prosodic phrasing of right-dislocation in Spanish, I compared the F_0 of sentences with a right-dislocated object with the F_0 of sentences with a focused constituent immediately followed by an in-situ "deaccented" object. I found the same kind of contrast (with respect to the F_0 transition) that B&P did between tags and focus-internal structures. The F_0 diagrams in figures 3.2a and 3.2b illustrate my results.[58] In figure 3.2a the subject bears NS and the object is right-dislocated.

(156) La   lavó   mamá, la mamadera.
 ACC.CL washed Mother the milk-bottle

In figure 3.2b, on the other hand, the subject has contrastive stress and the object is deaccented.

(157) Lavó   MAMÁ la mamadera.
 washed Mother the milk-bottle

To ensure that I was comparing similar objects, I recorded these sentences used in the same context—namely, in a context where the subject was interpreted as contrastively focused. More precisely, the sentences were to be understood as answers to the context question *Did Nina wash the mild bottle?* (I omitted the initial negative word *no* in the answers for the sake of simplicity.) Compare the transition between the second syllable of *mamá* (which is perceived as most prominent in both sentences) and the following material. In figure 3.2a *la* and the onset of the first phoneme of *mamadera* are not part of the fall of the stressed syllable of *mamá*. On the other hand, in figure 3.2b the fall following the stressed syllable of *mamá* continues through *la* and ends with the onset of the first [m] in *mamadera*. This suggests that in figure 3.2b, as in the English example in figure 3.1a, there is no prosodic boundary between the nuclear pitch-accented word and the material immediately following it. On the other hand, the F_0 transition in figure 3.2a suggests that the prosodic status of the right-dislocated object is comparable to some extent to that of English tags; compare figure 3.1b. Like a tag, the right-dislocated object constitutes a distinct prosodic phrase from the preceding material and it bears its own nuclear pitch accent. And, like that of tags, its pitch range is subordinate to that of the preceding prosodic phrase, and for this reason it is perceived as less

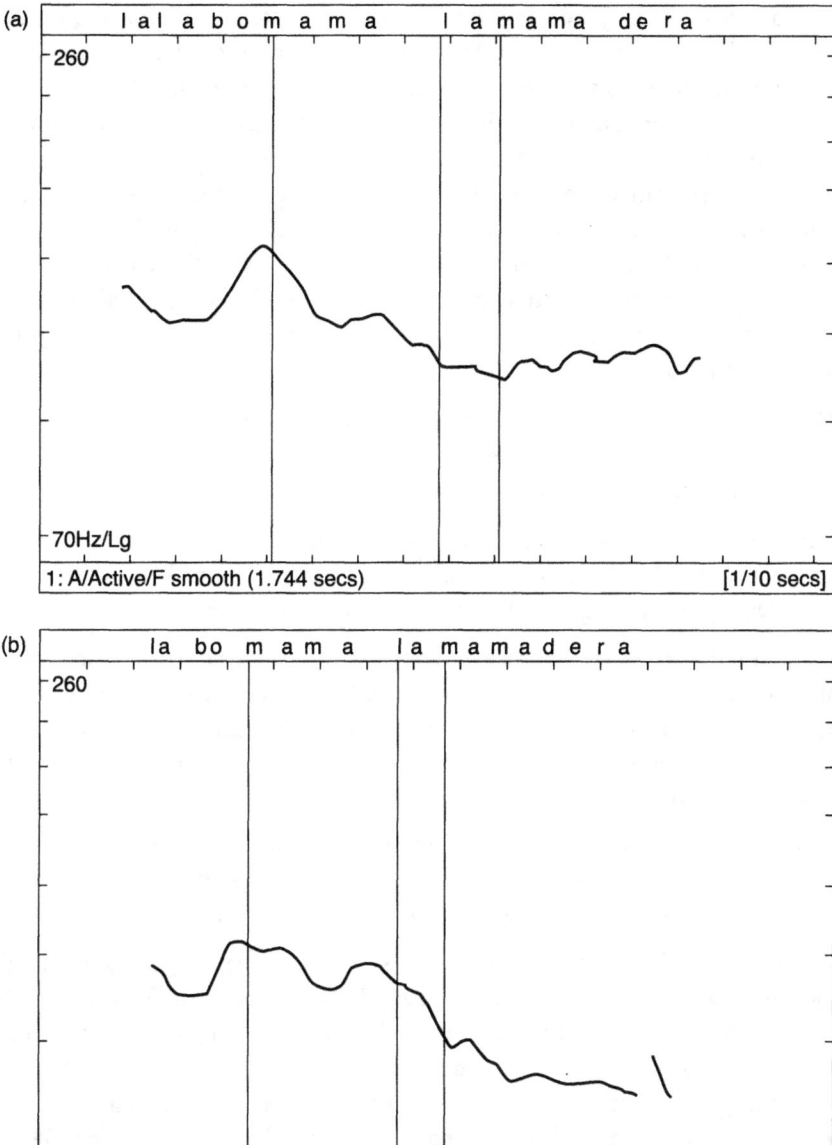

Figure 3.2
F₀ contours for a sentence with a right-dislocated object ((a), *La lavó mamá, la mamadera*) and for a sentence with a focused constituent immediately followed by an in-situ "deaccented" object ((b), *Lavó MAMÁ la mamadera*).

prominent than the preceding nuclear pitch-accented word. On the other hand, unlike tags, right-dislocated phrases may be preceded by a salient pause. I therefore conclude that (a) right-dislocated phrases, unlike focused phrases, constitute an independent prosodic unit and (b) this prosodic unit is the intonational phrase (rather than the intermediate phrase).

In-situ deaccented phrases can be distinguished from right-dislocated phrases not only prosodically, but also syntactically and interpretively. As shown below, a sentence can have more than one right-dislocated phrase. In such cases each dislocated phrase constitutes an intonational phrase. (The pound sign indicates the prosodic boundary preceding a right-dislocated phrase.)

(158) a. Le   envió un <u>regalo</u> # María # a mamá.
         DAT.CL sent   a   present   # María # to Mother
     b. Le envió un <u>regalo</u> # a mamá # María.

(159) a. Escondió el <u>libro</u> # el niño # debajo de la cama.
         hid   the book   # the boy # under   the bed
     b. Escondió el <u>libro</u> # debajo de la cama # el niño.

Although the order of right-dislocated phrases is free, as illustrated in (158) and (159), the order of in-situ "deaccented" phrases is determined by the syntax. This can be appreciated more clearly with locative structures than with dative structures because in the latter case there is interfering noise from the dative-shift form.[59] Consider the locative structure in (160a).

(160) a. Escondió el NIÑO *el libro debajo de la cama*.
         hid   the boy   the book under   the bed
     b. *Escondió el NIÑO *debajo de la cama el libro*.

The order of the deaccented phrases is the one given by the syntax of the embedded VP: [subj [V_1 [obj [V_2[PP]]]]]. The object is in [Spec, V_2] and must therefore precede the PP complement of V_2. This order cannot be reversed, as shown in (160b). Incidentally, note that this constitutes a strong argument against the hypothesis that postverbal subjects in Spanish are right-adjoined to VP (as assumed by Chomsky (1981) and Rizzi (1982) for pro-drop Romance languages in general). Since the order between the complements in (160) is fixed by the syntax of VP, the postverbal subject cannot be analyzed as right-adjoined to VP in such examples (nor, ceteris paribus, can it be in other VSO examples). Furthermore, in-situ deaccented lexical objects do not coexist with a clitic. This property follows directly from the fact that in configurations that are not those of clitic doubling, the clitic must be construed with a pronominal in argument position. On the other hand, with obligatorily transitive verbs, a right-dislocated DP is obligatorily construed with a clitic. Compare (161a) and (161b).

(161) a. Trajo   NINA *el* *vino.*
      brought Nina the wine
   b. Lo   trajo   <u>Nina</u> # el vino.
      ACC.CL brought Nina # the wine

This difference between in-situ deaccented phrases and right-dislocated phrases accounts for the paradigm in (162). (162a) is a case of deaccenting of the embedded VP constituent (*el Quijote al inglés*). (162b) and (162c) are cases of right-dislocation of the direct object and the PP complement. The ordering of these two constituents is free, as is typically the case with right-dislocated constituents. In Standard Spanish, which does not readily allow for null objects, the accusative clitic is obligatorily present (or highly preferred), as shown by the contrast between (162c) and (162d).[60]

(162) a. Tradujo   JUAN *el* *Quijote al inglés.*
      translated Juan   the Quixote to English
   b. Lo   tradujo <u>Juan</u> # el Quijote # al inglés.
      ACC.CL
   c. Lo tradujo <u>Juan</u> # al inglés # el Quijote.
   d. ??Tradujo <u>Juan</u> # al inglés # el Quijote.

In Spanish there are no pronominal forms for PPs (or for subjects). Therefore, it is not possible to distinguish syntactically an in-situ PP from a right-dislocated one, when the PP is part of a structure that respects the word order generated by the base. Thus, (163a) could have the structure in (163b) (where the PP is in situ and "deaccented") or the structure in (163c) (where the PP is syntactically right-dislocated and prosodically a tag). On the other hand, in (164a–b), where the object is right-dislocated (i.e., it coexists with a clitic), the PP must also be right-dislocated. Like that of (162d), the marginality of (164c) can be attributed to the absence of the accusative clitic.

(163) a. Escondió el niño el   libro debajo de la cama.
      hid   the boy the book under   the bed
   b. [Escondió el niño [el LIBRO *debajo de la cama*]].
   c. [[Escondió el niño el <u>libro</u>] debajo de la cama].

(164) a. Lo   escondió el <u>niño</u> # el libro # debajo de la cama.
         ACC.CL
     b. Lo escondió el <u>niño</u> # debajo de la cama # el libro.
     c. ??Escondió el <u>niño</u> # debajo de la cama # el libro.

Finally, as noted earlier, structures involving right-dislocation of complements and structures involving in-situ "deaccented" complements can be distinguished with respect to their possible focus structures. Recall that a word with contrastive stress must be dominated by every F-marked constituent in the structure (see section 2.4). Thus, (160a), (161a), and (162a) may only be interpreted with narrow focus on the subject and (163b) may only be interpreted with narrow focus on the object. On the other hand, in (161b), (162b–c), (163c), and (164a–b), both narrow and wide focus interpretations are available.

Notes

Chapter 1

1. For a review of the many discourse-related terms such as *focus/presupposition, focus/ground, focus/topic, rheme/theme, topic/comment, dominant/nondominant, categorical/thetic judgments,* see Vallduví and Engdahl 1995. This review shows that in many cases different scholars use the same terms to mean different things or different terms to mean the same thing. See also Prince 1981.

As will soon become obvious, I will take the position that the grammatical notion of focus is grounded in the discourse notion of presupposition. Furthermore, I will claim that, although the dichotomy *focus/presupposition* is grammatically relevant, *new* and *old information* (as defined in Rochemont 1986) are discourse notions with no direct grammatical import; they have at best a very superficial relation to the grammar. (See note 4. See also Suñer 1982 for a similar view of the distinction between *old* and *new* information.) I will also claim (following Reinhart (1982) and others) that the notions *topic/comment*, not to be confused with the dichotomy *focus/presupposition*, are represented in the Assertion Structure of the sentence in terms of a subject/predicate relation.

2. See Wilson and Sperber 1979 for a proposal that the notion of presupposition be rethought in terms of ordered entailments.

3. The standard argument against defining focus in terms of presupposition is due initially to Schmerling (1976, 77) and is endorsed by other authors (see, e.g., Rochemont 1986, 44). They note that the complement of factive predicates, although logically presupposed, may be focused. Thus, in the sentence *I didn't realize that Mary was bald*, the proposition denoted by the complement is presupposed to be true. But, the argument goes, in the following discourse the complement in (iB) is prosodically prominent and consequently must also function as the semantic focus of the sentence (see section 2.2). We therefore seem to have a contradiction: the complement is logically presupposed, but it functions as the focus of the sentence.

(i) A: I thought you realized that Mary has a husband.
    B: I did! But I didn't realize that Mary was báld.

If we think about the meaning of (iB), it becomes clear that what constitutes the assertion in this sentence is not the proposition denoted by the complement; rather, it is the denial that the proposition expressed by the complement was previously part of the presuppositional set of the interlocutors. It is saying, 'The proposition *Mary has a husband* was part of our shared assumptions, but *that Mary is bald* was not (although it is now)'. This example shows that, although the notion of presupposition relevant to the definition of focus is context dependent, the notion of presupposition that factive verbs give rise to is not. In Wilson and Sperber's (1979) terms, lexically determined presuppositions "neither entail nor are entailed by the background"; rather, "they form part of the increments of information that have to be added to the background" (p. 321).

4. Elaborating on work by Culicover and Rochemont (1983), Rochemont (1986) defines focus in terms of the dichotomy *new* versus *old* (or *given*) *information*: the material in a sentence S that corresponds to the new information in a given discourse context constitutes the focus in S. New information is that which is not old information. Old information is defined in terms of the notion *c-construable* (Rochemont 1986, 47).

(i) A string P is c-construable in a discourse D if P has a semantic antecedent in D.

The notion *semantic antecedent* is in turn defined as follows:

(ii) A string P has a semantic antecedent in a discourse D, $D = \{D_1, \ldots, D_n\}$, if, and only if, there is a prior and readily available string P' in D, such that the uttering of P' either formally or informally entails mention of P.

The most interesting cases are those of informal entailment, which is based on the meaning of nonlogical vocabulary. Thus, in the example *Harry wants a VW, but his wife would prefer an AMERICAN car* (where capitals indicate that the word is pitch-accented), the mention of a VW suffices to render the mention of cars c-construable (Rochemont 1986, 49). Similarly, two nominal expressions that have the same extension are informally entailed by each other. Rochemont notes that the characterization of a string P as old information, which is ultimately defined in terms of the notion "mention of P" (rather than in terms of "reference" or "definiteness" or "specificity" or "familiarity"), seems to be accurate in that nonreferential DPs (like nonspecific indefinites, for instance) may function as old information. As an example, consider the following discourse, where the nonspecific indefinite objects in (iiiB) and (iiiB′) are defocalized (Rochemont 1986, 50):

(iii) A: I saw some GORILLAS in the SUBWAY today.
B: Oh, really? We saw some gorillas at the ZOO today.
B′: Oh, really? We saw some animals at the ZOO today.

Part-whole relations should also be subsumed under the notion "informally entails mention of." More precisely, mention of the "whole" may informally entail mention of the corresponding "part," as in the following discourse, where *legs* functions as old information by virtue of being in a part-whole relation with *cat*:

(iv) Poor cat! It has only THREE legs.

Although the notion "mention of" is relevant in defining the notion "c-construable," it is insufficient. Clearly, a perceptually salient or familiar referent may function as "c-construable" even if it has not been previously mentioned. For example, if two people see a cat, one of them may say, *How strange! It has only THREE legs*. Although it has not been linguistically mentioned, the cat is present in the discourse. Therefore, it is "c-construable" and may be referred to by a deictic pronoun. By the same token, *legs* functions as "c-construable" (by informal entailment). The conclusion is then that the notion "c-construable information" is not uniquely definable in linguistic terms; it involves other cognitive (or perceptual) modes as well.

Given the above characterization of "old information," the question is, does the notion "old/new information" underlie the grammatical notion of focus? As has frequently been pointed out since Schmerling 1976, the difficulty in defining focus as new information is that old information may also be focused, as the often-cited example in (v) shows. (vi) illustrates the same point.

(v) John hit Mary, and then SHE hit HIM.

(vi) A: Did John eat a hamburger or did John eat a hot dog?
 B: He ate a HAMBURGER.

In light of such examples, Rochemont proposes to abandon a unitary semantic definition of focus. Instead, he proposes to distinguish two types of focus: presentational and contrastive. A unitary definition of focus is a priori desirable; see below in the text for further discussion of this point.

5. I exclude cases in which a negative phrase in the answer substitutes for the *wh*-phrase in the context question; see (i). In such cases the answer negates the presupposition of the context question; see (ii). I consider such question-answer pairs to be of a different nature.

(i) Q: Who did you see?
 A: I saw no one.

(ii) Q: there is an x, such that you saw x
 A: there is no x, such that I saw x

6. Note, however, that the question/answer test is not always straightforward because discourse allows for "accommodation of presuppositions" on the basis of common knowledge and inferences, as illustrated by Lakoff's (1968) famous example in (i) (slightly modified to better illustrate my point). The answer to the question in (i) is appropriate only to the extent that the discourse participants can readily accommodate the inference in (ii), of which (iii) is a particular instantiation, as part of the speaker/hearer's presuppositional set (or common assumptions) on the basis of common knowledge.

(i) A: John called Mary a Republican. [What did Mary do then?]
 B: Then Mary insulted John.

(ii) If X calls Y a Republican, then X insults Y.

(iii) John insulted Mary.

Another example of accommodation is provided by the following discourse segment (from Williams 1997, 599–600).

(iv) A: Gee, they don't make brightly colored shirts anymore, do they?
B: I saw a convict with a RED shirt yesterday.

In the sentence uttered by B, there is narrow focus on RED. If we follow Chomsky (1971) and Jackendoff (1972), the presuppositional structure of B's statement is roughly as in (v).

(v) I saw a convict with an x shirt (where x ranges over bright colors).

The set over which x ranges (provided by the context) is the set of bright colors: red, blue, green, and so on. (v) is a particular instantiation of a more general presupposition entailed by the utterance of speaker A. More precisely, the utterance of speaker A in (iv) entails that

(vi) Speaker A's assumption (namely, that they don't make brightly colored shirts anymore) can be contradicted if speaker B has knowledge (by direct or indirect perception) that someone who meets any description whatsoever (the description being irrelevant) has recently been in possession (the manifestation of POSS being irrelevant) of a brightly colored shirt.

(v) is a particular instantiation of (vi) in that it states that speaker B has "seen" (a case of knowledge by virtue of direct perception) someone (with the irrelevant description of "convict") "wearing" (which is a particular manifestation of the POSS relation) a "shirt" (of the relevant type) recently (namely, "yesterday"). Given that (v) is a particular instantiation of (vi), it can be accommodated as part of the speaker/hearer's presuppositional set as well.

The above examples show that particular instantiations of a general presuppositional structure entailed by the context can be accommodated within the set of assumptions shared by speaker and hearer within a cooperative act of communication. See Wilson and Sperber 1979, Sperber and Wilson 1986.

7. We will see at the end of chapter 2 (see the appendix in particular) that we must assume a three-way distinction: [+F], [−F], and unmarked for [F].

(i) a. A constituent C is marked [+F] iff C is focused or part of the focus.
b. A constituent C is marked [−F] iff C is presupposed or part of the presupposition.
c. A constituent C is unmarked for the feature [F] if it dominates both [+F] and [−F] constituents.

Unless the three-way distinction is relevant to the discussion at hand, I will use the simplified notation given in the text.

8. There is a preference to use a pronoun in the answer to refer back to the DP in the context question, rather than to repeat the lexical content of the DP. I abstract away from this constraint.

9. For alternative views, see Rooth 1985, Kratzer 1991, Tancredi 1992.

10. Note that the sentence in (i) is ambiguous, depending on whether the assertion is attributed to the speaker or the subject of the matrix clause, as shown in (ii) and (iii), respectively. In other words, focus extraction is not clause bound.

(i) Bill thinks that John ate the pie.

(ii) the x, such that Bill thinks that John ate x, is the pie

(iii) Bill thinks that the x, such that John ate x, is the pie

11. See also Matsuda 1997. Matsuda proposes that the focus is extracted (as in a clefting operation) and that the presupposed proposition is then topicalized, giving rise to an LF representation comparable to that of pseudoclefts. This analysis inherits that same problem with respect to (5e) as Chomky's (1976) analysis.

12. On the constituency problem, see also Tancredi 1992.

13. See Heycock and Kroch 1996 for an analysis of pseudocleft constructions that reaches a similar conclusion.

14. This proposal thus integrates the notion of "order" introduced by Wilson and Sperber (1979) in their account of presuppositions in terms of ordered entailments.

15. For an alternative event-based notation, see Herburger 1993, 1997.

16. The semantic property of "symmetry" that distinguishes weak determiners from strong determiners is illustrated in (i) and (ii).

(i) Few cats yawn. ↔ Few yawners are cats.

(ii) Every cat yawns. ∼ ↔ Every yawner is a cat.

17. Note incidentally that focus extraction via QR at LF fails to account for Herburger's contrast.

18. The context for contrastive focus can be provided by a yes/no question as well (e.g., *Did John wear a blue shirt today?*). I consider the yes/no question to be a type of statement, namely, a statement embedded under the yes/no operator (the statement *John is wearing a blue shirt today* in (14)).

19. In my view, every sentence S is associated with a context (the minimal context being "there is an x, such that x ($= S$) happened"). If a sentence is provided out of context in an experimental setting, the hearer will automatically and arbitrarily attach a context to it. This is confirmed by Reinhart's experiment below. Therefore, the PPA of S should be interpreted as the set of possible *in-context* assertion structures associated with S.

20. On the relation between sentence structure and sentence topics, see also Kuroda 1992, chap. 1. In Japanese, sentences with a *wa*-phrase (which functions as a sentence topic) express a "categorical judgment," whereas sentences with a *ga*-phrase are topicless and express a "thetic judgment."

21. Some authors refer to the topic/comment distinction as theme versus rheme; see Vallduví and Engdahl 1995.

22. The following sentences also contrast with respect to the intended binding relation:

(i) [$_F$ A párent] will accompany every boy, namely, his mother.

(ii) [$_F$ A párent] will accompany everybody, namely, his mother.

23. This is supported by the contrast between (i) and (ii). Although for some speakers of English, a QP topic in a left-dislocation construction is marginal (languages differ in this respect: English and French contrast with Arabic and Spanish), all speakers agree that there is a clear contrast between the two sentences.

(i)   (?)Each boy/Every boy, the doctor examined him.

(ii) *Everybody, the doctor examined him.

24. This difference between *personne/aucun enfant* and *aucun de ces enfants* can also be appreciated with respect to left-dislocation.

(i)   *Personne/Aucun enfant, Pierre l'a   accompagné.
       no one/no child   Pierre it has accompanied

(ii) Aucun de ces enfants, Pierre ne les a   accompagnés.
      none of these children Pierre NEG them has accompanied

25. The awkwardness of a postverbal subject as sentence topic is illustrated by the contrast between (i) and (ii) (adapted from Calabrese 1990). The second sentence of the discourse in (ii) is awkward because *la carta* is a sentence topic and must therefore be fronted.

(i)   Juan me   escribió una carta. *La carta* llegó   ayer.
       Juan to-me wrote   a   letter the letter arrived yesterday

(ii) Juan me escribió una carta. ??Llegó *la carta* ayer.

26. Thus, a negative phrase may not be left-dislocated.

(i)   *Ningún padre, María dice que asistió a la ceremonia.
       no   father María says that assisted at the ceremony

(ii) *A ningún niño, María dice que el médico lo   examinó.
       ACC no   child María says that the doctor ACC.CL examined

27. As mentioned in note 8, there is a discourse-governed preference for using pronouns to refer back to an immediate topic. Therefore, (39d) is preferred if the context question is either (40b) or (40c), (39e) is preferred if the context question is (40e), and (39f) is preferred if the context question is (40f).

28. Although (41a) and (42a) are both compatible with a wide focus interpretation (i.e., as an answer to *What happened?*), they differ with regard to what aspect of the information is highlighted. In effect, prominence also serves to highlight the relevant part of the information being conveyed, within the limits imposed by the F-structure (see the Focus Prominence Rule below in the text). The same comments apply to the German examples in (43a) and (44a) in the text.

29. The ancestor of the FPR is the principle in (i), first formulated by Chomsky (1971) and Jackendoff (1972), which I will call the *Focus Prosody Correspondence Principle*.

(i)   *Focus Prosody Correspondence Principle (FPCP)*
       The focused constituent (or F-marked constituent) of the phrase must contain the intonational nucleus of that phrase.

30. See also Rivero 1995, where it is argued that certain cases of head movement are prosodically motivated.

31. In the earlier discussion of the grammatical representation of focus, I appealed to representations that are derived from LF by interpretive mechanisms, namely, AS (see section 1.1). If this is correct, then AS and not LF functions as the interface level to the C-I system.

32. Following Chomsky (1995, 220), I adopt the hypothesis that there are no PF-LF interactions relevant to convergence; call this the *Modularity of Convergence Hypothesis (MCH)*. At first sight, the MCH appears to be invalidated by the existence of a rule such as the FPR (see section 1.2). In general, the MCH is invalidated whenever properties of "surface structure" play a role in determining semantic interpretation; see Chomsky 1971. I return to this question in section 1.3.3.

33. It is assumed that an unergative verb as in the sentence *Mary laughed* is analyzed as a hidden transitive (see Hale and Keyser 1991, 1993).

34. It is called *Move f* here rather than *Move F* as in Chomsky 1995 because here *F* is used for *focus*.

35. Chomsky's formulation actually is, "Move F [Move f] carries along just enough material for convergence." I have adopted the more general formulation because, as I will argue, not all instances of Move reduce to Move f. Thus, an important distinct subcase of Move is p-movement, mentioned in section 1.2 and discussed in chapter 3.

36. But see Fiengo and May 1994 for a potential counterexample (i.e., cases in which covert movement seems to void a condition C violation).

37. Note that the revision of c-command proposed here solves the problem raised by the configuration Specifier-X' without requiring that that relation be identified with adjunction (see Kayne 1994, 16).

38. In essence, I adopt the proposals made in Hale and Keyser 1993. A verb with two arguments (i.e., a transitive or an unergative) is analyzed as composed of two elementary verbs. An accusative verb will involve movement of the argument to the subject position, so that the category X' in the text will dominate two nodes. See chapter 2.

39. In the case of a head and its sister complement as in (i), the contradiction entailed by the formulation of the NSR in (37) is not removed by the revision of the notion of c-command proposed in (93).

(i) [$_X$ X YP]

I return to this structure in chapter 2, note 9. I will show that this case can usually be resolved by taking advantage of the presence of "metrically invisible" categories.

Chapter 2

1. When there is a mismatch between the syntactic phrasing and the intonational phrasing, it is assumed that the syntactic tree has undergone restructuring at PF either because of length, as in Chomsky and Halle's (1968, 372) example *(This is*

the cát) (that chased the rát) (that stole the chéese), or because of discourse considerations, such as the theme/rheme (or topic/comment) partitioning of the sentence. On the latter, see Jackendoff 1972, Liberman and Pierrehumbert 1984, Steedman 1991. An illustrative example is given in (i)–(ii). See Steedman 1991 for a detailed description of the intonation patterns for such examples.

(i)   Q: Well, what about the BEANS? Who ate THEM?
     A: (FRED) (ate the BEA-NS).
          rheme   contrastive theme

(ii) Q: Well, what about FRED? What did HE eat?
     A: (FRED ate)   (the BEANS).
        contrastive theme   rheme

2. The numbers are to be interpreted in terms of the *SPE* convention: 1 = primary, 2 = secondary, and so on.

3. Selkirk (1995) cites an example (which she attributes to Bruce Hayes) in which secondary stress appears at the beginning of the DP subject, rather than at the end.

(i) Nìneteen thousand linguists síng.

According to native speakers' intuition, secondary stress cannot be retracted if the VP is heavier, which shows the relevance of length is determining the location of nonprimary stress.

(ii) Nineteen thousand lìnguists sign the Marseilláise.
    vs. *Nìneteen thousand linguists sing the Marseilláise.

Nor can secondary stress be retracted if the DP subject contains a complement.

(iii) Nineteen thousand linguists from Grèece síng.
     vs. *Nìneteen thousand linguists from Greece síng.

(iv) Linguists from Grèece síng.
    vs. *Lìnguists from Greece síng.

This shows that some sort of syntax-based constraint governs the relation between the syntactic tree and the prosodic tree on the basis of which the metrical grid is constructed. See Dell 1984 for relevant discussions, as well as Martin 1975, 1978, 1981, 1982, 1987 and Martin and Vergnaud, in preparation.

4. According to (12) in the text, then, if a constituent is metrically invisible (i.e., dominates only metrically invisible heads), the NSR does not assign relative prominences to that constituent and its sister. In such a case relative prominence is established by another rule. See below in the text and section 2.7.

5. Alternatively, one might postulate the following convention:

(i) The structural description of the NSR is applied to a *virtual metrical tree* obtained from the syntactic tree by deleting all metrically invisible constituents and their mothers.

For example, the virtual metrical tree corresponding to the structure in (13) is that in (ii) (the labels on the brackets have been preserved for ease of identification).

Notes to Pages 42–43

(ii) $[_{C_1}\ C_1\ [_{C_2}\ C_4\ [_{C_2}\ C_2\ C_3]]]$

Given some syntactic tree T, two constituents in T would then be defined to be metrical sisters just in case they were sisters in the virtual metrical tree associated with T. An advantage of this formalization over the one in the text is that the condition in (12) ("Relative prominence between two constituents is established iff they are both metrically visible") would not be required as an independent constraint, since it would follow from (i). Nevertheless, this approach has fundamental drawbacks; see note 6.

6. Note that the alternative approach to metrical invisibility sketched in note 5, which is based on the notion of virtual metrical tree defined in (i) in that note, could not dispense with the independent notion of metrical nondistinctness defined in the text in (15) and (17). To see this, consider again the structure in (13). I repeat in (i) the central convention of the formal system sketched in note 5.

(i) The structural description of the NSR is applied to a *virtual metrical tree* obtained from the syntactic tree by deleting all metrically invisible constituents and their mothers.

The virtual metrical tree corresponding to the structure in (13) is that in (ii) (the labels on the brackets have been preserved for ease of identification).

(ii) $[_{C_1}\ C_1\ [_{C_2}\ C_4\ [_{C_2}\ C_2\ C_3]]]$

The constituent C_4 in (ii) c-commands, but fails to asymmetrically c-command, $[C_2\ C_3]$. In order for the NSR to correctly assign prominence to $[C_2\ C_3]$, it must be the case that asymmetric c-command is inherited in some way from the syntactic tree. The required convention would read as follows, where metrical nondistinctness is defined as in (15) and (17):

(iii) Constituent X is defined to asymmetrically c-command constituent Y in the virtual metrical tree iff there exists an analysis of the syntactic tree ..., Z, ..., W, ... such that (a) Z asymmetrically c-commands W in that tree and (b) the analysis ..., Z, ..., W, ... is metrically nondistinct from the analysis ... X, ..., Y, ... at (Z, X) and at (W, Y).

It appears, then, that a proper treatment of the NSR must incorporate a notion of metrical nondistinctness of analyses, regardless of whether it includes a notion of virtual metrical tree or not. But, then, the construct of virtual metrical tree is redundant, since the notion of metrical sisterhood may be subsumed under the more general concept of metrically nondistinct analyses, as has been done in the text. This point will be strengthened when the NSR is revised in section 2.3; see note 24.

7. Note that (19) must be understood strictly as a convention governing the interpretation of the structural description of the NSR; it cannot be viewed as an instance of some general principle stating that two metrically nondistinct categories are analyzed as equivalent for all relations. This would have absurd consequences—for example, taking a category that is metrically nondistinct from a dominating category to derivatively dominate itself. When the convention is understood restrictively as suggested, such unwanted consequences are avoided.

The convention might be formalized as follows. Given some tree T, a first step is to abstract away from T the sisterhood and the c-command relations at play within T. Concretely, let $\{\alpha_1, \alpha_2, \ldots, \alpha_k, \ldots, \alpha_n\}$ be the set of nodes in T. Now, set up two tables S(T) and K(T) consisting of pairs of nodes (α_i, α_j) such that

(i) a. the unordered pair (α_i, α_j) belongs to S(T) iff α_i and α_j are sisters in T
   b. the ordered pair (α_i, α_j) belongs to K(T) iff α_i c-commands α_j in T

Thus, S(T) represents the sisterhood relation between nodes in T, and K(T) represents the c-command relation between nodes in T. As an illustration, consider the tree T_0 in (ii), where Y is a metrically invisible category (written as $[_Y e]$):

(ii)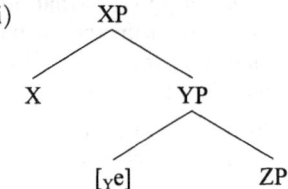

The tables $S(T_0)$ and $K(T_0)$ associated with the tree T_0 in (ii) are displayed in (iii) and (iv), respectively.

(iii) $S(T_0)$ *(the sisterhood relation)*
    (X, YP)
    (Y, ZP)

(iv) $K(T_0)$ *(the c-command relation)*
    (X, YP), (X, Y), (X, ZP)
    (YP, X)
    (Y, ZP)
    (ZP, Y)

If (α_i, α_j) is in K(T) and (α_j, α_i) is not, then, by definition α_i asymmetrically c-commands α_j in T, and reciprocally. Also, sisterhood holds between α_i and α_j in T if both pairs (α_i, α_j) and (α_j, α_i) are in K(T).

(v) (α_i, α_j) and (α_j, α_i) are in K(T) $\Longrightarrow$ (α_i, α_j) is in S(T)

The converse is not necessarily true, though, given the restricted definition of c-command introduced in section 1.3.4. Recall that, by that definition, only "computationally visible" nodes (i.e., heads and maximal projections) can c-command or be c-commanded. Given that restriction, sisterhood cannot be equated with mutual c-command. For example, in the tree in (vi), where XP is a specifier or an adjunct, XP and $Y^{(n)}$ are sisters although $Y^{(n)}$ does not c-command XP.

(vi)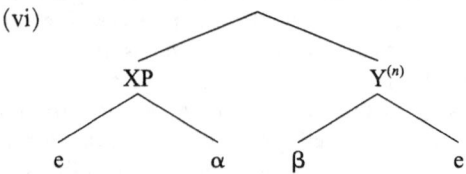

Note to Page 43

A second step in formalizing the convention (19) consists in associating a "derivative" table to each one of the relational tables S(T) and K(T) for every pair of metrically nondistinct nodes (α_p, α_q) in T. Those derivative tables are denoted by $S[\alpha_p \to \alpha_q](T)$ and by $K[\alpha_p \to \alpha_q](T)$, respectively, and are constructed by the rule in (vii).

(vii) The table $S[\alpha_p \to \alpha_q](T)$ (resp. $K[\alpha_p \to \alpha_q](T)$), where (α_p, α_q) is a pair of metrically nondistinct nodes in T, is derived from S(T) (resp, K(T))
   a. by first eliminating all pairs containing α_q from S(T) (resp, K(T)), when they exist
   b. by replacing α_p by α_q in the table derived by (a).

This rule yields two families of derivative tables, denoted by S'(T) and K'(T). We call the primitive relations represented by K(T) and by S(T) *0-relations*, and the derivative relations represented by tables in the families K'(T) and S'(T), *1-relations*. We take each 1-relation to be an extension of the corresponding 0-relation. Thus, the relation represented by a table in the family S'(T) is taken to be an extension of the sisterhood relation (0-sisterhood) and is called a *1-sisterhood relation*. Similarly, the relation represented by a table in the family K'(T) is taken to be an extension of the c-command relation (0-c-command) and is called a *1-c-command relation*. There are as many 1-sisterhood relations as there are tables in S'(T), and there are as many 1-c-command relations as there are tables in K'(T). As an illustration, consider again the tree T_0 in (ii). We are assuming that Y is the only metrically invisible category in that tree. Thus, T_0 contains only one class of metrically nondistinct nodes, namely, the pair (YP, ZP). The 0-sisterhood table $S(T_0)$ in (iii) then gives rise to the two 1-sisterhood tables $S[YP \to ZP](T_0)$ and $S[ZP \to YP](T_0)$ in (viii) and (ix).

(viii) *S[YP → ZP](T_0) (1-sisterhood)*
   (X, ZP)

(ix) *S[ZP → YP](T_0) (1-sisterhood)*
   (Y, YP)

Similarly, the 0-c-command table $K(T_0)$ in (iv) gives rise to the two 1-c-command tables $K[YP \to ZP](T_0)$ and $K[ZP \to YP](T_0)$ in (x) and (xi).

(x) *K[YP → ZP](T_0) (1-c-command)*
   (X, ZP), (X, Y)
   (ZP, X)

(xi) *K[ZP → YP](T_0) (1-c-command)*
   (X, Y), (X, YP)
   (Y, YP)
   (YP, Y)

An effect of constructing derivative tables in the example above is to define the node YP in T_0 as a 1-sister to Y in the same tree. This is of no consequence, since Y is metrically invisible and the NSR applies only to metrically visible pairs of nodes.

Given some tree T, a 0-relation over T and a 1-relation derived from it then constitute disjoint relations in the sense that they cannot be consolidated into any single consistent table associated to T or some transform of T. Indeed, although 0-relations are realized in a real tree, by construction, there is no sense in which a class of distinct 1-relations is directly reflected in any tree: such a class in general has no direct "geometric" interpretation, but may only be construed as an immediate symbolic extension of some class of 0-relations derived by the rule in (vii). For example, the node ZP in the tree T_0 in (ii) 1-c-commands X by virtue of the fact that it is metrically nondistinct from YP, which 0-c-commands X. In other words, the instantiation (ZP, X) of the 1-c-command relation in (x) is derived from the instantiation (YP, X) of the 0-c-command relation in (iv) by identifying ZP with its metrical equivalent YP. It is important to note that the instantiation (ZP, X) of the 1-c-command relation in (x) is *not* derived from—nor does it bear any direct relation to—the instantiation (X, ZP) of the 1-sisterhood relation in (viii). Indeed, the sense of the formalization just sketched is that *a 1-relation may only arise as an immediate "extension" of some 0-relation and has no independent interpretation or definition in terms of other 1-relations defined over the tree*. This is the intent behind the convention in (19). I can now define the algorithm for applying the NSR more precisely.

(xii) A pair of nodes (α_i, α_j) in T meets the structural description of the NSR $=_{def}$ the sisterhood condition of the NSR is met by (α_i, α_j) in S(T) or in some table in S'(T) and the asymmetric c-command condition of the NSR is met by (α_i, α_j) in K(T) or in some table in K'(T).

Note that the definitions and conventions above give rise to an indeterminacy in the case of a configuration such as that in (vi) if XP and $Y^{(n)}$ c-command each other. If $Y^{(n)}$ 0-asymmetrically c-commands α and XP 0-asymmetrically c-commands β in (vi), then β 1-asymmetrically c-commands α and reciprocally. But this situation actually never arises, because all configurations with the geometry in (vi) involve either a specifier or an adjunction relation, in which $Y^{(n)}$ is either a nonmaximal projection or a segment and therefore does not qualify as a c-commander (see section 1.3.4).

We will see below in the text that the convention (19) for applying the NSR extends to the relation that I will call *selection*. This means that, in addition to the tables K(T) and S(T) and their derivatives in K'(T) and S'(T), one must define a table $\Sigma(T)$ (a pair (α_i, α_j) is in $\Sigma(T)$ iff α_i selects α_j in T) and the derivatives of $\Sigma(T)$, constructed from $\Sigma(T)$ by a rule analogous to that in (vii).

8. The stricter version of asymmetric c-command assumed in this work (see section 1.3.4) appears necessary. Consider again the structure in (13) (repeated in (i)), in particular, the pair of sister constituents in (14d), repeated in (ii).

(i) $[_{C_1} C_1 [_{C_e} C_e [_{C_e} [_{C_4} C_4 C_e] [_{C_e} C_e [_{C_2} C_2 [_{C_3} C_3 C_e]]]]]]$

(ii) $[_{C_4} C_4 C_e]$ and $[_{C_e} C_e [_{C_2} C_2 [_{C_3} C_3 C_e]]]$

Under the classical definition of asymmetric c-command (see section 1.3.4), the pair of sister constituents in (ii) would give rise to an indeterminacy in the application of the NSR to the structure in (13). In effect, under the classical definition, it is the case both that $[_{C_4} C_4 C_e]$ asymmetrically c-commands $[_{C_2} C_2 [_{C_3} C_3 C_e]]$ and that $[_{C_e} C_e [_{C_2} C_2 [_{C_3} C_3 C_e]]]$ asymmetrically c-commands C_4. No indeterminacy arises under the stricter definition adopted in this work, because the constituent $[_{C_e} C_e [_{C_2} C_2 [_{C_3} C_3 C_e]]]$ in (ii) is not a maximal projection and hence cannot c-command. See also the penultimate paragraph in note 7.

9. As remarked in note 39 of chapter 1, in the case of a head and its sister complement as in (i), the requirements of sisterhood and asymmetric c-command in the formulation of the NSR in (20) are contradictory under the strict interpretation of these relations.

(i) $[_X$ X YP]

The NSR will not be able to apply to the structure in (i) unless the complement YP is metrically nondistinct from some constituent that it dominates. In general, the syntactic structure will include metrically invisible elements that allow both structural requirements of sisterhood and asymmetric c-command to be met at the same time, under the interpretation provided by the convention in (19) (see also note 7). As an illustration, consider (ii). Here, we will have to assume that the DP *Mary* is in fact branching, as shown in (iii) (see Longobardi 1994). Thus, *Mary* will both be a metrical sister of the preposition and be asymmetrically c-commanded by it.

(ii) John talked near Mary.

(iii) [John [talked near $[_{DP}[_D$ e $[_{NP}$ Mary]]]]]]

Generally, we will assume that the situation never arises where metrical sisterhood and syntactic sisterhood coincide for the structure in (i) (a situation of metrical serendipity). This might be interpreted as suggesting that the text formalization is inadequate in some respect. Alternatively, it might suggest that the ordering relation "asymmetric c-command" should be defined not in terms of asymmetry, but in some other terms. Perhaps asymmetric c-command should be defined to hold primitively between a head and the constituents c-commanded by that head.

10. In such cases, stress must be purely metagrammatical and not focus-related, if, as I assume, variables range solely over propositions, phrasal arguments such as DPs and PPs, and predicates such as VPs and APs, but not over prepositions, functional categories (such as auxiliaries and determiners), and subparts of words (such as affixes).

11. Gussenhoven notes that, in English, relational prepositions are characterized by obligatory accentuation, whereas case prepositions are optionally accented (in the appropriate contexts). Thus, *Have you héard from him?* and *Have you heard fróm him?* are equally possible, as well as *I gave it tó it* and *I gáve it to it*. On the other hand, in (36a) and (36e) the accent on the preposition is obligatory. This means that case prepositions may or may not be metrically invisible, whereas relational prepositions are never metrically invisible.

12. Another example cited by Ladd in which stress has a purely metagrammatical function is (i), in which B's statement reasserts a presupposed proposition, namely, that it will be hot all day.

(i) A: Man, it's hot! Doesn't fell like it'll cool off till tomorrow at least.

    B: Yeah, they SAID it would be hot all day.

13. It has been noticed that certain time adverbials (in particular, those that are deictic in nature) are "deaccented" (metrically invisible in our terms) when placed at the end of the sentence, although they are part of the focus (Bing 1979, Firbas 1980, Gussenhoven 1984; examples from Gussenhoven 1984, 113).

(i) I booked his dád *today*.

(ii) Special occásion *tonight*.

(iii) I was reading the páper *the other day*.

(iv) Do you cóat up *while you are in here*.

Possibly, it can be argued that such time adverbials are anaphoric in nature and it is for this reason that they are metrically invisible. Like pronouns, when these time adverbials bear main prominence, they are interpreted contrastively. This suggests that main prominence in such cases is assigned by the Emphatic/Contrastive Stress Rule, rather than by the NSR.

(v) I am leaving TODAY (not tomorrow).

(vi) I saw HER (not him).

14. I would like to thank Gerhard Brugger and Roland Hinterhölzl for extensive discussion of the German data in this section.

15. Defocalized objects may stay in situ or they may undergo scrambling to the higher part of the middle field (*Mittelfeld*; this term refers to the region between the finite verb and the nonfinite verb or verb particle in case there is no auxiliary). Scrambling to the higher part of the middle field (i.e., long scrambling) must not be confused with scrambling to the lower part of the middle field (i.e., short scrambling), which is movement of complements to licensing positions (generally obligatory). The border between the higher part and the lower part of the middle field is signaled by high adverbs such as *oft*. See (i) and (ii), where the position of the direct object with respect to the high adverb *oft* indicates whether or not the object has undergone long scrambling. If the object has undergone long scrambling (as in (i)), it precedes the adverb. In this case NS falls on the verb and the focus may include both the subject and the verb. Compare (i) with (ii), in which the object has not undergone long scrambling. If the object is not defocalized or anaphoric, NS falls on the object.

(i) Der Artz   wird den Patienten *oft*   úntersuchen.
    the doctor will the patient   often examine
    [What about the patient?]

(ii) Der Artz   wird *oft*   den Patiénten untersuchen.
    the doctor will often the patient   examine
    [What will the doctor do?]

Long-scrambled objects must be specific. Therefore, in structures with nonspecific indefinite objects, NS falls unambiguously on the object (as indicated in the text), unless defocalized as in the context *What does a doctor do with a patient?* For a comparative study of the higher part of the middle field in Germanic and Romance, see Zubizarreta, in preparation.

16. Note that the claim here is that both (a) and (b) in (48) and (49) are possible with the same focus structure (i.e., the entire sentence is focused, as in an out-of-the-blue context). That does not mean that the (a) and (b) examples have the same communicative value. In effect, stress is also used to highlight information that the speaker intends as relevant (within the limits allowed by the NSR). Thus, if the speaker chooses to put NS on the subject, it is because he or she intends to convey to the listener that the lexical content of the subject (*Junge*) is informationally relevant.

17. Gussenhoven (1984, 87) cites Dutch data that illustrate the same kind of contrast with respect to the position of NS. Notice the change of auxiliaries that goes hand in hand with the argument versus adjunct status of the PP.

(i) Hij is   naar Amérika gevaren.
    he has to   America sailed

(ii) Hij heeft in Amerika geváren.
    he has   in America sailed

Another argument/adjunct contrast cited by Gussenhoven (1984, 39) is given in (iii) and (iv).

(iii) Hij is   naar de stád gefietst.
     he has to   the town cycled

(iv) Hij heeft uren   gefíetst.
     he has hours cycled

18. Note that, within the formalization adopted here, the selection relation is taken to hold between V_i and the associated DP_i, and not between V_i and NP_i.

19. Note that, where the ordering relation in (57) holds between sequences that are lexical items, it corresponds to the notion of *government* advanced in Chomsky 1981. Thus, the maximal verbal sequence $V_1, \ldots, V_m$ preceding the argument D_m corresponds to a lexical item and, correspondingly, that sequence governs the argument D_m. On the other hand, no government relation holds between the incomplete lexical item $V_1 \ldots, V_i, i < m$, and D_i.

20. Of course, a preposition that is not an elementary predicate of a lexical item, such as the preposition in *John talked near Mary*, will not be a member of the selectional chain.

21. This choice is made on the basis of the assumption that accusative Case is licensed by an internal AspP, located between the two Vs, along the lines proposed by Travis (1991). See also Borer 1994 for relevant discussion.

22. Presumably, in (65) [*ein* Junge$_1$ [$_{V_1}$ [$_{V_2}$ gelacht]]] has left-adjoined to I (which dominates *hat*). But see Hinterhölzl 1996 for a different view.

23. Such structures show that it is indeed necessary to generalize the notion of metrically nondistinct analyses to relations other than sisterhood as in (67) (= (19)). If the analysis ..., [$_{D_2}$ *ein Buch*], [$_{V_2}$ *gekauft* [e_2]], ... were not defined to meet the structural description of the S-NSR derivatively, then there would be an indeterminacy in the application of the revised NSR. Namely, two metrically

nondistinct analyses would satisfy incompatible conditions for the application of the revised NSR: the analysis ..., [$_{D_2}$ *ein Buch*], [$_{V_2}$ *gekauft*], ... would satisfy both the description of the C-NSR and that of the S-NSR, and the analysis ..., [$_{D_2}$ *ein Buch*], [$_{V_2}$ *gekauft* [e_2]], ... would satisfy the structural description of the C-NSR but not that of the S-NSR.

24. The alternative formalization mentioned in note 5 encounters the same problem with selectional ordering as it does with asymmetric c-command (see note 6). Recall that the formalization sketched in note 5 was based on the following convention:

(i) The structural description of the NSR is applied to a virtual metrical tree obtained from the syntactic tree by deleting all metrically invisible constituents and their mothers.

Consider in this light the structure in (72a), the "lower part" of which is represented in (ii).

(ii) [*ein* Buch$_2$ [$_{V_2}$ gekauft [e_2]]]

The virtual metrical tree for the substructure represented in (ii) is given in (iii).

(iii) [$_{V_2}$ Buch$_2$ gekauft$_2$]

Given (i), NS should be assigned to *gekauft$_2$* by the C-NSR, because *gekauft$_2$* and *Buch$_2$* are not selectionally ordered (selectional ordering does hold between *gekauft$_2$* and *ein$_2$*, but *ein$_2$* is not present in the virtual metrical tree). See note 18. However, this result is wrong, as we have just seen: NS is assigned to *Buch$_2$* in such a case. It appears that the relation of selectional ordering, like that of asymmetric c-command, must be "projected" from the syntactic tree onto the metrical tree. The relevant convention can be stated as follows:

(iv) Constituent X is defined to select constituent Y in the virtual metrical tree iff there exist a constituent Z and a constituent W in the syntactic tree such that (a) Z selects W in that tree and (b) the analysis (Z, W) is metrically nondistinct from the analysis (X, Y) in that tree.

Obviously, positing the convention in (iv) will solve the problem raised by a structure such as (ii). Again, and independently of the problem raised by asymmetric c-command, it appears that a proper treatment of the NSR must incorporate the notion "metrically nondistinct analyses" defined in (15) and (17) regardless of whether the formalization includes the notion "virtual metrical tree" or not. This renders the latter notion redundant.

25. The dative construction is exceptional in its behavior. If the scope of the focus is intended to include both the dative and the verb but not the direct object, the defocalized direct object must be scrambled; compare (iii) with (iv) and (v). I assume that this fact is to be attributed to the intrinsic focus structure of the dative construction, and not to the NSR. (The paradigm in (i)–(v) was brought to my attention by Gerhard Brugger, who attributes it to Höhle (1981).)

(i) Hans *hat dem Kind das Geld* gegében.
     Hans has the   child the money given

(ii) ... daß Hans *das Geld dem Kind* gegében *hat*.
(iii) ... daß Hans *das Geld* [_F_ *dem* Kind gegeben *hat*].
(iv) *... daß Hans [_F_ *dem* Kind] *das Geld* [_F_ gegeben *hat*].
(v) *... daß Hans [_F_ *dem* Kind] *das Geld* [_F_ gegében *hat*].

26. Although both (a) and (b) in (75), (76), and (77) have the same focus structure, they do not have the same communicative value. If the speaker chooses to put NS on the subject, it is because he or she intends to highlight the fact that the lexical content of the subject is relevant. This is generally the case when the position of NS is grammatically ambiguous. See note 16.

27. Recall once more that the specifier asymmetrically c-commands its sister; see section 1.3.4.

28. It seems that manner adverbs are amenable to the same sort of analysis. Gussenhoven (1984, 86) notices the peculiar behavior of manner adverbs in Dutch, such as *(niet) goed* '(not) well'.

(i) Dit més snijdt niet goed.
    this knife cuts not well
    [What are you mooning about for like that?]

He also notes that within the predicate *goed snijden*, the verb is the accentable part.

29. As noted by Abraham (1993), in the following Adj-final structure, the Adjective rather than the PP argument attracts NS:

(i) Er ist auf seine Kinder stólz.
    he is of his children proud

The same is true in (ii), where the argument is a dative nominal phrase.

(ii) Ja, er kann keiner Frau tréu sein.
    yes he can no woman(DAT) faithful be
    [Has Peter a bad property?]

These facts would seem to indicate that the PP *auf seine Kinder* and the dative *keiner Frau* are internal arguments of the copula+adjective, and not of the adjective itself.

30. A DP topic must be specific. The fact that generics may undergo long scrambling (i.e., scrambling to the higher part of the middle field) shows that generics are specific. For example:

(i) Ich weiß nur, daß Hans (die) Frauen immer líebt.
    I know only that Hans women always loves

For a brief discussion of long scrambling of objects in German, see note 15.

31. Recall from section 1.1.2 that if, in the Assertion Structure of the sentence, the sentence topic is the subject of predication and the focus is part of the predicate, then the sentence topic cannot be part of the focus.

32. As in German (see 77), both (i) and (ii) are well-formed answers to the question in (iii). And, as in German, the communicative value of (i) and the

communicative value of (ii) are not identical. In (i) the informational relevance of the lexical content of the subject is highlighted (see notes 16 and 26).

(i) Jóhn's fixing it.

(ii) John's fíxing it.

(iii) What happened to your car?

In this respect, (i) and (ii) as answers to (iii) are no different than (iv) and (v) as answers to (vi); (iv) highlights the informational relevance of the content of the subject.

(iv) The báby's crying.

(v) The baby's crýing.

(vi) What's happening?

33. Only one of the five speakers consulted accepted both options with unaccusative verbs (NS on the subject or on the verb).

34. Another minimal contrast of the same sort is given in (i), which contains a predicate that is in all likelihood unaccusative. Schmerling comments:

(i) a. The statue's héad is missing.
     b. The statue's head is míssing.

[(ia)] is, again, a news sentence: it might be a report of vandalism, for example. Example [(ib)], on the other hand, sounds like part of a description of the statue. It must thus be uttered by a guide in a museum who was trying to tell the addressee what the statue in question looked like so that the addressee could identify it. (p 91)

In other words, in (ib) the subject is the sentence topic and therefore defocalized.

35. The analysis of the (b) examples in (i) and (ii) is less straightforward. Such examples seem to indicate that redundant information is metrically invisible in English. (These examples are also from Bolinger 1972.)

(i) a. Those are cràwling ínsects.
     b. Those are cràwling thìngs.

(ii) a. I'm going over to the dòctor's bárn.
      b. I'm going over to the dóctor's plàce.

36. Although it appears that there is another option for the second example as well. Given its heaviness, *digitalisieren* can also form an intonational unit of its own, in which case it would carry its own NS.

37. There seems to be a difference between the prosody of resultative adjectives and that of depictive adjectives. Although the former may be "destressed," the latter may not; compare (i) and (ii).

(i) John watered the plánts flat.

(ii) John ate the meat ráw.

I attribute this to the fact that the object is an argument of the complex predicate V+Adj in (i), but not in (ii). In other words, there is a selectional ordering relation between the object and the adjective in (i), but not in (ii). The S-NSR may therefore apply to the metrical sisters *(the plants, flat)* and assign NS to *the plants*. On the other hand, the S-NSR will fail to apply to the metrical sisters *(eat, raw)*. The C-NSR applies instead and assigns NS to *raw*.

38. Work in progress by Marcello Modesto on Brazilian Portuguese (Seminar in Linguistics, University of Southern California, fall 1996) suggests that this language is similar to French with respect to the location of NS.

39. François Dell has provided me with the following example, in which the anaphoric object is destressed:

(i) T'as   vú   ce   *film*?
    You have seen this movie

40. Italian seems to be comparable to Standard Spanish in this respect. See Cinque 1993.

41. In testing for metrical invisibility in Standard Spanish, it is important to avoid phrase-final PPs, since these can be analyzed as right-dislocated, in which case they are part of a distinct intonational grouping (although pronounced with a reduced pitch range and therefore easily confused with destressed material by the layperson's ear). See the appendix to chapter 3 for further discussion of the prosody of right-dislocation in Spanish.

42. Principle 1 is equivalent to the rule in the system proposed here according to which defocalized material is metrically invisible.

43. It is not clear, though, how Selkirk's system would account for Gussenhoven's (1984, 27) contrast in (105), repeated here.

(i) Our dóg's disappeared.

(ii) Our dog's mysteriously disappéared.

44. See note 15 on defocalized objects in German.

45. Following work by Beckman and Pierrehumbert (1986), in Zubizarreta 1995b, 1996 I present evidence, based on the shape of the fundamental frequency (F_0), that in examples with contrastive focus or emphasis the "accented" and "deaccented" portions of the sentence are part of the same intonational grouping. More precisely, I compared the F_0 properties of the transition between the subject and the object in the example in (i), where the subject is contrastively focused, with those in (ii), where the object is right-dislocated. The F_0 properties indicate that there is an intonational hiatus in (ii) (which can be attributed to an intonational boundary between the subject and the object), but not in (i). See the appendix to chapter 3 for further discussion.

(i) Lavó   MAMÁ   la   mamadera.
     washed Mother(S) the milk-bottle(O)

(ii) La   lavó   *mamá*   # la   mamadera.
     ACC.CL washed Mother(S)   the milk-bottle(O)

See also Sosa 1991 for evidence along similar lines.

46. Interestingly, Mota (1995) has provided phonetic evidence from Peninsular Spanish that seems to support the hypothesis that the accents associated with contrastive and noncontrastive focus have different properties. She shows that, although pitch height and syllable lengthening do not necessarily distinguish the two types of accent, the location of the peak of pitch does so. In Peninsular Spanish the realization of the peak of the pitch accent is usually displaced, but in contexts of contrastive focus or emphasis, this displacement is inhibited.

47. See note 38. In work in progress, Marcello Modesto (University of Southern California) has also shown that in Brazilian Portuguese (as in Spanish) a focused phrase may form part of the same intonational unit as the defocalized part of the sentence.

48. Selkirk (1984, 1995) and Gussenhoven (1984) both discuss a fact that I have ignored here. A difference has been noticed between (i) and (ii).

(i) John teaches Clássics.

(ii) John teaches in Lóndon.

Although the verb may be "deaccented" in (i), it may not be in (ii). In other words, the stress level on the verb in (i) may be lower than in (ii). Selkirk claims that this is because in (ii) focus cannot project to the VP from the (pitch-accented) adjunct; it must project from the pitch-accented verb. On the other hand, in (i) focus may project to the VP from the pitch-accented argument; therefore, the verb may be "deaccented." Similarly, in Gussenhoven's system the verb and the argument form a focus domain in (i); therefore, it is sufficient for the argument to be accented. On the other hand, in (ii) the verb and the adjunct do not form a focus domain; the verb and the adjunct constitute independent focus domains and therefore both must be pitch-accented. I an skeptical of this analysis because, according to native speakers' intuitions, in (iii) where the relation between the verb and the argument is not pragmatically predictable, both the verb and the argument must be "accented." This is reminiscent of Bolinger's (1972) contrasts (e.g., *próblems to solve* vs. *problems to compúterize*).

(iii) John raises ánts (for a living).

49. Note that (155b) and (155c) are not clear-cut counterexamples to Cinque's analysis, given that syntactic movement can separate the verb from the particle in the case of *wéggefahren* and the verb from the noun in the case of *skífahren*.

50. But note that, if an object in German checks the Case feature of a verb V overtly, and it does so by virtue of occupying [Spec, V] or [Spec, Asp] (see section 1.3.1), then an object cannot be distinguished from an adjunct simply in terms of sisterhood.

51. In chapter 3 I will postulate the existence of a functional feature "focus," not to be confused with the feature [F]. Whereas the F-marking of major categoreis encodes the focus/presupposition partitioning of the syntactic structure, the functional feature "focus" marks the syntactic positon of an F-marked constituent in certain constructions (but it has no semantic import). More precisely, the functional feature "focus" attracts a constituent marked [F] to its specifier, just as the *wh*-feature on a functional category attracts a *wh*-phrase to its specifier.

(i) El VINO   trajo   Pedro.
   the wine(O) brought Pedro(S)

But there is an important difference between the functional feature "focus" and the functional feature *wh*. Whereas checking by the *wh*-feature is sufficient to license an F-marked phrase, checking by the "focus" feature is not. In the latter case the F-marked phrase must contain main phrasal prominence as well: it must be prosodically licensed. This difference, I suggest, is related to the distinction between the extrinsically grammatical (or discourse-based) nature of the "focus" feature and the intrinsically grammatical nature of the *wh*-feature.

52. I assume that (168) holds of Romance as well. I leave German out of the discussion because I have not been able to determine what the facts are in this language; the native speakers I consulted have provided contradictory judgments.

53. Consider examples (i) and (ii) (cited by Selkirik (1984), who attributes them to Bresnan (1971)). In cases in which the fronted *wh*-phrase contains a restrictor NP, main prominence may fall either on the restrictor or on the rightmost constituent.

(i) Which bóok did Helen review?

(ii) Which book did John revíew?

We can accommodate such contrasts by assuming that in such cases there may be a mismatch between the scope of the "focus" feature and the scope of the *wh*-feature. Recall that we assumed that propositions, phrasal arguments such as DPs and PPs, and predicates such as VPs and APs—but not functional categories such as auxiliaries and determiners (or subparts of words)—may function as semantic focus (i.e., as a variable); see note 10. Therefore, in the case of *which book*, the DP and not the determiner is marked [+F]. On the other hand, the formal feature [wh] on the determiner may or may not percolate onto the DP. We thus obtain two possible representatios:

(iii) [$_F$[$_{wh}$ Which] bóok] did Helen review?

(iv) [$_{F/wh}$ Which book] did Helen revíew?

The analysis in (iv) is similar to cases with a bare *wh*-phrase, such as (165a) in the text. Consider next the structure in (iii). The scope mismatch between the two features allows this structure to escape the constraint in (168). Given that *which book* is unmarked for the *wh*-feature, the FPR in (170) applies to the metrical sister nodes [$_F$ *which book*] and [$_{-F}$ *did Helen review*] and assigns main prominence to *which book*. Since [$_{-F}$ *did Helen review*] is metrically invisible, the FPR does not conflict with the NSR (i.e., the NSR fails to apply to the above metrical sister nodes).

No prosodic pattern comparable to (i) can be found in French (although in this language a [−F] constituent may be analyzed as metrically invisible). This is probably due to the fact that the *wh*-determiner agrees with the NP in this language (as in other Romance languages); consequently, the entire DP is obligatorily analyzed as +*wh*. The FPR in (170) will therefore fail to apply to such structures.

(v) [$_{F/wh}$ Quel livre] as-tu <u>acheté</u>

54. A similar logic applies to cases of discontinuous F-marked constituents, such as the German example in (i) (discussed in section 2.3.1), where the subject and the verb are marked [+F], but the oject is marked [−F]. The constituent *das Buch genommen hat* is unmarked for the F-feature, because it dominates both a [+F] and a [−F] constituent. But note that the refinement of the notation is irrelevant in this case with respect to the end result because [_−F_ *das Buch*] is metrically invisible for the NSR. Therefore, [*das Buch genommen hat*] is metrically nondistinct from [_F_ *genommen hat*].

(i) a. Ich glaube, daβ [[_+F_ ein Júnge] [[_−F_ *das Buch*] [_F_ genommen hat]]].
    b. Ich glaube, daβ [[_+F_ ein Junge] [[_−F_ *das Buch*] [_F_ genómmen hat]]].
    [What happened to the book?]

The same comment applies to *John tóok it*, as an answer to *What happened to the book?*

55. Cases of superiority in multiple *wh*-questions also violate the "Shortest Movement" Condition (see Reinhart 1995). In effect, the *wh*-feature in C attracts the closest *wh*-phrase that it c-commands, giving rise to (i) in lieu of (ii).

(i) [who_i [e_i [bought what]]]
(ii) [what_i [who [bought [e_i [V e_i]]]]]

56. As has often been remarked, in the case of *which N*, superiority effects are considerably attenuated.

(i) (?)Which book did which boy buy?
(ii) (?)I wonder which girl which boy lent the book to.

Given the discussion in note 53, the DP subject may be analyzed as [_F_ [_wh_ *which*] N], giving rise to the stress patterns in (iii) and (iv).

(iii) Which book did which bóy buy?
(iv) I wonder which girl which bóy lent the book to.

It is unclear that this corresponds to the facts. Furthermore, note that *quel N* in French does not behave like *which N* in English. Compare (ii) with (v).

(v) *Je me demenade à quelle fille quel garçon a prêté le livre.
    I wonder   to which girl which boy   lent   the book

I leave the problem unresolved.

57. See also Bolinger's (1978, 108, 115) examples in (i)–(iii), which involve multiple (emphatic) stresses. (Except for the underlining, the notation is Bolinger's.)

(i) I know that among all the disasters in that kitchen, Jane scorched the beans and Lydia put salt in the ice tea; but whát did whó bréak? I know somebody broke something, so please stop evading my question.

(ii) I've asked you and asked you, and I'll repeat is again: to whóm did you give whát?

(iii) Enough of your evasions. Now just kindly tell me whére whó wént.

Notes to Pages 95–97   181

58. Example (176) (repeated in (i)) may only have the meaning 'for which $\langle x,y\rangle x$ knows what y bought'. This meaning is not available in the alternative derivation in (ii).

(i) Who knows what whó bought?

(ii) Who knows who bought whát?

The possibility of violating "Shortest Movement" in (i) could then be attributed to the fact that (i) and (ii) are associated with distinct semantic representations, an analysis that requires that "Shortest Movement" function as a derivational (or global) economy principle (see Reinhart 1995). But Chomsky (1995) argues that (i) is simply a case of "association of likes," thus avoiding giving "Shortest Movement" the status of a global economy principle. See section 1.3.2.

59. The examples in (177) are well formed with respect to PF, but are they well formed syntactically? What can we say about these examples with respect to the "Shortest Movement" Condition?

An analysis that assumes that the object moves above VP_1 (which contains the postverbal subject) in order to check its Case, before moving on to [Spec, T], would comply with "Shortest Movement." (See Mahajan 1990a,b, 1991.)

(i) [qué$_i$ [compró [e$_i$ [$_{VP_1}$ quién$_j$ [V [$_{VP_2}$ V e$_i$]]]]]]

But this cannot be the correct explanation. If the *wh*-phrase object is fronted through an intermediate A-position, then we would expect such structures not to give rise to weak crossover. But this is incorrect. As is well known, binding of the pronoun by the *wh*-phrase in C gives at best marginal results.

(ii) a. A   quién   repudió su madre?
       ACC whom(O) rejected his mother(S)
       [Binding: ??]
    b. A   quién   despidió su jefe?
       ACC whom(O) fired   his boss(S)
       [Binding: ??]

The examples in (ii) contrast with those in (ii). Indeed, binding becomes possible when an accusative clitic is inserted in dialects that allow for accusative clitic doubling.

(iii) a. A   cuál   de ellos   lo   repudió su madre?
        ACC which of them(O) ACC.CL rejected his mother(S)
        [Binding: OK]
     b. A   cuál   de ellos   lo   despidió su jefe?
        ACC which of them(O) ACC.CL fired   his boss(S)
        [Binding: OK]

Furthermore, speakers generally judge the sentences in (177) as less than perfect, which suggests that, although prosodically well formed, such sentences nonetheless violate the "Shortest Movement" Condition.

60. As with the English examples, it seems that there is a contrast between the French examples (i) and (ii). It is also predicted that *Je me demande à qui qui a*

prêté ce livre (with main prominence on the *wh*-subject) should be closer in acceptability to (i) than to (ii).

(i)   ?Je me demande à qui   qui a prêté quoi.
       I wonder   to whom who lent   what

(ii) *Je me demande à qui   qui a prêté ce livre.
      I wonder   to whom who lent   that book

Chapter 3

1. I use the term *Modern Standard Spanish* in a loose way. It is not meant to be associated with a specific geographical area. Judgments have been reproduced with speakers of Castilian Spanish as well as with speakers from the Rio de la Plata area (Argentina and Paraguay). Unless otherwise stated, the term *Spanish* will be used to mean Modern Standard Spanish.

2. I use quotation marks to distinguish features that are discourse-based from those that are not.

3. The "focus" feature that heads a functional projection and participates in the feature-checking algorithm is not to be confused with the [F] feature used in chapters 1 and 2 to mark the phrases that are part of the assertion of a sentence. "Focus" is a morphosyntactic feature with no semantic import. Its presence is optional, at least in the languages under discussion, and its function is to characterize the syntactic position of a fronted F-marked constituent in certain structures. In effect, when present in the structure, the functional feature "focus" attracts an F-marked constituent to its specifier position.

4. For example:

(i) Estoy segura que a María le   regalará su abuelo   un caballo de
    (I) am sure that to María DAT.CL will-give her grandfather a horse of
    pura raza.
    pure breed

(ii) Dudo/Lamento que a María le   haya   regalado su abuelo
    (I) doubt/regret that to María DAT.CL have(SUBJ) given her grandfather
    un caballo de pura raza.
    a horse of pure breed

5. Piera (1987) also provides relevant examples such as those in (i) and (ii), with different types of adverbs in preverbal position.

(i) a. Temprano salía   Julía de   casa.
     early   went-out(HABITUAL) Julía of-the house
  b. Por la noche salía   Julía de   casa.
     during the night went-out(HABITUAL) Julía of-the house
  c. En esta ciudad salía   Julía todas las noches.
     in this city   went-out(HABITUAL) Julía every night
  d. Con poco dinero salía   Julía de   casa.
     with little money went-out(HABITUAL) Julía of-the house
  e. Cansada salía   Julía de   casa.
     tired   went-out(HABITUAL) Julía of-the house

(ii) a. Supe   que bajo ningún pretexto conseguiría   Juan acercarse
       (I) knew that under no   conditions would-manage Juan to-approach
       a   nosotros.
       ACC us
   b. Limpia como una patena tenía Eduardo la   casa.
      as clean as a whistle   had Eduardo the house
   c. Cantando en la   ducha   estaba Edelmira cuando llegué.
      singing   in the shower was   Edelmira when   (I) arrived

6. For example:
(i) a. Estoy segura que a NADIE le devolvió María su manuscrito.
    b. Dudo/Lamento que a NADIE le haya devuelto María su manuscrito.
(ii) a. Estoy segura que las ESPINACAS detesta Pedro (y no las papas).
     b. Dudo/Lamento que las ESPINACAS deteste Pedro (y no las papas).

7. As remarked in section 1.1.1, the example in (i) is not a case of multiple foci. The focus in such cases is the paired variables $\langle x, y \rangle$ with their associated values.

(i) Q: Who bought what?
       for which $\langle x, y \rangle$, x bought y
    A: John bought the book, Mary the newspaper, and Ann the magazine.

8. The assumption that a verb must move to the head of the Focus/Emphasis projection also seems implausible on crosslinguistic grounds. Szabolsci (1996) argues that this is not the case in Hungarian, contra Brody (1995).

9. The argument that [Spec, T] may host a *wh*-phrase is not affected by the data discussed in Suñer 1991. (Examples (i), (ii) are from pages 294, 288.)

(i) Me pregunto que *proqué* el   gobernador no firma   ese proyecto en
    (I) wonder   what why   the governor   doesn't sign that project into
    ley.
    law
(ii) Mara me   preguntó que *qué libros* había comprado yo en Rusia.
     Mara to-me asked   that what books had   bought   I in Russia
     'Mara asked me what books I had bought in Russia.'

On the basis of data such as (i)–(ii) and other facts, Suñer argues that indirect question verbs select for a double complementizer. More precisely, Suñer argues that a (semantic) *WH-feature* must be distinguished from a (syntactic) *wh-feature* (in the spirit of Grimshaw's (1979) proposal). The former requires a Q-operator in its specifier, and the latter a *wh*-phrase. The *WH*-C is realized phonologically as *que* in Spanish and is phonologically null in English. Thus, given Suñer's analysis, the *wh*-adjunct *porqué* in (i) and the *wh*-argument *qué libros* in (ii) are located in the specifier of the lower *wh*-C (whereas *que* is the phonological realization of the higher *WH*-C in both cases).

Within the generalized TP analysis discussed in the text, Suñer's analysis can be maintained with a few adjustments: the *wh*-phrases in (i) and (ii) are located in distinct positions. The *wh*-adverb in (i) is in the specifier of the *wh*-C (situated between the *WH*-C and T), and the *wh*-argument in (ii) is in the specifier of the syncretic category T/wh (situated immediately below the *WH*-C).

In certain idiolects of Standard Spanish (reported by Suñer), the functional category that hosts the Q-operator and the functional category that hosts the *wh*-phrase may be separated by a functional category that hosts a topic; see (iii) and (iv).

(iii) Me preguntaron que *a Juan*, qué le habría prometido el
to-me (they) asked that to Juan what DAT.CL could-have promised the
decano.
dean
'They asked me what the dean could have promised Juan.'

(iv) Me preguntaron que a *mi hijo*, dónde lo iban a mandar
to-me (they) asked that ACC my son where ACC.CL were-going to send
los militares.
the militaries
'They asked me where the military was going to send my son.'

10. The *wh*-Q differs from emphatics and focused phrases in that it must obligatorily move, at least in nonisland configurations; compare (i) and (ii).

(i) Juan hizo qué cosa? [only echo interpretation available]
Juan did what

(ii) Ese trabajo es para hacer qué cosa?
that job is in-order to-do what

This suggests that a question obligatorily carries a functional *wh*-feature. On the other hand, a sentence that contains a focused or emphatic constituent does note obligatorily carry a functional "focus" or "emphasis" feature in this language. Perhaps this is to be attributed to the fact that the *wh*-phrase, unlike focus and emphasis, is a scope-taking element.

11. Note the difference between (i)/(ii) and (iii). This contrast can probably be attributed to the fact that temporal adverbs (such as *nunca*) are TP modifiers; therefore, they appear in [Spec, T] for reasons quite independent of feature checking. In other words, more than one specifier of T is allowed, but at most one of them may enter into a feature-checking relation with T.

(i) a. *Nunca nadie* llama.
never no-one calls
'No one ever calls.'
b. *Nadie nunca* llama.

(ii) a. *Nunca nada* diré que te pueda ofender.
never nothing will-say that DAT.CL could offend
'Never will I say anything that could offend you.'
b. ?*Nada nunca* diré que te pueda ofender.

(iii) a. *Nada nadie dijo.
nothing no-one said
b. *Nadie nada dijo.

The same analysis can be extended to (iv), cited in Suñer 1994. Compare (iv) with (v).

(iv) A quién jamás ofenderías   tú   con tus   acciones?
      whom never would-offend you with your actions
      'Whom would you never offend with your actions?'
(v) *A quién nadie   ofendería   con sus acciones?
      whom nobody would-offend with his actions
      'Whom would nobody offend with his actions?'

12. Single-argument VS structures such as *Llamó Juan* 'Juan called' (lit, 'called Juan') are not relevant in considering the status of [Spec, T], since (as I will show in section 3.2) there are reasons to believe that single-argument VS structures in Italian are cases of covert locative constructions, as suggested by Pinto (1994) (building on insights due originally to Paola Benincà). If Pinto is correct, then VS structures in Italian are reminiscent of the locative construction in French.

(i) a. Il a dormi beaucoup de rois   dans ce   lit.
       it slept   many   kings in   this bed
    b. Dans ce   lit   ont dormi beaucoup de rois.
       in   this bed slept   many   kings

The difference between the two languages is that French, but not Italian, exhibits a definiteness effect and, furthermore, in Standard Italian the verb and the postverbal subject always agree and the locative may be covert (at least in some cases).

13. This question arises to the extent that we assume that specifier-head and head-head relations are licensing relations (as in Chomsky 1995) but "government" is not (contra Chomsky 1981). If government is assumed, we can define nominative Case checking in terms of the government relation that holds between $V + T$ and the subject in [Spec, VP_1] (as in Koopman and Sportiche 1991).

14. See Contreras 1986 and Longobardi 1994 for an ECP-based account and Zubizarreta and Vergnaud 1992 for an analysis in terms of complex-predicate formation at LF, based on insights due originally to Lois (1989).

15. This fact was brought to my attention by Joseph Aoun.

16. In structures where the object is a clitic-doubled strong pronoun that bears phrasal stress, the object is obligatorily emphatic (a fact that remains to be explained). Compare (ia–b) with (ii).

(i) a. María lo   castigó   a ÉL.
       María ACC.CL punished ACC him
    b. Lo castigó María a ÉL.

(ii) Lo castigó a él MARÍA.

As brought to my attention by Liliana Sanchez, if the clitic-doubled pronoun is emphatic, the effects of Condition C disappear. Compare (iii) with (iv).

(iii) Esta mañana lo$_i$ castigó   la madre de Juan$_i$.
      this morning ACC.CL punished the mother of Juan
      [Coreference: *]

(iv) Esta mañana lo$_i$ castigó   la madre de Juan$_i$ a ÉL$_i$.
     this morning ACC.CL punished the mother of Juan ACC him
     [Coreference: OK]

Independent data show that emphasis can nullify the effects of Condition C under certain conditions; see Evans 1980, which is the source of (v) (where there is intended coreference between *he* and *Oscar*).

(v) Everyone has finally realized that Oscar is incompetent. Even HE has realized that Oscar is incompetent.

As I will show in section 3.1, in the case of VOS the subject receives NS (as indicated by the underlining) and is interpreted as focused. In this case the effects of Condition C reappear.

(vi) Esta mañanan lo$_i$ castigó   a   él   [$_F$ la madre de Juan$_i$].
    this morning ACC.CL punished ACC him   the mother of Juan
    [Coreference: *]
    [Who punished him this morning?]

17. Note the relevance of the distinction between specifiers and adjuncts in this analysis. Also note that it is assumed that a head may adjoin only to another head and that a phrase may adjoin only to another phrase, not to a head. To the extent that feature checking is established via a relation to a head, there can be no feature checking via "overt" adjunction to a head in the cases under discussion, because these are cases of XP-movement.

18. More precisely, Fontana argues that OS was an obligatory V2 language, comparable to Yiddish and Icelandic (as argued in Diesing 1990, Santorini 1989, Rögnvaldsson and Thráinsson 1990). Fontana claims that cases of V1 should be analyzed as instances of V-to-T-to-C movement (as in yes/no questions and narrative inversion). But see his footnote (p. 134) for possible counterexamples.

19. Here I disagree with Fontana, who claims that XPVSO structures are no longer available in MS.

20. Within a theory in which the distinction between heads and phrases is not a primitive one (Chomsky 1995), we would have to assume that pronouns in OS were syntactically branching structures and were therefore analyzed unambiguously as phrases.

21. For a different point of view on OS clitics, see Wanner 1991.

22. Since Standard Spanish and Standard Italian do not have nominative clitics, I do not include them in the discussion. As is well known, many northern Italian dialects have nominative clitics, and perhaps to some extent so does French. Sportiche (1993) argues that the nominative Cl is located above TP. This hypothesis will not bear one way or another on what I have to say here. What is important to retain is that Case is not licensed in the specifier of the Cl projection. Nor do I assume a Case (or Agr) projection. If nominative, accusative, and oblique Cases are functional features, then they are intrinsic to (and inseparable from) the categories T, V (or Asp), and P, respectively.

I will not discuss the issue of in-situ clitic doubling. See Aoun 1991, Sportiche 1992, Franco 1993, and references cited therein for relevant discussion.

23. In this note I review briefly the properties of the so-called clitic left-dislocation construction (CLLD).

CLLD is sensitive to strong islands, as observed by Cinque (1983, 1990) for Italian and Dolci (1986) for Spanish.

(i) *Relative clause*
  *Estoy segura que *a Pedro*, conocemos a la mujer que *lo*
  (I) am sure that ACC Pedro (we) know ACC the woman that ACC.CL
  traicionó.
  betrayed

(ii) *Adjunct*
  *Me parece mejor que *a Pedro*, terminemos la tarea antes de
  to-me (it) seems better that ACC Pedro (we) finish the task before
  llamar*lo*.
  calling ACC.CL

(iii) *Sentential subject*
  *Estoy segura que *a Pedro*, que María *lo* haya invitado
  (I) am sure that ACC Pedro that María ACC.CL had invited
  sorprendió a todo el mundo.
  surprised ACC everyone

As Iatridou (1990b) notes, such facts provide strong evidence that the topic in CLLD originates within the minimal clause that contains the clitic to which it is related. From there it may move to a higher clause, an operation subject to standard bounding conditions on movement.

When testing for island effects, it is very important not to confuse CLLD with hanging topic constructions (see Cinque 1983, 1990, Dolci 1986). The topic in CLLD has distinct properties. It may be adjoined to a root clause or an embedded clause. It must be related to a position in the clause via a pronominal clitic in the case of direct and indirect objects, and via a gap in the case of oblique objects or adjuncts (for which there are no clitic forms in Spanish). It may not be construed with an epithet. A Case marker or preposition may precede the topic DP as determined by the verb to which it is grammatically related. These properties are illustrated in (iv) and (v).

(iv) a. *A sus amigos*, Pedro *los* invitó a cenar.
     ACC his friends Pedro ACC.CL invited to dine
  b. *A sus amigos, Pedro invitó a cenar a *esos idiotas*.
     ACC his friends Pedro invited to dine ACC those idiots

(v) a. Estoy segura que *de María*, Pedro siempre habla bien.
     (I) am sure that of María Pedro always speaks well
  b. *Estoy segura que *de María*, Pedro siempre habla bien *de esa idiota*.
     (I) am sure that of María Pedro always speaks well of that idiot

The so-called hanging topic is the expression, such as *en cuanto a DP* 'as for DP' or *con respecto a DP* 'with respect to DP', that serves the function of changing topics in an ongoing discourse. The hanging topic also has well-defined properties. It may be related to a position in the sentence occupied by a pronoun (see (via)) or an epithet (see (vib)), or it may simply bear an inalienable relation to a phrase in the sentence (see (vii)), comparable to the *wa*-topic in Japanese.

(vi) a. [Context: Discussion of Juan's unhappy relation with his parents]
... En cuanto a *su hermano*, parece que los padres hablan de
as for his brother (it) seems that the parents speak about
él todo el tiempo.
him all the time

b. ... (En cuanto a) *Pedro*, parece que *el desgraciado* se lleva con
as for Pedro (it) seems that the bastard gets along with
todo el mundo, inclusive con el enemigo.
everybody even with the enemy

(vii) [Context: Discussion of Mr. Gonzales's social abilities]
... En cuanto a la habilidad científica del Sr. Gonzales, basta con
as for Mr. Gonzales's scientific abilities it-is-sufficient
mencionar que acaba de ganar un premio de renombre internacional.
to-mention that (he) has won a prestigious international prize

But a hanging topic need not be preceded by *en cuanto a, con respecto a*, as illustrated in (viii). In this example *Bernardo* has the structure of a hanging topic: it exhibits no grammatical connection to the verb in the clause, as attested by the lack of a Case marker or a preposition on the DP topic.

(viii) [Context: Discussion of possible candidates for a certain job]
Sin embargo, Bernardo, estoy segura que nadie confía en
on the other hand Bernardo (I) am sure that nobody has confidence in
ese idiota.
that idiot

A hanging topic can appear only at the leftmost edge of the root clause.

(ix) *Sin embargo, estoy segura que, Bernardo, nadie confía en ese idiota.

Hanging topics are note sensitive to islands of any kind.

(x) *Extraction out of a relative clause*
(En cuanto a) el Sr. Gonzales, conocemos a la mujer que lo traicionó.
'(As for) Mr. Gonzales, we know the woman that ACC.CL betrayed.'

(xi) *Extraction out of a sentential adjunct*
(En cuanto a) el Sr. Gonzales, terminaremos la tarea antes de llamarlo.
'(As for) Mr. Gonzales, we will finish the task before ACC.CL calling.'

(xii) *Extraction out of a sentential subject*
(En cuanto a) el Sr. Gonzales, que María lo haya invitado sorprendió a todo el mundo.
'(As for) Mr. Gonzales, that María ACC.CL had invited surprised everyone.'

24. Aoun and Benmamoun (1998) report the same contrasts in Arabic. See also Cecchetto 1995 and Guasti 1996 for similar contrasts in Italian—although the relevance of the Italian examples is less clear because in this language (unlike in Spanish and Arabic) the postverbal subject in the relevant construction is unambiguously interpreted as focused (see section 3.3) and focus may affect quantifier binding (see section 1.1.3).

Notes to Pages 114–116

25. I consider clauses with modals, which are restructuring verbs in Spanish, to be monoclausal.

26. Note that (i) is also well formed.

(i) A   cada niño$_i$, su$_i$ madre lo$_i$ acompañará   el primer día de
    ACC each child   his mother ACC.CL will-accompany the first   day of
    escuela.
    school

We may interpret the absence of weak crossover in such sentences as indicating that the fronted topic functions as an A-position (whether it is in [Spec, T] or above TP) and that reconstruction from A-positions is possible but not obligatory. On reconstruction from A-positions, see Hornstein 1995. The A-status of the topic in such cases is to be attributed to the fact that it functions as the subject of predication with respect to the clause to which it is attached.

Note, however, that if the topic that originates in an embedded clause is moved to a higher clause, the topic cannot bind a pronoun in the matrix clause (see (ii)). The weak crossover effect would follow from the fact that the topic attached to the matrix clause has an Ā-status, given that it does not function as the subject of predication with respect to the matrix clause.

(ii) *A   cada niño$_i$, su$_i$ madre piensa que María lo$_i$ acompañará   el
     ACC each child   his mother thinks that María ACC.CL will-accompany the
     primer día de escuela.
     first   day of school

Alternatively, the contrast between (i) and (ii) could be attributed to the fact that a quantifier can only bind a pronoun within its quantificational domain (rather than to the A versus Ā distinction). In (ii) the domain of quantification of *cada niño* is the embedded clause. The question then is how to define the domain of quantification for each quantifier type; see Beghelli 1995 for relevant discussion.

27. In languages like Italian that have PP clitics, these are probably not functional projections at all. In fact, PP clitics are optional in cases of PP left-dislocation in this language.

28. Why does the empirical generalization in (46) hold? A possibility that can be explored is that "Shortest Movement" functions as an economy condition on derivations in such cases. More precisely, "Shortest Movement" may compare derivations in the case of movements triggered by discourse-based features like "topic." In effect, it could be that the "topic" chain is sufficiently local and does not interact with other types of chains so that "Shortest Movement" can function as an economy condition on derivations in such cases without giving rise to a computational explosion. The analysis would then be that the structure containing the clitic involves a movement with shorter steps than the structure containing no clitic. In order for this analysis to work, the two structures must have the same initial array. We could assume that the clitic is simply the copy of the φ-features of the DP with which it agrees and therefore does not count as a distinct lexical item. In the case of an accusative topic, the two competing analyses are those in (ia) and

(ib); in the case of a dative topic, the two competing analyses are those in (iia) and (iib) (I disregard the details of the analysis of datives).

(i) a. $[_{TP} \_\_\_i\ T\ [_{ClP}\ e_i\ [acc\ Cl_i\ [_{VP_1}\ V_1\ [_{VP_2}\ V_2\ e_i\ \ldots$
 b. $[_{TP} \_\_\_i\ T\ [_{VP_1}\ V_1\ [_{VP_2}\ V_2\ e_i\ \ldots$

(ii) a. $[_{TP} \_\_\_i\ T\ [_{VP_1}\ V_1\ [_{ClP}\ e_i\ [dat\ Cl_i\ [_{VP_2}\ [V_2\ [_{PP}\ P\ e_i\ \ldots$
 b. $[_{TP} \_\_\_i\ T\ [_{VP_1}\ V_1\ [_{VP_2}\ V_2\ [_{PP}\ P\ e_i\ \ldots$

If the length of the movement is computed in terms of c-commanding maximal projections that separate any two links in a chain created by movement, then the "topic" feature in T will prefer attracting a topic from [Spec, Cl] than from a position within VP_2. In effect, ClP is closer to T than VP_2 or PP is. More precisely, one maximal projection separates [Spec, T] from [Spec, acc Cl] in (ia) (namely, accusative ClP), whereas two maximal projections separate [Spec, T] from [Spec, VP_2] in (ib) (namely, VP_1 and VP_2). Two maximal projections separate [Spec, T] from [Spec, dat Cl] in (iia) (namely, dative ClP and VP_1), whereas three maximal projections separate [Spec, T] from [Spec, PP] in (iib) (namely, VP_1, VP_2, and PP). Note that the structure selected by "Shortest Movement" is more complex than the alternative (owing to the presence of the Cl), thus contradicting the Minimize Structure Principle in (49). We must therefore assume that when a head is a copy of another head (in the case under discussion, the Cl is the copy of the D with which it is associated), the copy is "invisible" to the Minimize Structure Principle. In other words, in computing structural complexity, the Minimize Structure Principle looks only at heads that dominate distinct items in the initial array and at the projections of such heads.

29. Some evidence in favor of the hypothesis that *clitic/e* functions as a predicate-variable is provided by the well-known observation that fronted emphatics and focused phrases do not cooccur with an accusative clitic. See (i). This follows immediately from the fact that neither emphatics nor focused phrases can function as the subject of predication; only topics can do so (and topics must furthermore be specific). See section 1.1.2.

(i) a. ALGO debe haberte (*lo) dicho María para que
 something(O) must have (*ACC.CL) said María(S) for
 te hayas enojado tanto.
 (you) to be angry so-much
 'Maria must have said something to you in order for you to be so angry.'
 b. NADA (*lo) comió el niño.
 nothing(O) (*ACC.CL) ate the boy(S)
 'The boy didn't eat anything.'
 c. Las ESPINACAS (*la) detestan los niños y no las
 the spinach(O) (*ACC.CL) hate the children(S) and not the
 papas.
 potatoes
 'The children detest spinach (and not potatoes).'

As is well known, the dative clitic differs from the accusative clitic in MS in that a dative clitic may cooccur with a fronted emphatic or focused phrase, as well as with a *wh*-phrase. See (ii). We may assume that in such cases the clitic functions purely as an agreement marker (see Suñer 1988, Franco 1993), and not as a predicate-variable. In other words, in MS the functional status of the dative clitic is ambiguous, a point that merits further investigation.

(ii) a. A NADIE le habló Pedro.
 to nobody DAT.CL spoke Pedro
 'Pedro didn't speak to anybody.'
 (cf. No le habló Pedro a nadie)
 b. A JUAN le habló María (y no a Pedro).
 to Juan DAT.CL spoke María (and not to Pedro)
 'María spoke to Juan (and not to Pedro).'
 c. A quién le habló Pedro?
 to whom DAT.CL spoke Pedro
 'To whom did Pedro speak?'

30. On the other hand, as suggested by Chomsky (1995), it might be the case that a phrase may check more than one formal feature in a given specifier-head configuration (the "free ride" situation). Also, in some languages a formal feature may be checked by more than one phrase via the specifier-head relation (as in the case of the double accusative in Japanese).

31. I have not addressed the position of negation within the generalized TP analysis. Though I will not enter into details, a few remarks are in order. As is well known, a negative phrase in postverbal position, unlike a negative phrase in preverbal position, must be licensed by an overt negative morpheme in Spanish as well as in Italian (compare (i) and (ii)).

(i) a. Nadie vino.
 no-one came
 b. No vino nadie.
 NEG came no-one

See Arnaiz 1996 for a review of the literature on licensing of negative polarity items and a discussion of the theoretical issues involved.

I assume, contra Laka (1990), that the functional projection NegP is located between TP and VP. The preverbal negative polarity item morphologically merges with the feature *neg* when it moves through the [Spec, Neg] on its way to [Spec, T]. I assume furthermore that, in Spanish as well as in Italian, when the feature *neg* does not undergo morphological merging, it adjoins to T and, in such cases, *neg* licenses any negative polarity item within the scope of T.

32. Barbosa (1995) suggests that in the Romance pro-drop languages, lexical subjects never occupy [Spec, T] ([Spec, I] in her terms); only a pro subject may move to this position. A fronted lexical subject is analyzed as left-dislocated (i.e., above TP). See also Barbosa 1997 for an analysis along similar lines. My analysis of preverbal subjects in Standard Spanish is incompatible with Barbosa's analysis.

33. The restriction against VSO order in Italian holds regardless of whether the subject is a name or a pronoun (Anna Cardinaletti, personal communication).

(i) *Iero   ha detto Gianni/lui la verità.
  yesterday has said Gianni/he the truth
  'Gianni/he told the truth yesterday.'

34. Speakers seem to vary with respect to which predicates allow an implicit locative argument. Thus, whereas Belletti and Shlonsky (1995, 498) judge (i) grammatical, Pinto (1994, 178) judges (ii) ungrammatical if the locative is not overtly present.

(i) Hanno lavorato molti operai.
     have   worked many workers
     'Many workers have worked.'

(ii) *(In questo albergo) hanno lavorato molte donne straniere.
     (in this hotel)   have worked many women foreign
     'Many foreign women have worked in this hotel.'

35. Savoia and Manzini (in preparation) provide data from northern Italian dialects that support Pinto's analysis of Standard Italian. In many dialects in northern Italy (Piedmont, Liguria, Lombardy, and Emilia), VS constructions cooccur with an expletive nominative clitic and a locative clitic. The following examples are from Montaldo:

(i) Ur e mort-je yn veje.
     EXPL is died-LOC an old-man
     'An old man died.'

(ii) U   i(e) mwera y galinne.
     EXPL LOC dies   chickens
     'Chickens die.'

36. The Italian native speakers consulted did not accept the Italian counterparts of Piera's (1987) examples in note 5 either.

37. The relevance of the tense/aspect property of the construction is also indicated by the following contrasts with respect to *ne*-cliticization in Italian, cited by Levin and Rappaport Hovav (1996) (who attribute them to Lonzi (1985)):

(i) a. *Di ragazze, ne   hanno lavorato molte nelle fabbriche di Shanghai.
        of girls   of-them have worked   many in-the factories of Shanghai
        (complex tense, with auxiliary *avere*)
     b. Di ragazze, ne lavorano molte nelle fabbriche di Shanghai.
        (simple tense)

(ii) a. *Di ragazzi, ne   hanno russato molti nel   corridoio del   treno.
        of boys   of-them have snored   many in-the corridor of-the train
        (complex tense, with auxiliary *avere*)
     b. Di ragazzi, ne   russavano molti nel   corridoio del   treno.
        of boys   of-them snore   many in-the corridor of-the train
        (simple tense)

38. Italian also differs from MS with respect to embedded questions. Although Italian does not allow a topic to intervene between the *wh*-phrase and the verb in matrix questions, it does so marginally in embedded questions.

(i) ?Mi domando a chi, il premio Nobel, lo potrebbero dare.
 (I) wonder to whom the Nobel Prize ACC.CL (they) could give
 (Rizzi 1995, n. 18)

The MS counterpart of (i) is ill formed.

(ii) *Me pregunto a quién, el premio Nobel, se lo pueden dar.

39. Also see Poletto 1995 for relevant discussion of the preverbal field in Italian.

40. The construction involving "anaphoric preposing" (see Cinque 1990, 86–94), similar to the VP-preposing cases of English, can be analyzed in the same way as VOS. In this construction the subject is focused as well. See note 48 for further discussion.

(i) a. Arrestati per ubriachezza, sono stati anche loro.
 arrested for drunkenness were too they
 b. *Arrestati per ubriachezza, anche loro sono stati.

(ii) a. ... e questo disse anche il Sottosegretario.
 and this said too the Vice-Minister
 b. *... e questo anche il Sottosegretario disse.

41. In the case of right-dislocation, there is an intonational hiatus between the dislocated phrase and the material that precedes it, which may or may not be accompanied by a salient pause. See the appendix to this chapter for further discussion of this issue.

42. As expected, the focus-sensitive operator *solo* 'only' must associate with the subject in the VOS order.

(i) Solo probó el pastel Juan.
 only tasted the cake Juan
 'Only Juan tasted the cake.'

43. Note that within this type of analysis, the fact that traces are not properly bound at Spell-Out is without consequence. But see section 3.6.

44. This fact was also noticed by Ordoñez (1995).

45. Some "exceptional" cases are discussed by Rizzi (1991, 20). Compare the examples in (i) with those in (ii).

(i) a. Non parla più nessuno.
 not speaks anymore anyone
 b. Vince sempre Gianni.
 wins always Gianni
 c. Ha fatto tutto Gianni.
 has done all Gianni

(ii) a. ??Ha telefonato ieri Gianni.
 has telephoned yesterday Gianni
 b. ??Ti contatterà domani Gianni.
 you will-contact tomorrow Gianni
 c. ??Ha fatto questo Gianni.
 has done this Gianni

Rizzi mentions that the adverbs in (ia–b) and the quantifier in (ic) are higher in the tree than the adverbs in (iia–b) and the object in (iic). This is suggested by the fact that *più*, *sempre*, and *tutto* can precede the "low" adverb *bene* 'well'. Compare (iii) with (iv).

(iii) a. Gianni non parla   più   bene.
         Gianni does not speak anymore well
      b. Gianni gioca sempre bene.
         Gianni plays always well
      c. Gianni ha   fatto tutto   bene.
         Gianni has   done everything well

(iv) a. *Gianni ha   fatto questo bene.
         Gianni has done this   well
      b. *Gianni ha   parlato ieri   bene.
         Gianni has spoken yesterday well
      c. *Gianni giocherà domani   bene.
         Gianni will-play tomorrow well

Given the analysis proposed in the text, a possible solution might be to assume that the syntax of (i) and (ii) is more complex. As shown in (v), movement in such cases might occur in two steps. In (i) the high adverb or Q is fronted above FP (pied-piping VP_1 as a result of the "Shortest Movement" Condition), followed by p-movement of the TP. Given this syntactic derivation, each of the constituents that has moved across the subject (i.e., VP_1 and TP) is metrically nonbranching; therefore, the Relative Weight Constraint is met.

(v) a. $[[_{TP}\ e_q\ [\text{non parla}\ e_k]]_j\ [\ \textit{più}\ [_{VP_1}\ e_q\ [v_1\ldots]]]_k\ [_{FP}\ \text{nessuno}_q\ e_j]]$
    b. $[[_{TP}\ e_q\ [\text{vince}\ e_k]]_j\ [\textit{sempre}\ [_{VP_1}\ e_q\ [v_1\ldots]]]_k\ [_{FP}\ \text{Gianni}_q\ e_j]]$
    c. $[[_{TP}\ e_q\ [\text{ha fatto}\ e_k]]_j\ [\textit{tutto}_j\ [_{VP_1}\ e_q\ [v_1\ [_{VP_2}\ [e_j\ pro]\ [v_2]]]]]_k\ [_{FP}\ \text{Gianni}_q\ e_k]]$

On the other hand, in (ii) the two-step derivation will be blocked if we assume that V_2 cannot move separately from V_1. In effect, as shown in (vi), if the lower adverb (such as *ieri* or *domani*) is fronted above FP (pied-piping VP_2 as a result of "Shortest Movement"), followed by p-movement of TP, the derivation is blocked because the two lexical components of the verb are separated.

(vi) $[[_{TP}\ e_q\ [\text{ha telefonato}\ [_{VP_1}\ e_q\ [v_1\ [_{VP_2}\ e]_k]]]]_j\ [\textit{ieri}\ [_{VP_2}\ [v_2\ldots]]]_k\ [_{FP}\ \text{Gianni}_q\ e_j]]$

The only other available derivation for the examples in (ii) is one in which the adverb has moved along with the TP, as shown in (vii). But this derivation violates the Relative Weight Constraint.

(vii) $[[_{TP}\ e_q\ [\text{ha telefonato}\ [_{VP_1}\ e_q\ [v_1\ [\textit{ieri}\ [_{VP_2}\ v_2]]]]]]_j\ [_{FP}\ \text{Gianni}_i\ e_q]]$

The question, then, is what triggers the fronting of adverbs (as in (v)). Clearly, it cannot be p-movement, because p-movement is strictly local: it affects only metrical sister nodes. See section 3.5.1 for further discussion of this point. I leave the question open for future research.

46. Belletti and Shlonsky (1995, 499) note the contrast between (ia) and (ib).

(i) a. *?Ne   ho   dato a Gianni uno.
         of-them (I) have given to Gianni one

Notes to Page 138

 b. Ne ho dato a Gianni uno solo.
         only

This contrast suggests that in Italian "light" functional categories, such as bare determiners, are metrically invisible for the NSR. In effect, the ill-formedness of (ia) could be attributed to the fact that the bare determiner *uno* is metrically invisible and therefore cannot trigger p-movement. In (ib) the DP is modified, rendering it metrically visible. A similar type of contrast is found in French, as illustrated in (ii); also see the contrast in (iii). (On p-movement in French, see section 3.6.)

(ii) a. *?J'en ai donné à Marie un.
   I of-them have given to Marie one
  b. J'en ai donné à Marie un grand nombre.
           a large number

(iii) a. J'ai donné l'autre à Marie.
   I have given the other to Marie
  b. *?J'ai donné à Marie l'autre.

Belletti and Shlonsky (1995, 507) also note the following contrast, which involves a light dative object *loro* and a prepositional object *a loro*:

(iv) a. Ne ho dato loro uno.
   of-them (I) have given them one
  b. ?*Ne ho dato a loro uno.
   of-them (I) have given to them one

(ivb) is ungrammatical, as is (ia). On the other hand, (iva) is well formed. This is due to the fact that the movement of the light dative object *loro* is syntactically, not prosodically, motivated (see Cardinaletti 1992, Corver and Delfitto 1993).

47. I have not discussed the ungrammaticality of the word order VPPOS exemplified in (i), with two [+F] constituents (the subject and the object).

(i) *(?)Ha messo sul tavolo il libro Maria.
   has put on-the table the book Maria
  (Belletti and Shlonsky 1995, 501)

Cases of multiple [+F] constituents give rise to a linked or paired focus reading. Italian is not the best language for studying such cases because it lacks multiple *wh*-questions. Still, let us examine the F-structure in (ii).

(ii) $[_{FP}$ Maria$_i$ $[_{TP}$ e$_i$ $[[_{-F}$ ha messo$]$ $[_{VP_1}$ $[$e$_i$ v$_1$ $[_{VP_2}$ $[_{+F}$ il libro$]$ v$_2$ $[_{-F}$ sul tavolo$]]]]]]]]$

Note that TP is unmarked for the feature [F] because it dominates both [+F] and [−F] material. Consequently, the FPR will fail to apply to the nodes (FP, TP). Recall that the FPR only applies to two metrical sister nodes, when one is specified as [+F] and the other as [−F] (see the appendix to chapter 2). On the other hand, the FPR does apply to the metrical sister nodes ($[_{+F}$ il libro$]$, $[_{-F}$ sul tavolo$]$). At this point p-movement can and must apply (to avoid to conflict between the FPR and the C-NSR): $[_{-F}$ sul tavolo$]$ is adjoined to VP$_2$. Thus, the word order in (123b) in the text is generated, but not the word order in (i).

48. In note 40 I mentioned the structures in (i) and (ii), discussed by Cinque (1990).

(i) a. Arrestati per ubriachezza, sono stati anche loro.
        arrested for drunkenness   were   too   they
    b. *Arrestati per ubriachezza, anche loro sono stati.

(ii) a. ... e   questo disse anche il   Sottosegretario.
         and this said   too   the Vice-Minister
     b. *... e questo anche il Sottosegretario disse.

It is reasonable to assume that in (ia) and (iia) the postverbal subject is in [Spec, F]. The derivation of (ia) and of (iia) will then take place in two steps: movement of TP above FP, followed by movement of the VP, as shown in (iii) (details omitted).

(iii) a. [[$_{VP}$ e$_j$ arrestati per ubriachezza]$_i$ [[$_{TP}$ e$_j$ sono stati e$_i$]$_k$ [$_{FP}$ anche loro$_j$ [e$_k$]]]]
      b. [[$_{VP}$ e$_j$ v$_1$ [questo v$_2$]]$_i$ [$_{TP}$ e$_j$ disse e$_i$]$_k$ [$_{FP}$ anche il Sottosegretario$_j$ [e$_k$]]]]

The first movement is clearly a case of p-movement. It is less clear what motivates the second movement, although it is definitely not feature checking. Possibly, this movement occurs as a way of ensuring an intonationally more balanced analysis of the sentence. For further discussion of this point, see section 3.6.2 on English heavy NP shift.

49. If β in (124) is a nonmaximal projection and therefore invisible to the syntactic computation, then the rule in (125) may affect α and a node γ immediately dominated by β, which is both metrically visible and visible to the syntactic computation. But this is possible only to the extent that γ is metrically nondistinct from β.

As an illustration, consider the Italian SVO/VOS structures in (i) and (ii) in which the subject is focused.

(i) [$_{FP}$ S [$_{F'}$ F [$_{TP}$ [V [...O...]]]]]
(ii) [[$_{TP}$ [V [...O...]]] [$_{FP}$ S [$_{F'}$ F [$_{TP}$ e]]]]

In (i), α = [Spec, F] and β = F'. Given that F' is invisible to the syntactic computation, the rule will affect [Spec, F] and the node immediately dominated by F'—namely, TP—giving rise to the structure in (ii). This extended interpretation of the rule Affect is possible only to the extent that F is phonologically empty. Because F is phonologically empty, F' and TP are metrically nondistinct and therefore [Spec, F] and TP are derivatively defined as metrical sisters.

50. One should be careful not to treat the negative polarity items *nadie* or *ningún N* as covert partitives.

51. It is not possible to control thoroughly for cases with a noncontrastive focus interpretation given that this interpretation is controlled with the question/answer test. In some cases—namely, those involving a strong QP (see (130) in the text)—the intended binding relation is available in the question; but in other cases—namely, those such as (i) in which the intended binder is a negative phrase—it is not.

(i) Quisiera saber quién no acompañó a nadie / ninguno niño /
I-would-like to-know who not accompanied ACC nobody no child
a ninguno de estos niños el primer día de escuela.
ACC none of those children the first day of school
'I would like to know who did not accompany anybody/any child/any of those children the first day of school.'

52. Locatives are generally inanimate, and inanimate possessive pronouns are not very felicitous (at least in some dialects of Spanish). But if we can abstract away from the noise created by this constraint, the expected parallelism obtains.

53. As mentioned in note 31, I assume that the functional projection NegP is located between TP and VP. The preverbal negative polarity item morphologically merges with the feature *neg* when it moves through the [Spec, Neg] on its way to [Spec, T]. I assume furthermore that, in Spanish as well as in Italian, when the feature *neg* does not undergo morphological merging, it adjoins to T and, in such cases, *neg* licenses any negative polarity item in the scope of T.

54. In French, not only defocalized phrases but also anaphoric phrases are treated optionally as metrically invisible. Compare (i) and (ii) (from Ronat 1982, 34–35; cited in section 2.4) with (iii) and (iv), which are equally well formed.

(i) Paul regarde les informations tous les soirs; Marie est jalouse <u>de la</u>
    Paul watches the news every evening Marie is jealous of the
    télévision.
    television

(ii) A: Le professeur Dupont veut être élu à l'Académie Française.
        Professor Dupont wants to-be elected to the Académie Française
    B: Oui. Il aime <u>énormément</u> *les habits verts.*
        Yes he likes a-lot the suits green
    'Yes. He likes green suits a lot.'

(iii) Paul regarde les informations tous les soirs; Marie est jalouse de la <u>télévision</u>.

(iv) A: Le professeur Dupont veut être élu à l'Académie Française.
     B: Oui. Il aime énormément les habits <u>verts</u>.

On the other hand, it is highly unnatural to pronounce the English example in (v) (from Ladd 1980, 81; cited in section 2.2) as in (vi), with NS on the object of *denounced.*

(v) A bill was sent to Congress today by President Carter which would require peanut butter sandwiches to be served at all government functions. At a press conference today, a group of Senators led by Republican Barry Goldwater of Arizona denóunced *the measure.* Goldwater said ...

(vi) A bill was sent to Congress today by President Carter which would require peanut butter sandwiches to be served at all government functions. At a press conference today, a group of Senators led by Republican Barry Goldwater of Arizona denounced the méasure. Goldwater said ...

Similarly, whereas the pronoun is interpreted obligatorily as contrastive in the English example in (vii), this is not the case in its French counterpart in (viii).

(vii) Mary talked about hím.

(viii) Marie a parlé de lui.

55. Binding in (i) and (ii) is unavailable. This is expected since binding is unavailable in the corresponding question as well; see (iii).

(i) On n'a déposé {son avis de mission} chez personne.
we not delivered his assignment at anyone's place
[Binding: *]

(ii) On n'a déposé chez personne {son avis de mission}.
[Binding: *]

(iii) Qu'a-t-on déposé chez personne?
what did we deliver at nobody's place
[Binding: *]

56. For a discussion of this construction from a different perspective, see Hawkins 1994.

57. I use the term *right-dislocation* in a theory-neutral sense. Given the antisymmetry line of analysis, right-dislocation must find its source in the left-dislocation construction. This is achieved be leftward movement of TP across the left-dislocated constituent.

58. These F_0 diagrams were done in collaboration with Alfredo Arnaiz and Gorka Elordieta.

59. In the dative-shifted construction in Spanish, the dative clitic is obligatorily present but either order (ACC DAT or DAT ACC) is possible with a wide focus interpretation.

(i) a. Le devolvió su manuscrito a cada autor.
    DAT.CL (he) returned his manuscript to each author
b. Le devolvió a cada autor su manuscrito.

See Strozer 1976, Demonte 1993, 1995 for discussion.

60. The contrast is less clear with dative structures, because for some not-yet-understood reason, it is easier to drop the object when a dative clitic is present. See, for example, the contrast between (iii) and (iv), which is very weak.

(i) Le envió MARÍA *el regalo a mamá.*
    DAT.CL sent María the present to Mother

(ii) Le envió el regalo # María # a mamá.

(iii) (?)Le envió a mamá # María # el regalo.

(iv) Se lo envió a mamá # María # el regalo.
    DAT.CL ACC.CL

Bibliography

Abraham, W. 1993. Structural properties of information packaging in German and in Universal Grammar. *Groninger Arbeiten zur germanistischen Linguistik* 35, 1–36.

Adger, D. 1996. Economy and optionality: Interpretations of subjects in Italian. *Probus* 8, 117–136.

Antinucci, F., and G. Cinque. 1977. Sull' ordine delle parole in italiano: L'emarginazione, *Studi di Grammatica Italiana* 6. Accademia della Crusca, Florence.

Aoun, J. 1991. The syntax of doubled arguments. Ms., Department of Linguistics, University of Southern California, Los Angeles. Revised version in Johnson and Roberts, to appear.

Aoun, J., and E. Benmamoun. 1998. Minimality, reconstruction, and PF movement. *Linguistic Inquiry* 29.

Aoun, J., and Y.-H. A. Li. 1989. Scope and constituency. *Linguistic Inquiry* 20, 141–172.

Arnaiz, A. 1992. On word order in *wh*-questions in Spanish. In A. Kathol and J. Beckman, eds., *MIT working papers in linguistics 16: Papers from the Fourth Student Conference in Linguistics*. MITWPL, Department of Linguistics and Philosophy, MIT, Cambridge, Mass.

Arnaiz, A. 1996. N-words and *wh*-in-situ. Doctoral dissertation, Department of Linguistics, University of Southern California, Los Angeles.

Barbosa, P. 1995. Null subjects. Doctoral dissertation, Department of Linguistics and Philosophy, MIT, Cambridge, Mass.

Barbosa, P. 1997. A new look at the null subject parameter. In J. Costa, R. Goedemans, and R. van de Vijver, eds., *Console IV Proceedings*. SOLE, HIL/Leiden University, The Netherlands.

Berckman, M., and J. Pierrehumbert. 1986. Intonational structure in Japanese and English. *Phonology Yearbook* 3, 255–309.

Beghelli, F. 1995. The phrase structure of quantifier scope. Doctoral dissertation, Department of Linguistics, UCLA, Los Angeles, Calif.

Belletti, A., and U. Shlonsky. 1995. The order of verbal complements: A comparative study. *Natural Language & Linguistic Theory* 13, 489–526.

Bing, J. 1979. Aspects of English prosody. Doctoral dissertation, Department of Linguistics, University of Massachusetts, Amherst.

Bolinger, D. 1958. A theory of pitch accent in English. *Word* 14, 109–149.

Bolinger, D. 1972. Accent is predictable (if you are a mind reader). *Language* 48, 633–644.

Bolinger, D. 1978. Asking more than one question at a time. In H. Hiz, ed., *Questions*. Dordrecht: Reidel.

Borer, H. 1984. *Parametric syntax*. Dordrecht: Foris.

Borer, H. 1994. The projection of arguments. In E. Benedicto and J. Runner eds., *University of Massachusetts occasional papers in linguistics 17: Functional projections*. GLSA, University of Massachusetts, Amherst.

Branigan, P. 1992. Subjects and complementizers. Doctoral dissertation, Department of Linguistics and Philosophy, MIT, Cambridge, Mass.

Brody, M. 1995. Focus and checking theory. In I. Kenesei, ed., *Approaches to Hungarian*. Vol. 5, *Levels and structures*. Szeged: JATE.

Burzio, L. 1986. *Italian syntax: A government-binding approach*. Dordrecht: Reidel.

Calabrese, A. 1990. Some remarks on focus and logical structures in Italian. In *Harvard working papers in linguistics 1*. Department of Linguistics, Harvard University, Cambridge, Mass.

Cardinaletti, A. 1992. On pronoun movement: The Italian dative *loro*. *Probus* 3, 127–153.

Cardinaletti, A. 1995. Subject positions. Ms., Seminario di Linguistica, Università di Venezia.

Carlson, G. 1977. Reference to kinds in English. Doctoral dissertation, Department of Linguistics, University of Massachusetts, Amherst.

Cecchetto, C. 1995. Reconstruction in clitic left dislocation. Ms., Department of Cognitive Science, Instituto scientifico San Raffaele, Milan.

Chierchia, G. 1991. Functional WH and weak crossover. In D. Bates, ed., *Proceedings of the Tenth West Coast Conference on Formal Linguistics*. Stanford, Calif.: CSLI Publications. [Distributed by Cambridge University Press.]

Chomsky, N. 1971. Deep structure, surface structure and semantic interpretation. In D. Steinberg and L. Jakobovits, eds., *Semantics: An interdisciplinary reader in philosophy, linguistics and psychology*. Cambridge: Cambridge University Press.

Chomsky, N. 1973. Conditions on transformations. In S. R. Anderson and P. Kiparsky, eds., *A festschrift for Morris Halle*. New York: Holt, Rinehart and Winston.

Chomsky, N. 1976. Conditions on rules of grammar: *Linguistic Analysis* 2, 303–351.

Chomsky, N. 1981. *Lectures on government and binding*. Dordrecht: Foris.

Chomsky, N. 1982. *Some concepts and consequences of the theory of government and binding*. Cambridge, Mass.: MIT Press.

Chomsky, N. 1986. *Barriers*. Cambridge, Mass.: MIT Press.

Chomsky, N. 1991. Some notes on economy of derivation and representation. In R. Freidin, ed., *Principles and parameters in comparative grammar*. Cambridge, Mass.: MIT Press.

Chomsky, N. 1993. A minimalist program for linguistic theory. In K. Hale and S. J. Keyser, eds., *The view from Building 20*. Cambridge, Mass.: MIT Press.

Chomsky, N. 1994. Bare phrase structure. MIT Occasional Papers in Linguistics 5. Department of Linguistics and Philosophy, MIT, Cambridge, Mass. [Also in G. Webelhuth, ed., *Government and Binding Theory and the Minimalist Program*. Oxford: Blackwell, 1995.]

Chomsky, N. 1995. Categories and transformations. In *The Minimalist Program*. Cambridge, Mass.: MIT Press.

Chomsky, N., and M. Halle. 1968. *The sound pattern of English*. New York: Harper and Row.

Chomsky, N., and H. Lasnik. 1993. The theory of principles and parameters. In J. Jacobs, A. von Stechow, W. Sternefeld, and T. Vennemann, eds., *Syntax: An international handbook of contemporary research*. Berlin: Walter de Gruyter.

Cinque, G. 1983. Topic constructions in some European languages and "connectedness." In K. Ehlich and H. van Riemsdijk, eds., *Connectedness in sentence, discourse, and text*. Katholieke Hogeschool, Tilburg.

Cinque, G. 1990. *Types of $\bar{A}$-dependencies*. Cambridge, Mass.: MIT Press.

Cinque, G. 1993. A null theory of phrase and compound stress. *Linguistic Inquiry* 24, 239–298.

Cinque, G., J. Koster, J.-Y. Pollock, L. Rizzi, and R. Zanuttini, eds. 1995. *Paths towards Universal Grammar*. Washington, D.C.: Georgetown University Press.

Contreras, H. 1976. *A theory of word order with special reference to Spanish*. Amsterdam: North-Holland.

Contreras, H. 1983. *El orden de palabras en español*. 2nd ed. Madrid: Cátedras.

Contreras, H. 1986. Spanish bare NPs and the ECP. In I. Bordelois, H. Contreras, and K. Zagona, eds., *Generative studies in Spanish syntax*. Dordrecht: Foris.

Corver, N., and D. Delfitto. 1993. Feature asymmetry and the nature of pronoun movement. Ms., OTS, Universiteit Utrecht.

Culicover, P., and M. Rochemont. 1983. Stress and focus in English. *Language* 59, 123–165.

Dell, F. 1984. L'accentuation des phrases en français. In F. Dell, D. Hirst, and J.-R. Vergnaud, eds., *Forme sonore du langage*. Paris: Hermann.

Demonte, V. 1993. Ditransitivity in Spanish: Syntax and semantics. Ms., Universidad Autónoma de Madrid.

Demonte, V. 1995. Dative alternation in Spanish. *Probus* 7, 5–30.

Diesing, M. 1990. Verb movement and the subject position in Yiddish. *Natural Language & Linguistic Theory* 8, 41–79.

Diesing, M. 1992a. Bare plural subjects and the derivation of logical representations. *Linguistic Inquiry* 23, 353–380.

Diesing, M. 1992b. *Indefinites*. Cambridge, Mass.: MIT Press.

Dobrovie-Sorin, C. 1990. Clitic doubling, *wh*-movement, and quantification in Romanian. *Linguistic Inquiry* 21, 351–397.

Dolci, R. 1986. Algunas construcciones con anteposición de constituyentes oracionales en español: Su determinación y análisis sintáctico. Tesi di laurea, Università di Venezia.

Elordieta, G. 1997. Morphosyntactic feature chains and phonological domains. Doctoral dissertation, Department of Linguistics, University of Southern California, Los Angeles.

Enç, M. 1991. The semantics of specificity. *Linguistic Inquiry* 22, 1–25.

Erteschik-Shir, N. 1986. WH-questions and focus. *Linguistics and Philosophy* 9, 117–149.

Escobar, M. A. 1995. Lefthand satellites in Spanish. Doctoral dissertation, OTS, Universiteit Utrecht.

Evans, G. 1980. Pronouns. *Linguistic Inquiry* 11, 337–362.

Fernández Soriano, O. 1989. *Rección y ligamento en español: Aspectos del parámetro de sujeto nulo*. Doctoral dissertation, Universidad Autónoma de Madrid.

Fiengo, R., and R. May. 1994. *Indices and identity*. Cambridge, Mass.: MIT Press.

Firbas, J. 1980. Post-intonation-centre prosodic shade in modern English clause. In S. Greenbaum, G. Leech, and J. Svartvik, eds., *Studies in English linguistics for Randolph Quirk*. London: Longman.

Fontana, J. 1993. Phrase structure and the syntax of clitics in the history of Spanish. Doctoral dissertation, Department of Linguistics, University of Pennsylvania, Philadelphia.

Franco, J. 1993. On object agreement in Spanish. Doctoral dissertation, Department of Spanish and Portuguese, University of Southern California, Los Angeles.

Giorgi, A., and F. Pianesi. 1996. Verb movement in Italian and syncretic categories. *Probus* 8, 137–160.

Goodall, G. 1991. On the status of SPEC of IP. In D. Bates, ed., *Proceedings of the Tenth West Coast Conference on Formal Linguistics*. Stanford, Calif.: CSLI Publications. [Distributed by Cambridge University Press.]

Grimshaw, J. 1979. Complement selection and the lexicon. *Linguistic Inquiry* 10, 279–326.

Guasti, M. T. 1996. On the controversial status of Romance interrogatives. *Probus* 8, 161–180.

Guasti, M. T., and M. Nespor. 1996. Is syntax phonology free? Ms., Instituto scientifico San Raffaele, Milan and HIL/University of Amsterdam.

Guéron, J. 1989. On the syntax and semantics of PP extraposition, *Linguistic Inquiry* 11, 637–677.

Gussenhoven, C. 1984. *On the grammar and semantics of sentence accents.* Dordrecht: Foris.

de Haan, G., and F. Weerman. 1985. Finiteness and verb fronting in Frisian. In H. Haider and M. Prinzhorn, eds., *Verb second phenomena in Germanic languages.* Dordrecht: Foris.

Hale, K., and S. J. Keyser. 1991. On the syntax of argument structure. Center for Cognitive Science, MIT, Cambridge, Mass.

Hale, K., and S. J. Keyser. 1993. On argument structure and the lexical representation of syntactic relations. In K. Hale and S. J. Keyser, eds., *The view from Building 20.* Cambridge, Mass.: MIT Press.

Halle, M., and A. Marantz. 1993. Distributed Morphology and the pieces of inflection. In K. Hale and S. J. Keyser, eds., *The view from Building 20.* Cambridge, Mass.: MIT Press.

Halle, M., and J.-R. Vergnaud. 1987. *An essay on stress.* Cambridge, Mass.: MIT Press.

Halliday, M. A. K. 1967. Notes on transitivity and theme in English, Part II. *Journal of Linguistics* 3, 199–244.

Hawkins, J. 1994. *Performance theory of order and constituency.* Cambridge: Cambridge University Press.

Hayes, B., and A. Lahiri. 1991. Bengali intonational phonology. *Natural Language & Linguistic Theory* 9, 47–98.

Heim, I. 1982. The semantics of definite and indefinite noun phrases. Doctoral dissertation, Department of Linguistics, University of Massachusetts, Amherst. [Published by Garland Press, 1988.]

Herburger, E. 1993. Focus and the LF of NP quantification. In U. Lahiri and A. Wyner, eds., *Proceedings from Semantics and Linguistic Theory III.* Department of Modern Languages, Cornell University, Ithaca, N.Y.

Herburger, E. 1997. Focus and weak noun phrases. *Natural Language Semantics* 5, 53–78.

Hernanz, M. L., and J. M. Brucart. 1987. *La sintaxis* (1). Barcelona: Editorial Crítica.

Heycock, C., and A. Kroch. 1996. Pseudocleft connectivity: Implications for the LF interface level. Edinburgh Occasional Papers in Linguistics. University of Edinburgh.

Hinterhölzl, R. 1996. Coherent infinitives in German, Dutch, and West Flemish. Ms., Department of Linguistics, University of Southern California, Los Angeles.

Höhle, T. 1981. Explikation für "normale Betonung" und "normale Wortstellung." In W. Abraham, ed., *Erklärende syntax des Deutschen*. Tübingen: Narr.

Hornstein, N. 1995. *The grammar of Logical Form: From GB to Minimalism*. Oxford: Blackwell.

Horvath, J. 1986. *Focus in the theory of grammar and the syntax of Hungarian*. Dordrecht: Foris.

Iatridou, S. 1990a. About Agr(P). *Linguistic Inquiry* 21, 551–577.

Iatridou, S. 1990b. Clitics and island effects. Ms., Department of Linguistics and Philosophy, MIT, Cambridge, Mass.

Iatridou, S., and A. Kroch. 1991. The licensing of CP-recursion and its relevance to the Germanic verb-second phenomenon. In *Working papers in Scandinavian linguistics 50*.

Inkelas, S., and D. Zec, eds. 1990. *The phonology-syntax connection*. Chicago: University of Chicago Press.

Jackendoff, R. 1974. *Semantic interpretation in generative grammar*. Cambridge, Mass.: MIT Press.

Jaeggli, O. 1982. *Topics in Romance syntax*. Dordrecht: Foris.

Johnson, K., and I. Roberts. To appear. *Beyond principles and parameters*. Dordrecht: Kluwer.

Jonas, D., and J. Bobaljik. 1993. Spec for subjects: The role of TP in Icelandic. In J. Bobaljik and C. Phillips, eds., *MIT working papers in linguistics 18: Papers on Case and agreement I*. MITWPL, Department of Linguistics and Philosophy, MIT, Cambridge, Mass.

Kayne, R. S. 1983. *Connectedness*. Dordrecht: Foris.

Kayne, R. S. 1991. Romance clitics, verb movement, and PRO. *Linguistic Inquiry* 22, 647–686.

Kayne, R. S. 1994. *The antisymmetry of syntax*. Cambridge, Mass.: MIT Press.

Keenan, E. 1987. A semantic definition of definite NPs. In E. Reuland and A. ter Meulen, eds., *The representation of (in)definiteness*. Cambridge, Mass.: MIT Press.

Kitagawa, Y. 1994. Shells, yolks, and scrambled e.g.s. In M. Gonzàlez, ed., *NELS 24*, vol. 1. GLSA, University of Massachusetts, Amherst.

Koopman, H., and D. Sportiche. 1991. The position of subjects. *Lingua* 85, 211–258.

Kratzer, A. 1991. The representation of focus. In A. von Stechow and D. Wunderlich, eds., *Semantics: An international handbook of contemporary research*. Berlin: Walter de Gruyter.

Krifka, M. 1984. Focus, Topic, syntaktische Struktur und semantische Interpretation. Ms., Universität Tübingen.

Kroch, A. 1989. Reflexes of grammar in patterns of language change. *Journal of Language Variation and Change* 1, 199–244.

Kuno, S. 1982. The focus of the question and the focus of the answer. In *Papers from the Parasession on Nondeclarative Sentences, Chicago Linguistic Society.* Chicago Linguistic Society, University of Chicago, Chicago, Ill.

Kuroda, S.-Y. 1992. *Japanese syntax and semantics.* Dordrecht: Kluwer.

Ladd, D. R. 1980. *The structure of intonational meaning.* Bloomington: Indiana University Press.

Laka, I. 1990. Negation in syntax: On the nature of functional categories and projections. Doctoral dissertation, Department of Linguistics and Philosophy, MIT, Cambridge, Mass.

Lakoff, G. 1968. Pronouns and reference. Indiana University Linguistics Club, Bloomington.

Larson, R. 1988a. Light predicate raising. Lexicon Project Working Papers 27. Center for Cognitive Science, MIT, Cambridge, Mass.

Larson, R. 1988b. On the double object construction. *Linguistic Inquiry* 19, 335–391.

Lasnik, H., and M. Saito. 1992. *Move α.* Cambridge, Mass.: MIT Press.

Lebeaux, D. 1988. Language acquisition and the form of the grammar. Doctoral dissertation, Department of Linguistics, University of Massachusetts, Amherst.

Levin, B., and M. Rappaport Hovav. 1996. *Unaccusativity: At the syntax–lexical semantics interface.* Cambridge, Mass.: MIT Press.

Liberman, M. 1975. The intonational system of English. Doctoral dissertation, Department of Linguistics, MIT, Cambridge, Mass.

Liberman, M., and J. Pierrehumbert. 1984. Intonational invariance under changes in pitch range and length. In M. Aronoff and R. Oehrle, eds., *Language sound structure.* Cambridge, Mass.: MIT Press.

Liberman, M., and A. Prince. 1977. On stress and linguistic rhythm. *Linguistic Inquiry* 8, 249–336.

Lois, X. 1989. Aspects de la grammaire de l'espagnol et théorie de la grammaire. Doctoral dissertation, Université Paris 8, St-Denis.

Longobardi, G. 1994. Reference and proper names: A theory of N-movement in syntax and Logical Form. *Linguistic Inquiry* 25, 609–665.

Mahajan, A. 1990a. Th A/A-bar distinction and movement theory. Doctoral dissertation, Department of Linguistics and Philosophy, MIT, Cambridge, Mass.

Mahajan, A. 1990b. Clitic doubling, object agreement, and specificity. In T. Sherer, ed., *NELS 21.* GLSA, University of Massachusetts, Amherst.

Mahajan, A. 1991. Operator movement, agreement, and referentiality. In L. L. S. Cheng and H. Demirdache, eds., *MIT working papers in linguistics 15: More papers on* wh-*movement.* MITWPL, Department of Linguistics and Philosophy, MIT, Cambridge, Mass.

Martin, P. 1975. Analyse phonologique de la phrase française. *Linguistics* 146, 35–68.

Martin, P. 1978. Questions de phonosyntaxe et de phonosémantique en français. *Lingvisticæ Investigationes* 2, 93–126.

Martin, P. 1981. Pour une théorie de l'intonation: L'intonation est-elle une structure congruante à la syntaxe? In M. Rossi et al., eds., *L'intonation, de l'acoustique à la sémantique*. Paris: Klincksieck.

Martin, P. 1982. Phonetic realisations of prosodic contours in French. *Speech Communication* 1, 283–294.

Martin, P. 1987. Prosodic and rhythmic structures in French. *Linguistics* 25, 925–949.

Martin, P., and J.-R. Vergnaud. In preparation. On prosody. Ms., French Department, University of Toronto, and Department of Linguistics, University of Southern California, Los Angeles.

Matsuda, Y. 1997. A syntactic analysis of focus sentences in Japanese. In B. Bruening, ed., *MIT working papers in linguistics 31: Proceedings of the Eighth Student Conference in Linguistics*. MITWPL, Department of Linguistics and Philosophy, MIT, Cambridge, Mass.

May, R. 1984. *Logical Form*. Cambridge, Mass. MIT Press.

Meredith, S. 1990. Issues in the phonology of prominence. Doctoral dissertation, Department of Linguistics and Philosophy, MIT, Cambridge, Mass.

Mota, C. 1995. La representación gramatical de la información nueva en el discurso. Doctoral dissertation, Departamento de Filología Española, Universitat Autónoma de Barcelona.

Nespor, M., and I. Vogel. 1986. *Prosodic phonology*. Dordrecht: Foris.

Newman, S. S. 1946. On the stress system of English. *Word* 2, 171–187.

Ordoñcz, F. 1995. Postverbal asymmetries in Spanish. Ms., Graduate Center, City University of New York.

Pesetsky, D. 1987. *Wh*-in-situ: Movement and unselective binding. In E. Reuland and A. G. B. ter Meulen, eds., *The representation of (in)definiteness*. Cambridge, Mass.: MIT Press.

Piera, C. 1987. Sobre la estructura de las cláusulas de infinitivo. In V. Demonte and M. Fernández Lagunilla, eds., *Sintaxis de las lenguas románicas*. Madrid: El Arquero.

Pierrehumbert, J. 1980. The phonology and phonetics of English intonation. Doctoral dissertation, Department of Linguistics, MIT, Cambridge, Mass.

Pinto, M. 1994. Subjects in Italian: Distribution and interpretation. In R. Bok-Bennema and C. Cremers, eds., *Linguistics in the Netherlands*. Amsterdam: John Benjamins.

Poletto, C. 1995. Complementizer deletion and verb movement in Italian. In L. Brugè, ed., *Working papers in linguistics 5*. Centro Linguistico Interfacoltà, Università di Venezia.

Pollock. J.-Y. 1989. Verb movement, Universal Grammar, and the structure of IP. *Linguistic Inquiry* 20, 365–424.

Prince, E. 1981. Toward a taxonomy of given-new information. In P. Cole, ed., *Radical pragmatics*. New York: Academic Press.

Prinzhorn, M. 1994. Prosodic and syntactic structure: An outline. Handout, Department of Linguistics, Universität Wien and Università di Venezia.

Reinhart, T. 1982. Pragmatics and linguistics: An analysis of sentence topics. Distributed by the Indiana University Linguistics Club, Bloomington. Published in *Philosophica 27*, special issue on Pragmatic Theory, 1981.

Reinhart, T. 1983. Coreference and bound anaphora: A restatement of the anaphora questions. *Linguistics and Philosophy* 6, 47–88.

Reinhart, T. 1995. *Interface strategies*. Ms., OTS, Universiteit Utrecht.

Rivero, M. L. 1986. Parameters in the typology of clitics in Romance and Old Spanish. *Language* 64, 774–807.

Rivero, M. L. 1995. Diachrony and the status of Last Resort as an economy principle. Paper presented at the Fourth Diachronic Generative Syntax Conference, Université du Québec à Montréal.

Rizzi, L. 1982. *Issues in Italian syntax*. Dordrecht: Foris.

Rizzi, L. 1991. Residual verb second and the *Wh*-Criterion. Technical Reports in Formal and Computational Linguistics 2. Faculté des Lettres, Université de Genève.

Rizzi, L. 1995. The fine structure of the left periphery. Ms., Université de Genève.

Rochemont, M. 1986. *Focus in generative grammar*. Amsterdam: John Benjamins.

Rochemont, M., and P. Culicover. 1990. *English focus constructions and the theory of grammar*. Cambridge: Cambridge University Press.

Rögnvaldsson, E., and H. Thráinsson. 1990. On Icelandic word order once more. In J. Maling and A. Zaenen, eds., *Syntax and semantics*. Vol. 24, *Modern Icelanic syntax*. San Diego, Calif.: Academic Press.

Ronat, M. 1982. Logical Form and discourse islands. *Journal of Linguistic Research* 2, 33–48.

Rooth, M. 1985. Association with focus. Doctoral dissertation, Department of Linguistics, University of Massachusetts, Amherst.

Rooth, M. 1992. A theory of focus interpretation. *Natural Language Semantics* 1, 75–116.

Ross, J. R. 1967. Constraints on variables in syntax. Doctoral dissertation, Department of Linguistics, MIT, Cambridge, Mass.

Santorini, B. 1989. The generalization of the verb-second constraint in the history of Yiddish. Doctoral dissertation, Department of Linguistics, University of Pennsylvania, Philadelphia.

Savoia, L., and M. R. Manzini. In preparation. *I dialetti italiani*. Bologna: Il Mulino.

Schmerling, S. 1976. *Aspects of English sentence stress.* Austin: University of Texas Press.

Schneider-Zioga, P. 1993. The syntax of clitics in Modern Greek. Doctoral dissertation, Department of Linguistics, University of Southern California, Los Angeles.

Selkirk, E. 1980. Prosodic domains in phonology: Sanskrit revisited. In M. Aronoff and M. L. Kean, eds., *Juncture.* Saratoga, Calif.: Anma Libri.

Selkirk, E. 1984. *Phonology and syntax: The relation between sound and structure.* Cambridge, Mass.: MIT Press.

Selkirk, E. 1995. Sentence prosody: Intonation, stress, and phrasing. In J. Goldsmith, ed., *The handbook of phonological theory.* Oxford: Blackwell.

Solà, J. 1992. Agreement and subjects. Doctoral dissertation, Department of Linguistics, Universitat Autónoma de Barcelona.

Sosa, J. M. 1991. Fonética y fonología de la entonación del español hispanoamericano. Doctoral dissertation, Department of Spanish and Portuguese, University of Massachusetts, Amherst.

Sperber, D., and D. Wilson. 1986. *Relevance: Communication and cognition.* Oxford: Blackwell.

Sportiche, D. 1992. Clitic constructions. Ms., Department of Linguistics, UCLA, Los Angeles, Calif.

Sportiche, D. 1993. Subject clitics in French and Romance: Complex inversion and clitic doubling. Ms., Department of Linguistics, UCLA, Los Angeles, Calif. To be published in Johnson and Roberts, to appear.

Stalnaker, R. 1978. Assertion. In P. Cole, ed., *Syntax and semantics.* Vol. 9, *Pragmatics.* New York: Academic Press.

Steedman, M. 1991. Structure and intonation. *Language* 67, 260–296.

Stowell, T. 1981. Origins of phrase structure. Doctoral dissertation, Department of Linguistics, MIT, Cambridge, Mass.

Strawson, P. 1964. Identifying reference and truth values. *Theoria 30.* Reprinted in D. Steinberg and L. Jakobovits, eds., *Semantics: An interdisciplinary reader in philosophy, linguistics and psychology.* Cambridge: Cambridge University Press.

Stroik, T. 1990. Adverbs as V-sisters. *Linguistic Inquiry* 21, 654–661.

Strozer, J. 1976. Clitics in Spanish. Doctoral dissertation, Department of Spanish and Portuguese, UCLA, Los Angeles, Calif.

Suñer, M. 1982. *Syntax and semantics of Spanish presentational sentence-types.* Washington, D.C.: Georgetown University Press.

Suñer, M. 1988. The role of agreement in clitic-doubled constructions, *Natural Language & Linguistic Theory* 6, 391–434.

Suñer, M. 1991. Indirect questions and the structure of CP: Some consequences. In H. Campos and F. Martínez-Gil, eds., *Current studies in Spanish linguistics.* Washington, D.C.: Georgetown University Press.

Suñer, M. 1994. V-movement and the licensing of argumental *wh*-phrases in Spanish. *Natural Language & Linguistic Theory* 12, 335–372.

Szabolcsi, A. 1981. The semantics of topic-focus articulation. In T. Jansen and M. Stokhof, eds., *Formal methods in the study of language*. Amsterdam: Mathematisch Centrum.

Szabolcsi, A. 1996. Verb and particle movement in Hungarian. Ms., Department of Linguistics, UCLA, Los Angeles, Calif.

Tancredi, C. D. 1990. Not only EVEN, but even ONLY. Ms., Department of Linguistics and Philosophy, MIT, Cambridge, Mass.

Tancredi, C. D. 1992. Deletion, deaccenting, and presupposition. Doctoral dissertation, Department of Linguistics and Philosophy, MIT, Cambridge, Mass.

Thráinsson, H. 1985. V1, V2, V3 in Icelandic. In H. Haider and M. Prinzhorn, eds., *Verb second phenomena in Germanic languages*. Dordrecht: Foris.

Torrego, E. 1984. On inversion in Spanish and some of its effects. *Linguistic Inquiry* 15, 103–130.

Travis, L. 1991. Derived objects, inner aspect, and the structure of the VP. Paper presented at NELS 21, Université du Québec à Montreal.

Truckenbrodt, H. 1993. Syntax vs. phonology: Which gets the stress right? Ms., Department of Linguistics and Philosophy, MIT, Cambridge, Mass.

Truckenbrodt, H. 1995. Phonological phrases: Their relation to syntax, focus, and prominence. Doctoral dissertation, Department of Linguistics and Philosophy, MIT, Cambridge, Mass.

Tuller, L. 1992. The syntax of postverbal focus constructions in Chadic. *Natural Language & Linguistic Theory* 10, 303–334.

Uriagereka, J. 1995. Aspects of the syntax of clitic placement in Western Romance. *Linguistic Inquiry* 26, 79–123.

Vallduví, E. 1993. Catalan as VOS: Evidence from information packaging. In J. Ashby, M. Mithun, G. Perissinotto, and E. Raposo, eds., *Linguistic perspectives in the Romance languages*. Amsterdam: John Benjamins.

Vallduví, E. 1995. Structural properties of information packaging in Catalan. In K. Kiss, ed., *Discourse configurational languages*. Oxford: Oxford University Press.

Vallduví, E., and E. Engdahl. 1995. The linguistic realisation of information packaging. Ms., Centre for Cognitive Science and Human Communication Research Centre, University of Edinburgh.

Vikner, S. 1991. Verb movement and the licensing of NP-positions in Germanic languages. Doctoral dissertation, Faculté des Lettres, Université de Genève.

Wanner, D. 1991. The Tobler-Mussafia law in Old Spanish. In H. Campos and F. Martínez-Gil, eds., *Current studies in Spanish linguistics*. Washington, D.C.: Georgetown University Press.

Williams, E. 1980. Predication. *Linguistic Inquiry* 11, 203–238.

Williams, E. 1997. Blocking and anaphora. *Linguistic Inquiry* 28, 577–628.

Wilson, D., and D. Sperber. 1979. Ordered entailments: An alternative to presuppositional theories. In C.-K. Oh and D. Dinneen, eds., *Syntax and semantics*. Vol. 11, *Presupposition*. New York: Academic Press.

Zagona, K. 1993. Perfectivity and temporal arguments. In M. Mazzola, ed., *Issues and theory in Romance linguistics: Selected papers from the Symposium on Romance Languages 23*. Washington, D.C.: Georgetown University Press.

Zubizarreta, M. L. 1992a. The lexical encoding of scope relations among arguments. In T. Stowell and E. Wehrli, eds., *Syntax and semantics*. Vol. 26, *Syntax and the lexicon*. New York: Academic Press.

Zubizarreta, M. L. 1992b. Word order in Spanish and the nature of nominative Case. Ms., Department of Linguistics, University of Southern California, Los Angeles. To be published in Johnson and Roberts, to appear.

Zubizarreta, M. L. 1993. The grammatical representation of topic and focus: Implications for the structure of the clause. In *Cuadernos de lingüística 2*. Instituto Universitario Ortega y Gasset, Madrid. Also published in *University of Venice working papers in linguistics*, Centro Linguistico Interfacoltà, Università di Venezia.

Zubizarreta, M. L. 1994. El orden de palabras en español y el caso nominativo. *Nueva revista de filología hispánica VI* (special issue, ed. V. Demonte). Colegio de México.

Zubizarreta, M. L. 1995a. Some prosodically motivated movements. In G. Cinque, J. Koster, J.-Y. Pollock, L. Rizzi, and R. Zanuttini, eds., *Paths towards Universal Garmmar*. Washington, D.C.: Georgetown University Press.

Zubizarreta, M. L. 1995b. Prosody, focus, and word order (version 3). Ms., Department of Linguistics, University of Southern California, Los Angeles.

Zubizarreta, M. L. 1996. Prosody, focus, and word order (version 4). Ms., Department of Linguistics, University of Southern California, Los Angeles.

Zubizarreta. M. L. In preparation. Some comparative remarks on the higher middle field in Germanic and Romance. Ms., Department of Linguistics, University of Southern California, Los Angeles.

Zubizarreta, M. L., and J.-R. Vergnaud. 1992. Generics and existentials in French and English. Paper presented at the GLOW Colloquium, Lisbon.

Zwarts, J. W. 1993. Dutch syntax: A minimalist approach. Doctoral dissertation, Department of Linguistics, Rijksuniversiteit Groningen.

Index

Adger, D., 118–119
Anaphoric preposing, 123n40, 138n48
Antinucci, F., 121
Assertion Structure, 2–6, 11–12, 31–32
  background assertion, 4–6
  main assertion, 4–6, 14
  ordered assertions, 4–16
Asymmetric c-command, 34–36, 40, 43n7, 43–44, 52, 55, 63
  derivative asymmetric c-command, 43n7
Asymmetric c-command ordering, 44, 59. See also Asymmetric c-command and Linear ordering

Bare plurals in Spanish, 109
Beckman, M., 91, 152
Belletti, A., 119n34, 138n46
Bolinger, D., 67–70
Brody, M., 105n8

Calabrese, A., 114n25, 121–122
Categories, 27, 34, 36, 127, 136
  heads and maximal projections, 27, 36, 127, 136
Chomsky, N., 1, 3, 17, 24–30, 33–34, 37–38, 40–41, 44, 53, 67, 101, 108–109
Cinque, G., 37, 85, 87–88, 114n23, 121, 123n40, 138n48
Clitics and fronted focus construction in Spanish, 116n29
Clitic-doubled strong pronouns and Condition C, 109n16
Clitic left-dislocation and pronominal binding, 113–115
Clitic projection, 112, 114–116
Condition C, 109n16, 113
Context-question, 2, 4, 12. See also Focus-structure
Context-statement, 6–7. See also Emphasis
Contrastive stress, 45

Convention for the application of the NSR, 43, 56
Convergence, 23, 28
  convergent derivations, 23
  Modularity of Convergence Hypothesis (MCH), 30

Dative-shift construction in Spanish, 156n
Deaccented, 84n48, 85, 154, 157–158. See also Metrical invisibility
  deaccented time adverbials, 49n13
Defocalized and anaphoric constituents, 19, 41, 46–49, 59–60, 64, 74, 130–131
Dell, F., 38–39
Diesing, M., 100, 126
Discourse-based functional features: "emphasis," "focus," "topic," 100n3, 103–105, 116n29, 117, 123
Dolci, R., 114n23
Domination, 34

Echo/Non-echo Relative Prominence Rule (ERPR), 88
Emphatic stress, 48. See also Emphatic/Contrastive Stress Rule
Emphatic/Contrastive Stress Rule, 18, 44, 76, 125, 129, 134
Emphasis, 7, 20, 44, 102
Eurhythmicity, 39

Feature, 25. See also Discourse-based functional features
Case feature, 26
categorial feature, 25
D-feature, 112–113
feature-checking, 26, 100, 102, 107n11, 108, 112
feature [wh], 92, 93n53, 95n55, 107, 105n8, 105n9
formal feature, 25

Feature (cont.)
  0 feature, 26
  semantic feature, 25
  strong feature, 26
Feature [F], 30–31, 94, 100n3. *See also* Prosodic prominence and F-structure
Focus, 1–7, 37, 39. *See also* Presupposition
Focus/Contrastive Stress Correspondence Principle, 45, 77
Focus/Prominence Rule (FPR), 21, 88, 93, 124
Focus/Prosody Correspondence Principle (FPCP), 38, 88
Focus structure, 1, 3–4. *See also* Assertion Structure
  contrastive focus interpretation, 6, 20, 45, 106, 125
  focus neutral or wide focus interpretation, 11, 18–21, 125, 127–128, 149
Fontana, J., 110–112, 110n19
Franco, J., 112
Free-ride, 117n30
French stylistic inversion, 96
F-structure, 2–3, 16–17, 46. *See also* Feature [F]
Full Interpretation (FI), 23

Generalized TP analysis, 100, 117
Giorgi, A., 100
Goodall, G., 105
Guasti, M. T., 22, 121, 137
Gussenhoven, C., 17, 21, 37, 44, 48, 49, 68, 79, 82–84

Hale, K., 18, 53
Halle, M., 33, 38, 67
Hayes, B., 91
Heavy NP Shift, 148
Herburger, E., 4n15, 5
Höhle, T., 62
Hornstein, N., 12

Iatridou, S., 116
Inclusiveness Principle, 30
Interface levels, 30–33
Intermediate phrase, 91, 152, 156
Intonational nucleus, 38
Intonational phrase, 84, 91, 152, 156

Jackendoff, R., 1–2, 17, 37–38, 44
Jaeggli, O., 95

Kayne, R., 33, 40
Keyser, J., 18, 53

Ladd, D., 48–49
Lahiri, A., 91

Last Resort, 20, 32, 134, 140, 146, 150
Left-dislocation, 108, 110, 114n23, 126, 136
Liberman, M., 38, 40, 152
Linear ordering, 34, 40. *See also* Asymmetric c-command ordering
Locative construction, 107n12, 118–119n35, 120–121

Meredith, S., 46
Merge, 25
Metrically equivalent class, 42, 57, 60. *See also* Metrically nondistinct
Metrical invisibility, 34, 46, 48–49, 60, 64, 74, 147
Metrically nondistinct, 42–43, 56–61
Metrical nondistinctness of structural analysis, 42
Middle field and scrambling, 50n15
Minimal Link Condition, 29. *See also* Shortest Movement Condition
Minimalist Program, minimalist approach, 23, 29, 32, 117
Minimize Structure, 101, 117
Modifier/complement asymmetries, 50–52
Move, 26–28. *See also* P-movement
  Attract f., 29, 32
  covert movement, 26, 32, 108
  Move f, 28–29, 110
  overt movement, 27, 32
Multiple wh-questions, wh-in-situ, 3, 6, 93–96, 131

ne-cliticization, 120n
NegP, 117n31, 146n53
Nespor, M., 22, 39, 137
Nominative Case, 108, 110, 121, 123
Nuclear Stress Rule (NSR), 17, 38, 40
  Revised NSR, 19, 43, 56, 90, 124, 141

PF restructuring and nuclear stress, 90
Phrasal or prosodic prominence, 30–31, 37. *See also* Nuclear Stress Rule and Emphatic/Contrastive Stress Rule
  echo stress, 47, 84
  primary stress, 38, 39
  relative prominence, 40–41, 89, 139
  secondary stress, 38, 39, 47
Pianesi, F., 110
Pierrehumbert, J., 91, 152
Pinto, M., 118–119n34
Predication, 8–9, 160. *See also* Topic
Presupposition, 1–4. *See also* Focus structure
Preverbal/postverbal symmetries, 16, 109n16, 113–116, 114n25, 121–122
Prince, A., 38
Procrastinate, 26

Pro-drop, 148
P(rosodically)-motivated movement, 22, 99, 123–127, 130–132, 134, 136, 138–141, 146–148

Quantifier binding, quantifier scope, pronominal binding, 13–16, 114, 142–144, 147
Quantifier Raising (QR), 3

Reconstruction, 113–116, 141, 145
Reinhart, T., 7–9
Relative Weight Constraint, 22–23, 137–138, 137n, 151
  metrical heaviness, 137, 150–151
Right-dislocation, 151, 154
  emarginated or right-dislocated phrases, 121–122, 156–157
Rivero, M. L., 112, 116
Rizzi, L., 123, 135, 137n
Rochemont, M., 1n3, 1n4, 92
Rögnvaldsson, E., 100
Ronat, M., 73–74

Santorini, B., 100
Szabolsci, A., 105n8
Schmerling, S., 1n3, 37, 49, 67, 69, 78
Segments, 27, 34, 36
Selectional chain, 54, 57, 62, 65
Selectional ordering, 18, 52–53, 57, 63
  derivatively selectionally ordered, 57–60, 62–63
Selkirk, E., 2, 17, 21, 37–38, 48–49, 70–71, 79–82
Semantically light or highly predictable, 70
Shlonsky, U., 119n34, 138n46
Shortest Movement Condition, 23, 95n58, 95n59, 97, 116n28, 137n, 154n, 156n
Sisterhood, 34, 42–43n7
  derivative sisterhood, 43n7
  metrical sisterhood, 40–42, 56–58, 62, 64, 139
  syntactic sisterhood, 41, 43
Spell-Out, 22, 28, 41, 141
Sperber, D., 1n2, 2n6
Sportiche, D., 24, 112
Suñer, M., 105n 9
Superiority, 95–96
Syncretic categories, 100, 107, 118

Thráinsson, E., 100.,
Topic, 7–10, 14–16, 113–114, 116. *See also* Discourse-based functional features
  topic/comment, 9–10
Truckenbrodt, H., 50–51, 86., 92

Vergnaud, J. R., 38
Virtual metrical tree, 42n5, 42n6

Wh-adjuncts and word order in Spanish, 105–106
Wh-complements and word order in Spanish, 105–107, 105n9
Wh-phrases and word order in Italian, 121–122
Williams, E., 2n6, 48.,
Wilson, D., 1n2, 2n6

X-bar theory, 24

Zubizarreta, M. L., 11, 87, 100, 101, 114
Zwarts, J. W., 55

www.ingramcontent.com/pod-product-compliance
Lightning Source LLC
Chambersburg PA
CBHW061443300426
44114CB00014B/1819